VOICES OF FREEDOM

A Documentary History

Second Edition

Volume 1

VOICES OF FREEDOM

A Documentary History

Second Edition

EDITED BY

ERIC FONER

Volume 1

W.W. NORTON & COMPANY · NEW YORK · LONDON

W. W. Norton & Company has been independent since its founding in 1923, when William Warder Norton and Mary D. Herter Norton first published lectures delivered at the People's Institute, the adult education division of New York City's Cooper Union. The Nortons soon expanded their program beyond the Institute, publishing books by celebrated academics from America and abroad. By mid-century, the two major pillars of Norton's publishing program—trade books and college texts—were firmly established. In the 1950s, the Norton family transferred control of the company to its employees, and today—with a staff of four hundred and a comparable number of trade, college, and professional titles published each year—W. W. Norton & Company stands as the largest and oldest publishing house owned wholly by its employees.

Manufactured by Victor Graphics, Inc.
Book design by Antonina Krass
Composition by Binghamton Valley Composition

ISBN 13: 978-0-393-93106-8 (pbk.)

W. W. Norton & Company, Inc., 500 Fifth Avenue, New York, NY 10110
www.wwnorton.com
W. W. Norton & Company Ltd., Castle House, 75/76 Wells Street, London W1T 3QT

6 7 8 9 0

ERIC FONER is DeWitt Clinton Professor of History at Columbia University, where he earned his B.A. and Ph.D. In his teaching and scholarship, he focuses on the Civil War and Reconstruction, slavery, and nineteenth-century America. Professor Foner's publications include *Free Soil, Free Labor, Free Men: The Ideology of the Republican Party Before the Civil War; Tom Paine and Revolutionary America: Politics and Ideology in the Age of the Civil War; Nothing but Freedom: Emancipation and Its Legacy; Reconstruction: America's Unfinished Revolution, 1863–1877; Freedom's Lawmakers: A Directory of Black Officeholders During Reconstruction; The Story of American Freedom; Who Owns History? Rethinking the Past in a Changing World;* and *Forever Free: The Story of Emancipation and Reconstruction.* His history of Reconstruction won the *Los Angeles Times* Book Award for History, the Bancroft Prize, and the Parkman Prize. He has been co-curator for two historical exhibits, "A House Divided" at the Chicago Historical Society, and "America's Reconstruction" at the Virginia Historical Society. He served as president of the Organization of American Historians (1993–1994), the American Historical Association (2000), and the Society of American Historians (2006–2007).

Contents

Preface   *xv*

1

A New World

1. *Adam Smith, The Results of Colonization (1776)*   3
2. *Giovanni da Verrazano, Encountering Native Americans (1524)*   6
3. *Bartolomé de las Casas on Spanish Treatment of the Indians,*
   from History of the Indies (1528)   10
4. *The Pueblo Revolt (1680)*   14
5. *Father Jean de Brébeuf on the Customs and Beliefs*
   of the Hurons (1635)   17
6. *A Micmac Indian Replies to the French (1677)*   22

2

Beginnings of English America, 1607–1660

7. *Richard Hakluyt, an Argument for Colonization from* A Discourse
   Concerning Western Planting *(1584)*   25
8. *Sending Women to Virginia (1622)*   28

9. *Maryland Act Concerning Religion (1644)* — 30

10. *John Winthrop, Speech to the Massachusetts General Court (1645)* — 32

11. *The Trial of Anne Hutchinson (1637)* — 35

12. *The Levellers, The Agreement of the People Presented to the Council of the Army (1647)* — 42

13. *Henry Care, English Liberties, or the Free-Born Subject's Inheritance (1680)* — 46

3

Creating Anglo-America, 1660–1750

14. *New York Charter of Liberties and Privileges (1683)* — 49

15. *William Penn on Religious Liberty, from* England's Present Interests Discovered *(1675)* — 53

16. *Nathaniel Bacon on Bacon's Rebellion (1676)* — 56

17. *Letter by an Immigrant to Pennsylvania (1769)* — 61

18. *Gottlieb Mittelberger on the Trade in Indentured Servants (1750)* — 63

19. *Complaint of an Indentured Servant (1756)* — 66

20. *Women in the Household Economy (1709)* — 68

4

Slavery, Freedom, and the Struggle for Empire, to 1763

21. *Olaudah Equiano on Slavery (1789)* — 70

22. *Slave Conspiracy in Virginia (1709)* — 75

23. The Independent Reflector *on Limited Monarchy*
    and Liberty (1752) 78
24. *The Trial of John Peter Zenger (1735)* 81
25. *A Defense of George Whitefield (1739)* 85
26. *Pontiac, Two Speeches (1762 and 1763)* 87

5

The American Revolution, 1763–1783

27. *Virginia Resolutions on the Stamp Act (1765)* 90
28. *Petition of North Carolina Regulators (1769)* 92
29. *Association of the New York Sons of Liberty (1773)* 96
30. *Farmington, Connecticut, Resolutions on the Intolerable
    Acts (1774)* 100
31. *Thomas Paine,* Common Sense *(1776)* 102
32. *James Chalmers,* Plain Truth *(1776)* 109

6

The Revolution Within

33. *Abigail and John Adams on Women
    and the American Revolution (1776)* 111
34. *The Right of "Free Suffrage" (1776)* 114
35. *Thomas Jefferson, An Act for Establishing
    Religious Freedom (1785)* 117
36. *Noah Webster on Equality (1787)* 119
37. *Liberating Indentured Servants (1784)* 122
38. *Petition of Slaves to the Massachusetts Legislature (1777)* 123
39. *Pennsylvania Act for the Gradual Abolition of Slavery (1780)* 125

7

Founding a Nation, 1783–1789

40. Petition of Inhabitants West of the Ohio River (1785)   130

41. James Madison, The Federalist, No. 51 (1787)   132

42. James Winthrop on the Anti-Federalist Argument (1787)   135

43. A July Fourth Oration (1800)   139

44. Thomas Jefferson on Race and Slavery (1781)   142

8

Securing the Republic, 1790–1815

45. William Manning on the Nature of Free Government (1799)   147

46. Address of the Democratic-Republican Society of
    Pennsylvania (1794)   151

47. Judith Sargent Murray, "On the Equality of the Sexes" (1790) 154

48. George Washington, Farewell Address (1796)   158

49. George Tucker on Gabriel's Rebellion (1801)   164

50. Tecumseh on Indians and Land (1810)   167

51. Felix Grundy, Battle Cry of the War Hawks (1811)   168

9

The Market Revolution, 1800–1840

52. Josephine L. Baker, "A Second Peep at Factory Life" (1840)   171

53. Immigrants Arriving in New York City (1853)   174

54. Ralph Waldo Emerson, "The American Scholar" (1837)   176

55. *Henry David Thoreau,* Walden *(1854)*   *180*

56. *Charles G. Finney, "Sinners Bound to Change Their*
    Own Hearts" (1836)   *184*

57. *Orestes Brownson, "The Laboring Classes" (1840)*   *189*

10

Democracy in America, 1815–1840

58. *"The Memorial of the Non-Freeholders of the City of*
    Richmond" (1829)   *193*

59. *John Quincy Adams on the Role of the National*
    Government (1825)   *197*

60. *John C. Calhoun, the Concurrent Majority (ca. 1845)*   *201*

61. *Chief Sharitarish on Changes in Indian Life (1822)*   *204*

62. *Appeal of the Cherokee Nation (1830)*   *207*

63. *Andrew Jackson, Veto of the Bank Bill (1832)*   *209*

11

The Peculiar Institution

64. *Frederick Douglass on the Desire for Freedom (1845)*   *213*

65. *Rise of the Cotton Kingdom (1836)*   *216*

66. *J. D. B. De Bow, "The Non-Slaveholders of the*
    South" (1860)   *218*

67. *George Fitzhugh and the Proslavery Argument (1854)*   *222*

68. *Solomon Northup, The New Orleans Slave Market (1853)*   *225*

69. *Letter by a Fugitive Slave (1840)*   *229*

70. *Confessions of Nat Turner (1831)*   *231*

12

An Age of Reform, 1820–1840

71. Robert Owen, "The First Discourse on a New System
    of Society" (*1825*)   237
72. Philip Schaff on Freedom as Self-Restraint (*1855*)   241
73. Opening Editorial of The Liberator (*1831*)   244
74. Frederick Douglass on the Fourth of July (*1852*)   247
75. Catherine Beecher on the "Duty of American Females" (*1837*)   252
76. Angelina Grimké on Women's Rights (*1837*)   257
77. Declaration of Sentiments of the Seneca Falls Convention (*1848*) 261

13

A House Divided, 1840–1861

78. John L. O'Sullivan, Manifest Destiny (*1845*)   265
79. Henry David Thoreau, "Resistance to Civil Government" (*1849*) 269
80. George Henry Evans, "Freedom of the Soil" (*1844*)   273
81. William Henry Seward, "The Irrepressible Conflict" (*1858*)   275
82. Hinton R. Helper, "The Impending Crisis" (*1857*)   279
83. The Lincoln-Douglas Debates (*1858*)   283
84. South Carolina Ordinance of Secession (*1860*)   287

14

A New Birth of Freedom: The Civil War, 1861–1865

85. Alexander H. Stephens, The Cornerstone of the Confederacy (*1861*) 291
86. Marcus M. Spiegel, Letter of a Civil War Solider (*1864*)   296

87. Abraham Lincoln, The Gettysburg Address (1863)   299

88. Frederick Douglass on Black Soldiers (1863)   301

89. Letter by the Mother of a Black Solider (1863)   304

90. Abraham Lincoln, Address at Sanitary Fair, Baltimore (1864)   307

91. Mary Livermore on Women and the War (1883)   309

15

"What Is Freedom?": Reconstruction, 1865–1877

92. "Colloquy with Colored Ministers" (1865)   313

93. Petition of Committee on Behalf of the Freedmen to Andrew
    Johnson (1865)   316

94. The Mississippi Black Code (1865)   319

95. Sidney Andrews on the White South and Black Freedom (1866)   324

96. Elizabeth Cady Stanton, "Home Life" (ca. 1875)   328

97. Frederick Douglass, "The Composite Nation" (1869)   332

98. Robert B. Elliott on Civil Rights (1874)   338

Preface

Voices of Freedom is a documentary history of American freedom from the earliest days of European exploration and settlement of the Western Hemisphere to the present. It was prepared as a companion volume to *Give Me Liberty!*, my survey textbook of the history of the United States centered on the theme of freedom. But it can also stand independently as a documentary introduction to the history of American freedom. This second edition of *Voices of Freedom* is organized in chapters that correspond to those in the second edition of *Give Me Liberty!*. It has been expanded to include more than fifty documents not available in the first edition. Many of the new documents reflect revisions that were made in the textbook, in whose second edition considerable material was added strengthening discussions of the history of Native Americans, immigration and the controversies surrounding it, and the American West.

Thus, this edition of *Voices of Freedom* includes such new documents as Father Jean de Brêbeuf's account of the customs and beliefs of the Hurons in New France and Carlos Montezuma's 1914 critique of federal Indian policy; Gottlieb Mittelberger's description of the arrival of Geman indentured servants in eighteenth-century Philadelphia and Archbishop Roger Mahoney's explanation in 2006 of why he would refuse to obey a proposed law making it illegal to aid illegal immigrants; John L. O'Sullivan's 1845 defense of territorial expansion in the name of "manifest destiny" and James Watts's 1978

attack on the environmentalist movement and call for the development of western energy resources. I have also taken the opportunity
to add documents reflecting the diversity of the American experience, and of American ideals of freedom, including Frederick Douglass's plea for acceptance of Chinese immigrants in his "Composite
Nation" speech of 1869, Carrie Chapman Catt's address to Congress
calling for women's suffrage in 1917, and a condemnation of prejudice against Mexican-Americans from 1945.

No idea is more fundamental to Americans' sense of themselves as
individuals and as a nation than freedom, or liberty, with which it is
almost always used interchangeably. The Declaration of Independence lists liberty among humanity's inalienable rights; the Constitution announces as its purpose to secure liberty's blessings. "Every
man in the street, white, black, red or yellow," wrote the educator
and statesman Ralph Bunche in 1940, "knows that this is 'the land of
the free'... 'the cradle of liberty.' "

The very universality of the idea of freedom, however, can be mis-
leading. Freedom is not a fixed, timeless category with a single un-
changing definition. Rather, the history of the United States is, in
part, a story of debates, disagreements, and struggles over freedom.
Crises like the American Revolution, the Civil War, and the Cold
War have permanently transformed the idea of freedom. So too have
demands by various groups of Americans for greater freedom as they
understood it.

In choosing the documents for *Voices of Freedom*, I attempted to
convey the multifaceted history of this compelling and contested
idea. The documents reflect how Americans at different points in
our history have defined freedom as an overarching idea or have understood its many dimensions, including political, religious, economic, and personal freedom. For each chapter, I tried to select
documents that highlight the specific discussions of freedom that
occurred during that time period. I hope that students will gain an
appreciation of how the idea of freedom has expanded over time,
and how it has been extended into more and more areas of Ameri-

cans' lives. But, at the same time, the documents suggest how freedom for some Americans, at various times in our history, rested on lack of freedom—slavery, indentured servitude, the subordinate position of women—for others.

The documents that follow reflect the kinds of historical developments that have shaped and reshaped the idea of freedom, including war, economic change, territorial expansion, and international involvement. The selections try to convey a sense of the rich cast of characters who contributed to the history of American freedom. They include presidential proclamations and letters by runaway slaves, famous court cases and obscure manifestos, ideas dominant in a particular era and those of radicals and dissenters. They range from the John Peter Zenger case in colonial New York, which helped to establish the principle of freedom of the press, to Frederick Douglass's account of how he learned to cherish the idea of freedom while in slavery, Charlotte Perkins Gilman's discussion at the turn of the twentieth century of how expanding employment opportunities instilled a new spirit of freedom in American women, and Franklin D. Roosevelt's Four Freedom's speech of 1941, outlining Allied aims in World War II. I have been particularly attentive to how battles at the boundaries of freedom—the efforts of racial minorities, women, and others to secure greater freedom—deepened and transformed the concept of freedom and extended it into new realms.

All of the documents in this collection are "primary sources"; that is, they were written or spoken by men and women enmeshed in the events of the past rather than by later historians. They therefore offer students the opportunity to encounter ideas about freedom in the actual words of participants in the drama of American history. Some of the documents are reproduced in their entirety. Most are excerpts from longer articles or books. In editing the documents, I tried to remain faithful to the original purpose of the author, while highlighting the portion of a text that deals directly with one or another aspect of freedom. In most cases, I reproduced the wording of the original texts exactly, but I modernized the spelling and punctuation of some early documents to make them more understandable to the modern reader. Each document is preceded by a brief introduction that places it in historical context and is followed by two questions that highlight key elements of the argument and may help to focus students' thinking about the issues raised by the author.

A number of these documents were suggested by students in a U. S. history class at Juniata College in Huntingdon, Pennsylvania, taught by Professor David Hsiung. I am very grateful to these students, who responded enthusiastically to an assignment by Professor Hsiung asking them to locate documents that might be included in this second edition of *Voices of Freedom* and to justify their choices with historical arguments. I also wish to thank Professor Barbara Y. Welke of the University of Minnesota, who offered valuable suggestions for documents to be included.

Taken together, the documents suggest the ways in which American freedom has changed and expanded over time. But they also remind us that American history is not simply a narrative of continual progress toward greater and greater freedom. While freedom can be achieved, it may also be reduced or rescinded. It can never be taken for granted.

Eric Foner

VOICES OF FREEDOM

A Documentary History

Second Edition

Volume 1

CHAPTER 1

A New World

1. Adam Smith, The Results of Colonization (1776)

Source: Adam Smith, An Inquiry into the Nature and Causes of the Wealth of Nations *(London, 1776), Vol. 2, pp. 190–91, 235–37.*

"The discovery of America," the British writer Adam Smith announced in his celebrated work *The Wealth of Nations*, published in 1776, was one of "the two greatest and most important events recorded in the history of mankind." Smith is regarded as the founder of modern economics. It is not surprising that looking back nearly three centuries after the initial voyage of Christopher Columbus in 1492, Smith focused primarily on the economic results of the conquest and colonization of North and South America. The influx of goods from the New World, he insisted, greatly increased the "enjoyments" of the people of Europe and the market for European goods. Nonetheless, Smith did not fail to note the price paid by the indigenous population of the New World, who suffered a dramatic decline in population due to epidemics, wars of conquest, and the exploitation of their labor. "Benefits" for some, Smith observed, went hand in hand with "dreadful misfortunes" for others—a fitting commentary on the long encounter between the Old and New Worlds.

OF THE ADVANTAGES which Europe has derived from the Discovery of America, and from that of a Passage to the East Indies by the Cape of Good Hope

What are [the advantages] which Europe has derived from the discovery and colonization of America?

The general advantages which Europe, considered as one great
country, has derived from the discovery and colonisation of America, consist, first, in the increase of its enjoyments; and, secondly, in
the augmentation of its industry.

The surplus produce of America, imported into Europe, furnishes
the inhabitants of this great continent with a variety of commodities
which they could not otherwise have possessed; some for conve-
niency and use, some for pleasure, and some for ornament, and
thereby contributes to increase their enjoyments.

The discovery and colonization of America, it will readily be allowed, have contributed to augment the industry, first, of all the
countries which trade to it directly, such as Spain, Portugal, France,
and England; and, secondly, of all those which, without trading to it
directly, send, through the medium of other countries, goods to it of
their own produce; such as Austrian Flanders, and some provinces of
Germany, which, through the medium of the countries before mentioned, send to it a considerable quantity of linen and other goods.
All such countries have evidently gained a more extensive market
for their surplus produce, and must consequently have been encouraged to increase its quantity. . . .

• • •

The discovery of America, and that of a passage to the East Indies
by the Cape of Good Hope, are the two greatest and most important
events recorded in the history of mankind. Their consequences
have already been very great; but, in the short period of between
two and three centuries which has elapsed since these discoveries
were made, it is impossible that the whole extent of their consequences can have been seen. What benefits or what misfortunes to
mankind may hereafter result from those great events, no human
wisdom can foresee. By uniting, in some measure, the most distant
parts of the world, by enabling them to relieve one another's wants,
to increase one another's enjoyments, and to encourage one

another's industry, their general tendency would seem to be beneficial. To the natives however, both of the East and West Indies, all the commercial benefits which can have resulted from those events have been sunk and lost in the dreadful misfortunes which they have occasioned. . . .

• • •

In the meantime one of the principal effects of those discoveries has been to raise the mercantile system to a degree of splendour and glory which it could never otherwise have attained to. It is the object of that system to enrich a great nation rather by trade and manufactures than by the improvement and cultivation of land, rather by the industry of the towns than by that of the country. But, in consequence of those discoveries, the commercial towns of Europe, instead of being the manufacturers and carriers for but a very small part of the world (that part of Europe which is washed by the Atlantic Ocean, and the countries which lie round the Baltic and Mediterranean seas), have now become the manufacturers for the numerous and thriving cultivators of America, and the carriers, and in some respects the manufacturers too, for almost all the different nations of Asia, Africa, and America. Two new worlds have been opened to their industry, each of them much greater and more extensive than the old one, and the market of one of them growing still greater and greater every day.

Questions

1. According to Adam Smith, how did the "discovery and colonization" of America affect the economic development of Europe?

2. Why does Smith believe that the "benefits" of colonization outweigh the "misfortunes?"

2. Giovanni da Verrazano, Encountering Native Americans (1524)

Source: From The Voyages of Giovanni da Verrazano, *ed. Lawrence C. Wroth, translated by Susan Tarrow pp. 133–34, 137–38, 140–41. Copyright © 1970 Yale University Press. Reprinted with permission.*

One of the first European explorers to encounter the Indians of eastern North America was Giovanni da Verrazano, an Italian-born navigator who sailed in 1524 under the auspices of King Philip I of France. His voyage took him from modern-day Cape Fear, North Carolina, north to the coast of Maine. In the following excerpt from his diary, which he included in a letter to the king, Verrazano tries to describe the appearance, economic life, customs, and beliefs of some of the region's various Native American groups. Some, he reports, were friendly and generous; others warlike and hostile. He is particularly interested in their spiritual beliefs, concluding that they have "no religion." Verrazano found the east coast thickly populated. By the time English settlement began in the early seventeenth century, many of the groups he encountered had been all but destroyed by epidemic diseases.

════════════

... Since the storm that we encountered in the northern regions, Most Serene King, I have not written to tell Your Majesty of what happened to the four ships which you sent over the Ocean to explore new lands, as I thought that you had already been informed of everything—how we were forced by the fury of the winds to return in distress to Brittany with only the *Normandy* and the *Dauphine*, and that after undergoing repairs there, began our voyage with these two ships, equipped for war, following the coasts of Spain, Your Most Serene Majesty will have heard; and then according to our new plan, we continued the original voyage with only the Dauphine; now on our return from this voyage I will tell Your Majesty of what we found.

... Seeing that the land continued to the south we decided to turn and skirt it toward the north, where we found the land we had sighted earlier. So we anchored off the coast and sent the small boat in to land. We had seen many people coming to the seashore, but they fled when they saw us approaching; several times they stopped and turned around to look at us in great wonderment. We reassured them with various signs, and some of them came up, showing great delight at seeing us and marveling at our clothes, appearance, and our whiteness; they showed us by various signs where we could most easily secure the boat, and offered us some of their food. We were on land, and I shall now tell Your Majesty briefly what we were able to learn of their life and customs.

They go completely naked except that around their loins they wear skins of small animals like martens, with a narrow belt of grass around the body, to which they tie various tails of other animals which hang down to the knees; the rest of the body is bare, and so is the head. Some of them wear garlands of birds' feathers. They are dark in color, not unlike the Ethiopians, with thick black hair, not very long, tied back behind the head like a small tail. As for the physique of these men, they are well proportioned, of medium height, a little taller than we are. They have broad chests, strong arms, and the legs and other parts of the body are well composed. There is nothing else, except that they tend to be rather broad in the face: but not all, for we saw many with angular faces. They have big black eyes, and an attentive and open look. They are not very strong, but they have a sharp cunning, and are agile and swift runners. From what we could tell from observation, in the last two respects they resemble the Orientals, . . .

We reached another land 15 leagues from the island, where we found an excellent harbor; before entering it, we saw about boats full of people who came around the ship uttering various cries of wonderment. They did not come nearer than fifty paces but stopped to look at the structure of our ship, our persons, and our clothes; then all together they raised a loud cry which meant that they were joyful. We reassured them somewhat by imitating their gestures, and they came near enough for us to throw them a few little bells and mirrors and many trinkets, which they took and looked at, laughing, and then they confidently came on board ship. Among them were two kings, who were as beautiful of stature and build as I can possibly describe. The first was about 40 years old, the other a young man of 24, and they were dressed thus: the older man had on his naked body a stag skin, skillfully worked like damask with various embroideries; the head was bare, the hair tied back with various bands, and around the neck hung a wide chain decorated with many different-colored stones. The young man was dressed in almost the same way. These people are the most beautiful and have the most civil customs that we have found on this voyage. They are taller than we are; they are a bronze color, some tending more toward whiteness, others to a tawny color; the face is clear-cut; the hair is long and black, and they take great pains to decorate it; the eyes are black and alert, and their manner is sweet and gentle, very like the manner of the ancients. I shall not speak to Your Majesty of the other parts of the body, since they have all the proportions belonging to any well-built man.

Their women are just as shapely and beautiful; very gracious, of attractive manner and pleasant appearance; their customs and behavior follow womanly custom as far as befits human nature; they go nude except for stag skin embroidered like the men's, and some wear rich lynx skins on their arms; their bare heads are decorated with various ornaments made of braids of their own hair which hang down over their breasts on either side. Some have other hair arrangements such as the women of Egypt and Syria wear, and these women are older and have been joined in wedlock. Both men and women have various trinkets hanging from their ears as the Orientals do; and we saw that they had many sheets of worked copper which they prize more than gold. They do not value gold because of its color; they think it the most worthless of all, and rate blue and red above all other colors. The things we gave them that they prized the most were little bells, blue crystals, and other trinkets to put in the ear or around the neck. They did not appreciate cloth of silk and gold, nor even of any other kind, nor did they care to have them; the same was true for metals like steel and iron, for many times when we showed them some of our arms, they did not admire them, nor ask for them, but merely examined the workmanship. They did the same with mirrors; they would look at them quickly, and then refuse them, laughing.

They are very generous and give away all they have. We made great friends with them, and one day before we entered the harbor with the ship, when we were lying at anchor one league out to sea because of unfavorable weather, they came out to the ship with a great number of their boats; they had painted and decorated their faces with various colors, showing us that it was a sign of happiness. They brought us some of their food, and showed us by signs where we should anchor in the port for the ship's safety, and then accompanied us all the way until we dropped anchor. . . .

At a distance of 50 leagues, keeping more to the north, we found high country full of very dense forests, composed of pines, cypresses, and similar trees which grow in cold regions.

The people were quite different from the others, for while the previous ones had been courteous in manner, these were full of crudity and vices, and were so barbarous that we could never make any communication with them, however many signs we made to them. They were clothed in skins of bear, lynx, sea-wolf and other animals. As far as we could judge from several visits to their houses, we think they live on game, fish, and several fruits which are a species of root which the earth produces itself. They have no pulse, and we saw no sign of cultivation, nor would the land be suitable for producing any fruit or grain on account of its sterility. If we wanted to trade with them for some of their things, they would come to the seashore on some rocks where the breakers were most violent, while we remained in the little boat, and they sent us what they wanted to give on a rope, continually shouting to us not to approach the land; they gave us the barter quickly, and would take in exchange only knives, hooks for fishing and sharp metal. We found no courtesy in them, and when we had nothing more to exchange and left them, the men made all the signs of scorn and shame that any brute creature would make. Against their wishes, we penetrated 2 or 3 leagues inland with 25 armed men, and when we disembarked on the shore, they shot at us with their bows and uttered loud cries before fleeing into the woods. We did not find anything of great value in this land, except for the vast forests and some hills which could contain some metal: for we saw many natives with "paternostri" beads of copper in their ears. . . .

Due to the lack of [a common] language, we were unable to find out by signs or gestures how much religious faith these people we found possess. We think they have neither religion nor laws, that they do not know of a First Cause or Author, that they do not worship the sky, the stars, the sun, the moon, or other planets, nor do they even practice any kind of idolatry; we do not know whether they offer any sacrifices or other prayers, nor are there any temples or churches of prayer among their peoples. We consider that they have no religion and that they live in absolute freedom, and that everything they do proceeds from Ignorance; for they are very easily persuaded, and they imitated everything that they saw us Christians do with regard to divine worship, with the same fervor and enthusiasm that we had.

Questions

1. How much do Verrazano's observations seem to be affected by his own beliefs and experiences?

2. Why does he write that Indians live in "absolute freedom," and why does he consider this a criticism rather than a compliment?

---

3. Bartolomé de las Casas on Spanish Treatment of the Indians, from *History of the Indies* (1528)

Source: History of the Indies, *trans./ed. Andrée Collard. Copyright © 1971 by Andrée Collard, renewed 1999 by Joyce J. Contrucci. Reprinted by permission of Joyce Contrucci.*

Known as the "Apostle of the Indians," Bartolomé de las Casas, a Catholic priest, was the most eloquent critic of Spanish mistreatment of the New World's native population. Las Casas took part in the plunder of Peru and the exploitation of Indian labor on Hispaniola and Cuba. But, in 1514, he freed his Indian slaves and began to preach against the injustices of Spanish rule. In his *History of the Indies*, Las Casas denounced Spain for causing the deaths of millions of innocent people. The excerpt that follows details events on Hispaniola, the Caribbean island first conquered and settled by Spain. Las Casas called for the Indians to enjoy the rights of other subjects of Spain.

Largely because of Las Casas's efforts, Spain in 1542 promulgated the New Laws, ordering that Indians no longer be enslaved. But Spain's European rivals seized upon Las Casas's criticisms to justify their own ambitions. His writings became the basis for the Black Legend, the image of Spain as a uniquely cruel empire. Other nations would claim that their imperial ventures were inspired by the desire to rescue Indians from Spanish rule.

IN THAT YEAR of 1500, . . . the King determined to send a new governor to Hispaniola, which at the time was the only seat of government in the Indies. The new governor was fray Nicolás de Ovando, Knight of Alcántara, and at that time comendador of Lares.

• • •

At first, the Indians were forced to stay six months away at work; later, the time was extended to eight months and this was called a shift, at the end of which they brought all the gold for minting. The King's part was subtracted and the rest went to individuals, but for years no one kept a single peso because they owed it all to merchants and other creditors, so that the anguish and torments endured by the Indians in mining that infernal gold were consumed entirely by God and no one prospered. During the minting period, the Indians were allowed to go home, a few days' journey on foot. One can imagine their state when they arrived after eight months, and those who found their wives there must have cried, lamenting their condition together. How could they even rest, since they had to provide for the needs of their family when their land had gone to weeds? Of those who had worked in the mines, a bare 10 per cent survived to start the journey home. Many Spaniards had no scruples about making them work on Sundays and holidays, if not in the mines then on minor tasks such as building and repairing houses, carrying firewood, etc. They fed them cassava bread, which is adequate nutrition only when supplemented with meat, fish or other more substantial food. The minero killed a pig once a week but he kept more than half for himself and had the leftover apportioned and cooked daily for thirty or forty Indians, which came to a bite of meat the size of a walnut per individual, and they dipped the cassava in this as well as in the broth.

• • •

The comendador arranged to have wages paid as follows, which I swear is the truth: in exchange for his life of services, an Indian received 3 *maravedís* every two days, less one-half a *maravedí* in order not to exceed the yearly half gold peso, that is, 225 *maravedís*, paid them once a year as pin money or *cacona*, as Indians call it, which means bonus or reward. This sum bought a comb, a small mirror and a string of green or blue glass beads, and many did without that consolation for they were paid much less and had no way of mitigating their misery, although in truth, they offered their labor up for nothing, caring only to fill their stomachs to appease their raging hunger and find ways to escape from their desperate lives. For this loss of body and soul, then, they received less than 3 *maravedís* for two days; many years later their wages were increased to 1 gold peso by the order of King Hernando, and this was no less an affront, as I will show later.

I believe the above clearly demonstrates that the Indians were totally deprived of their freedom and were put in the harshest, fiercest, most horrible servitude and captivity which no one who has not seen it can understand. Even beasts enjoy more freedom when they are allowed to graze in the fields. But our Spaniards gave no such opportunity to Indians and truly considered them perpetual slaves, since the Indians had not the free will to dispose of their persons but instead were disposed of according to Spanish greed and cruelty, not as men in captivity but as beasts tied to a rope to prevent free movement. When they were allowed to go home, they often found it deserted and had no other recourse than to go out into the woods to find food and to die. When they fell ill, which was very frequently because they are a delicate people unaccustomed to such work, the Spaniards did not believe them and pitilessly called them lazy dogs, and kicked and beat them; and when illness was apparent they sent them home as useless, giving them some cassava for the twenty- to eighty-league journey. They would go then, falling into the first stream and dying there in desperation; others would hold on longer but very few ever made it home. I sometimes came upon dead bodies on my way, and upon others who were gasping and moaning in their death agony, repeating "Hungry, hungry." And this was the freedom, the good treatment and the Christianity that Indians received.

• • •

About eight years passed under the comendador's rule and this disorder had time to grow; no one gave it a thought and the multitude of people who originally lived on this island . . . was consumed at such a rate that in those eight years 90 per cent had perished. From here this sweeping plague went to San Juan, Jamaica, Cuba and the continent, spreading destruction over the whole hemisphere.

• • •

Questions

1. What do you think Las Casas hoped to accomplish by writing so critically about Spanish treatment of the Indians?

2. Why, after describing illness and starvation among the Indians, does Las Casas write,"this was the freedom, the good treatment and the Christianity that Indians received"?

4. The Pueblo Revolt (1680)

*Source: Charles W. Hackett, Declarations of Josephe and Pedro Naranjo,
Revolt of the Pueblo Indians of New Mexico and Otermín's Attempted
Reconquest 1680–1682, Volume 2, pp. 238–48, 1942. Reprinted with
permission of the University of New Mexico Press.*

In 1680, the Pueblo Indians of modern-day New Mexico revolted against Spanish rule. During the seventeenth century, governors, settlers, and missionaries
had sought to exploit the labor of an Indian population that declined from
about 60,000 in 1600 to some 17,000 eighty years later. Franciscan friars
worked diligently, often violently, to convert Indians to Catholicism. Some natives accepted baptism. But the friars' efforts to stamp out traditional religious
ceremonies in New Mexico—they burned Indian idols, masks, and other sacred objects—alienated far more Indians than they converted. Under the leadership of Popé, a local religious leader, the rebelling Indians killed 400
colonists, including twenty-one Franciscan missionaries. The Pueblo Revolt
was the most complete victory for native Americans over Europeans and the
only wholesale expulsion of settlers in the history of North America. The uprising, concluded a royal attorney who interviewed survivors in Mexico City,
arose from the "many oppressions" the Indians had suffered. In 1692, the Spanish launched an invasion that reconquered New Mexico.

―――――――――――

DECLARATION OF JOSEPHE, SPANISH-SPEAKING INDIAN.
[PLACE OF THE RIO DEL NORTE, DECEMBER 19, 1681.]

Asked what causes or motives the said Indian rebels had for re-
nouncing the law of God and obedience to his Majesty, and for committing so many kinds of crimes, and who were the instigators of the
rebellion, and what he had heard while he was among the apostates,
he said that the prime movers of the rebellion were two Indians of
San Juan, one named El Popé and the other El Taqu, and another from
Taos named Saca, and another from San Ildefonso named Francisco.
He knows that these were the principals, and the causes they gave

were alleged ill treatment and injuries received from the present secretary, Francisco Xavier, and the maestre de campo, Alonso García, and from the sargentos mayores, Luis de Quintana and Diego López, because they beat them, took away what they had, and made them work without pay. Thus he replies.

Asked if he has learned or it has come to his notice during the time that he has been here the reason why the apostates burned the images, churches, and things pertaining to divine worship, making a mockery and a trophy of them, killing the priests and doing the other things they did, he said that he knows and has heard it generally stated that while they were besieging the villa the rebellious traitors burned the church and shouted in loud voices, "Now the God of the Spaniards, who was their father, is dead, and Santa Maria, who was their mother, and the saints, who were pieces of rotten wood," saying that only their own god lived. Thus they ordered all the temples and images, crosses and rosaries burned, and this function being over, they all went to bathe in the rivers, saying that they thereby washed away the water of baptism. For their churches, they placed on the four sides and in the center of the plaza some small circular enclosures of stone where they went to offer flour, feathers, and the seed of maguey, maize, and tobacco, and performed other superstitious rites, giving the children to understand that they must all do this in the future. The captains and chiefs ordered that the names of Jesus and of Mary should nowhere be uttered, and that they should discard their baptismal names, and abandon the wives whom God had given them in matrimony, and take the ones that they pleased. He saw that as soon as the remaining Spaniards had left, they ordered all the estufas erected, which are their houses of idolatry, and danced throughout the kingdom the dance of the cazina, making many masks for it in the image of the devil. Thus he replied to this question. . . .

Asked if he knows, or whether it has come to his notice, that the said apostates have erected houses of idolatry which they call estufas in the pueblos, and have practiced dances and superstitions, he said there is a general report throughout the kingdom that they have done so and he has seen many houses of idolatry which they have built, dancing the dance of the cachina, which this declarant has also danced. Thus he replies to the question.

DECLARATION OF PEDRO NARANJO OF THE QUERES NATION.
[PLACE OF THE RÍO DEL NORTE, DECEMBER 19, 1681.]

Asked for what reason they so blindly burned the images, temples, crosses, and other things of divine worship, he stated that the said Indian, Popé, came down in person, and with him El Saca and El Chato from the pueblo of Los Taos, and other captains and leaders and many people who were in his train, and he ordered in all the pueblos through which he passed that they instantly break up and burn the images of the holy Christ, the Virgin Mary and the other saints, the crosses, and everything pertaining to Christianity, and that they burn the temples, break up the bells, and separate from the wives whom God had given them in marriage and take those whom they desired. In order to take away their baptismal names, the water, and the holy oils, they were to plunge into the rivers and wash themselves with amole, which is a root native to the country, washing even their clothing, with the understanding that there would thus be taken from them the character of the holy sacraments. They did this, and also many other things which he does not recall, given to understand that this mandate had come from the Caydi and the other two who emitted fire from their extremities in the said estufa of Taos, and that they thereby returned to the state of their antiquity, as when they came from the lake of Copala; that this was the better life and the one they desired, because the God of the Spaniards was worth nothing and theirs was very strong, the Spaniards's God being rotten wood. These things were observed and obeyed by all except some who, moved by the zeal of Christians, opposed it, and such persons the said Popé caused to be killed immediately. He saw to it that they at once erected and rebuilt their houses of idolatry which they call estufas, and made very ugly masks in imitation of the devil in order to dance the dance of the cacina; and he said likewise that the devil had given them to understand that living thus in accordance with the law of their ancestors, they would harvest a great deal of maize, many beans, a great abundance of cotton, calabashes, and very large watermelons and cantaloupes; and that they could erect their houses and enjoy abundant health and leisure.

Questions

1. What actions did Indians take during the Pueblo Revolt to demonstrate their new freedom from Spanish rule?

2. Why do you think religion played so large a role in the Pueblo Revolt?

5. Father Jean de Brébeuf on the Customs and Beliefs of the Hurons (1635)

Source: Reuben G. Thwaites, ed., The Jesuit Relations and Allied Documents: Travels and Explorations of the Jesuit Missionaries in New France, 1610–1791 *(Cleveland, 1896–1901), Vol. 12, pp. 117–24.*

With its small white population and emphasis on the fur trade rather than agricultural settlement, the viability of New France depended on friendly relations with local Indians. They neither appropriated substantial amounts of Indian land like the English nor conquered native inhabitants militarily and set them to forced labor, as in Spanish America. The Jesuits, a missionary religious order, sought to convert Indians to Catholicism. One of the Jesuit missionaries to the Huron people in modern-day Quebec, Jean de Brébeuf, left a vivid description of the lives and customs of the Indians. In the following excerpt, he dwells upon their religious beliefs, marriage customs, and gender relations—all aspects of Indian life that seemed very alien to Europeans—and describes how he tried to convert them. De Brébeuf was killed after being captured during a war between Hurons and Iroquois in 1649.

IT REMAINS NOW to say something of the country, of the manners and customs of the Hurons, of the inclination they have to the Faith, and of our insignificant labors.

As to the first, the little paper and leisure we have compels me to say in a few words what might justly fill a volume. The Huron country is not large, its greatest extent can be traversed in three or four days. Its situation is fine, the greater part of it consisting of plains. It is surrounded and intersected by a number of very beautiful lakes or rather seas, whence it comes that the one to the North and to the Northwest is called "fresh-water sea." [Lake Huron]... There are twenty Towns, which indicate about 30,000 souls speaking the same tongue, which is not difficult to one who has a master. It has distinctions of genders, number, tense, person, moods; and, in short, it is very complete and very regular, contrary to the opinion of many....

It is so evident that there is a Divinity who has made Heaven and earth that our Hurons cannot entirely ignore it. But they misapprehend him grossly. For they have neither Temples, nor Priests, nor Feasts, nor any ceremonies.

They say that a certain woman called *Eataensic* is the one who made earth and man. They give her an assistant, one named *Jouskeha*, whom they declare to be her little son, with whom she governs the world. This *Jouskeha* has care of the living, and of the things that concern life, and consequently they say that he is good. *Eataensic* has care of souls; and, because they believe that she makes men die, they say that she is wicked. And there are among them mysteries so hidden that only the old men, who can speak with authority about them, are believed.

This God and Goddess live like themselves, but without famine; make feasts as they do, are lustful as they are; in short, they imagine them exactly like themselves. And still, though they make them human and corporeal, they seem nevertheless to attribute to them a certain immensity in all places.

They say that this *Eataensic* fell from the Sky, where there are inhabitants as on earth, and when she fell, she was with child. If you ask them who made the sky and its inhabitants, they have no other reply than that they know nothing about it. And when we preach to them of one God, Creator of Heaven and earth, and of all things, and even when we talk to them of Hell and Paradise and of our other mysteries, the headstrong reply that this is good for our Country and not for theirs; that every Country has its own fashions. But having pointed out to them, by means of a little globe that we had brought, that there is only one world, they remain without reply.

I find in their marriage customs two things that greatly please me; the first, that they have only one wife; the second, that they do not marry their relatives in a direct or collateral line, however distant they may be. There is, on the other hand, sufficient to censure, were it only the frequent changes the men make of their wives, and the women of their husbands.

They believe in the immortality of the soul, which they believe to be corporeal. The greatest part of their Religion consists of this point. We have seen several stripped, or almost so, of all their goods, because several of their friends were dead, to whose souls they had made presents. Moreover, dogs, fish, deer, and other animals have, in their opinion, immortal and reasonable souls. In proof of this, the old men relate certain fables, which they represent as true; they make no mention either of punishment or reward, in the place to which souls go after death. And so they do not make any distinction between the good and the bad, the virtuous and the vicious; and they honor equally the interment of both, even as we have seen in the case of a young man who poisoned himself from the grief he felt because his wife had been taken away from him. Their superstitions are infinite, their feast, their medicines, their fishing, their hunting, their wars,—in short almost their whole life turns upon this pivot; dreams, above all have here great credit.

As regards morals, the Hurons are lascivious, although in two leading points less so than many Christians, who will blush some day in their presence. You will see no kissing nor immodest caressing; and in marriage a man will remain two or three years apart from his wife, while she is nursing. They are gluttons, even to disgorging;

it is true, that does not happen often, but only in some superstitious feasts,—these, however, they do not attend willingly. Besides they endure hunger much better than we,—so well that after having fasted two or three entire days you will see them still paddling, carrying loads, singing, laughing, bantering, as if they had dined well. They are very lazy, are liars, thieves, pertinacious beggars. Some consider them vindictive; but, in my opinion, this vice is more noticeable elsewhere than here.

We see shining among them some rather noble moral virtues. You note, in the first place, a great love and union, which they are careful to cultivate by means of their marriages, of their presents, of their feasts, and of their frequent visits. On returning from their fishing, their hunting, and their trading, they exchange many gifts; if they have thus obtained something unusually good, even if they have bought it, or if it has been given to them, they make a feast to the whole village with it. Their hospitality towards all sorts of strangers is remarkable; they present to them, in their feasts, the best of what they have prepared, and, as I have already said, I do not know if anything similar, in this regard, is to be found anywhere. They never close the door upon a Stranger, and, once having received him into their houses, they share with him the best they have; they never send him away, and when he goes away of his own accord, he repays them by a simple "thank you."

• • •

About the month of December, the snow began to lie on the ground, and the savages settled down into the village. For, during the whole Summer and Autumn, they are for the most part either in their rural cabins, taking care of their crops, or on the lake fishing, or trading; which makes it not a little inconvenient to instruct them. Seeing them, therefore, thus gathered together at the beginning of this year, we resolved to preach publicly to all, and to acquaint them with the reason of our coming into their Country, which is not for their furs, but to declare to them the true God and his son, Jesus Christ, the universal Saviour of our souls.

The usual method that we follow is this: We call together the people by the help of the Captain of the village, who assembles them all in our house as in Council, or perhaps by the sound of the bell. I use the surplice and the square cap, to give more majesty to my appearance. At the beginning we chant on our knees the *Pater noster*, translated into Huron verse. Father Daniel, as its author, chants a couplet alone, and then we all together chant it again; and those among the Hurons, principally the little ones, who already know it, take pleasure in chanting it with us. That done, when every one is seated, I rise and make the sign of the Cross for all; then, having recapitulated what I said last time, I explain something new. After that we question the young children and the girls, giving a little bead of glass or porcelain to those who deserve it. The parents are very glad to see their children answer well and carry off some little prize, of which they render themselves worthy by the care they take to come privately to get instruction. On our part, to arouse their emulation, we have each lesson retraced by our two little French boys, who question each other,—which transports the Savages with admiration. Finally the whole is concluded by the talk of the Old Men, who propound their difficulties, and sometimes make me listen in my turn to the statement of their belief.

Two things among others have aided us very much in the little we have been able to do here, by the grace of our Lord; the first is, as I have already said, the good health that God has granted us in the midst of sickness so general and so widespread. The second is the temporal assistance we have rendered to the sick. Having brought for ourselves some few delicacies, we shared them with them, giving to one a few prunes, and to another a few raisins, to others something else. The poor people came from great distances to get their share.

Questions

1. Which aspects of Indian practices and beliefs does de Brébeuf find admirable and which does he criticize most strongly?

2. How do Huron gender and family relations seem to differ from those of
Europeans?

6. A Micmac Indian Replies to the French (1677)

Source: William F. Ganong, trans. and ed., New Relation of Gaspesia, with
the Customs and Religion of the Gaspesian Indians, by Chrestien
LeClerq *(Toronto, 1910), pp. 104–06.*

Nearly all European colonizers were convinced of the superiority of their
own culture to that of the Indians. Many Indians, while anxious to benefit
from trade with the technologically more advanced Europeans, did not
share this view. In the excerpt that follows, Chrestien LeClerq, a French
priest who traveled among the Micmac Indians of the Gaspe peninsula of
Quebec, reproduces an Indian leader's response to French assertions of superiority, defending the Indian's way of life.

THOU REPROACHEST US, very inappropriately, that our country is
a little hell in contrast with France, which thou comparest to a terrestrial paradise, inasmuch as it yields thee, so thou sayest, every
kind of provision in abundance. Thou sayest of us also that we are
the most miserable and most unhappy of all men, living without religion, without manners, without honour, without social order, and,
in a word, without any rules, like the beasts in our woods and our
forests, lacking bread, wine, and a thousand other comforts which
thou hast in superfluity in Europe. Well, my brother, if thou dost not
yet know the real feelings which our Indians have towards thy country and towards all thy nation, it is proper that I inform thee at once.
I beg thee now to believe that, all miserable as we seem in thine eyes,
we consider ourselves nevertheless much happier than thou in this,

that we are very content with the little that we have; and believe also once for all, I pray, that thou deceivest thyself greatly if thou thinkest to persuade us that thy country is better than ours. For if France, as thou sayest, is a little terrestrial paradise, art thou sensible to leave it? And why abandon wives, children, relatives, and friends? Why risk thy life and thy property every year, and why venture thyself with such risk, in any season whatsoever, to the storms and tempests of the sea in order to come to a strange and barbarous country which thou considerest the poorest and least fortunate of the world? Besides, since we are wholly convinced of the contrary, we scarcely take the trouble to go to France, because we fear, with good reason, lest we find little satisfaction there, seeing, in our own experience, that those who are natives thereof leave it every year in order to enrich themselves on our shores. We believe, further, that you are also incomparably poorer than we, and that you are only simple journeymen, valets, servants, and slaves, all masters and grand captains though you may appear, seeing that you glory in our old rags and in our miserable suits of beaver which can no longer be of use to us, and that you find among us, in the fishery for cod which you make in these parts, the wherewithal to comfort your misery and the poverty which oppresses you. As to us, we find all our riches and all our conveniences among ourselves, without trouble and without exposing our lives to the dangers in which you find yourselves constantly through your long voyages. And, whilst feeling compassion for you in the sweetness of our repose, we wonder at the anxieties and cares which you give yourselves night and day in order to load your ship. We see also that all your people live, as a rule, only upon cod which you catch among us. It is everlastingly nothing but cod—cod in the morning, cod at midday, cod at evening, and always cod, until things come to such a pass that if you wish some good morsels, it is at our expense; and you are obliged to have recourse to the Indians, whom you despise so much, and to beg them to go a-hunting that you may be regaled. Now tell me this one little thing, if thou hast any sense: Which of these two is the wisest and happiest—he who labours without ceasing and only obtains, and that with great trouble, enough to live on, or he who rests in comfort and finds all that he needs in the pleasure of hunting and fishing? It is true, . . . that we have not always had the use of bread and of wine which your France produces; but, in fact, before the arrival of the French in these parts, did not the Gaspesians live much longer than now? And if we have not any longer among us any of those old men of a hundred and thirty to forty years, it is only because we are gradually adopting your manner of living, for experience is making it very plain that those of us live longest who, despising your bread, your wine, and your brandy, are content with their natural food of beaver, of moose, of waterfowl, and fish, in accord with the custom of our ancestors and of all the Gaspesian nation. Learn now, my brother, once for all, because I must open to thee my heart: there is no Indian who does not consider himself infinitely more happy and more powerful than the French.

Questions

1. Why does the Micmac leader claim that Indians consider themselves "infinitely more happy and more powerful than the French"?

2. How does the Indian leader interpret French migration from Europe to North America?

CHAPTER 2

Beginnings of English America, 1607–1660

7. Richard Hakluyt, an Argument for Colonization from *A Discourse Concerning Western Planting* (1584)

Source: Richard Hakluyt, "A Discourse Concerning Western Planting" [1584], Collections of the Maine Historical Society, Series 2, Vol. 2 (1877), pp. 152–61.

In *A Discourse Concerning Western Planting*, written in 1584, the Protestant minister and scholar Richard Hakluyt listed twenty-three reasons why Queen Elizabeth I should support the establishment of English colonies in North America. Hakluyt's arguments covered almost every possible benefit that might arise from colonization—economic, political, religious, nationalist, and social. Colonists would enrich the mother country and themselves by providing goods now supplied by foreigners and opening a new market for English products. America could be a refuge for England's "surplus" population. Hakluyt urged the government to settle "wandering beggars" in America, where they could become productive citizens, contributing to the nation's wealth.

For England, Hakluyt insisted, empire and freedom went hand in hand. English settlements would help to rescue the New World and its inhabitants from the influence of Catholicism and tyranny. Indians oppressed by Spain, he proclaimed, would welcome the British as bearers of "liberty."

A BRIEF COLLECTION of certain reasons to induce her Majesty and the state to take in hand the western voyage and the planting there.

1. The soil yields and may be made to yield all the several commodities of Europe. . . .

2. The passage thither and home is neither too long nor too short, but easy, and to be made twice in the year.

3. The passage cuts not near the trade of any prince, nor near any of their countries or territories, and is a safe passage, and not easy to be annoyed by prince or potentate whatsoever.

• • •

6. This enterprise may stay the Spanish king from flowing over all the face of that waste firmament of America, if we seat and plant there in time. . . . And England possessing the purposed place of planting, her Majesty may, by the benefit of the seat, having won good and royal havens, have plenty of excellent trees for masts, of goodly timber to build ships and to make great navies, of pitch, tar, hemp, and all things incident for a navy royal, and that for no price, and without money or request. How easy a matter may it be to this realm, swarming at this day with valiant youths, rusting and hurtful by lack of employment, and having good makers of cable and of all sorts of cordage, and the best and most cunning shipwrights of the world, to be lords of all those seas, and to spoil Philip's . . . navy, and to deprive him of yearly passage of his treasure to Europe, and consequently to abate the pride of Spain and of the supporter of the great Anti-christ of Rome, and to pull him down in equality to his neighbour princes, and consequently to cut off the common mischiefs that come to all Europe by the peculiar abundance of his Indian treasure, and this without difficulty.

7. This voyage, albeit it may be accomplished by bark or smallest pinnace for advice or for a necessity, yet for the distance, for burden and gain in trade, the merchant will not for profit's sake use it but by ships of great burden; so as this realm shall have by that means ships of great burden and of great strength for the defence of this realm.

• • •

✗ **10.** No foreign commodity that comes into England comes without payment of custom once, twice, or thrice, before it comes into the realm, and so all foreign commodities become dearer to the subjects of this realm; and by this course . . . foreign princes' customs are avoided; and the foreign commodities cheaply purchased, they become cheap to the subjects of England, to the common benefit of the people, and to the saving of great treasure in the realm; whereas now the realm becomes poor by the purchasing of foreign commodities in so great a mass at so excessive prices.

✗ **11.** At the first traffic with the people of those parts, the subjects of this realm for many years shall change many cheap commodities of these parts for things of high value there not esteemed; and this to the great enriching of the realm, if common use fail not.

• • •

13. By making of ships and by preparing of things for the same, by making of cables and cordage, by planting of vines and olive trees, and by making of wine and oil, by husbandry, and by thousands of things there to be done, infinite numbers of the English nation may be set on work, to the unburdening of the realm with many that now live chargeable to the state at home.

• • •

✗ **16.** We shall by planting there enlarge the glory of the gospel, and from England plant sincere religion, and provide a safe and a sure place to receive people from all parts of the world that are forced to flee for the truth of God's word.

• • •

18. The Spaniards govern in the Indies with all pride and tyranny; and like as when people of contrary nature at sea enter into galleys, where men are tied as slaves, all yell and cry with one voice, *Liberta, liberta,* as desirous of liberty and freedom, so no doubt whensoever the Queen of England, a prince of such clemency, shall seat upon that firmament of America, and shall be reported throughout all that tract to use the natural people there with all humanity, courtesy, and freedom, they will yield themselves to her government, and revolt clean from the Spaniard.

• • •

21. Many soldiers and servitors, in the end of the wars, that might be hurtful to this realm, may there be unladen, to the common profit and quiet of this realm, and to our foreign benefit there, as they may be employed.

22. The . . . wandering beggars of England, that grow up idly, and hurtful and burdenous to this realm, may there be unladen, better bred up, and may people waste countries to the home and foreign benefit, and to their own more happy state.

Questions

1. Why does Hakluyt think the Indians of North America will welcome English colonizers as bearers of liberty?

2. Why does Hakluyt seem to be so intent on reducing the power of Spain?

---

8. Sending Women to Virginia (1622)

Source: Susan Myra Kingsbury, ed., The Records of the Virginia Company of London *(Washington, D.C., 1906–35), Vol. 1, pp. 256–57.*

Early Virginia lacked one essential element of English society—stable family life. Given the demand for male servants to work in the tobacco fields, for most of the seventeenth century, men in the Chesapeake outnumbered women by four or five to one. The Virginia Company avidly promoted the immigration of women, sending "tobacco brides" to the colony in 1620 and 1621 for arranged marriages (so-called because the husband was ordered to give a payment in tobacco to his wife). The company preferred that the women marry only free, independent colonists. Unlike these women, however, the vast majority of women who emigrated to the region in the seventeenth century came as indentured servants. Since they usually had to complete their terms of service before marrying, they did not begin to form families until their mid-twenties. Virginia remained for many years a society with large numbers of single men, widows, and orphans rather than the family-oriented community the company desired.

———

WE SEND YOU in this ship one widow and eleven maids for wives for the people in Virginia. There hath been especial care had in the choice of them; for there hath not any one of them been received but upon good commendations, as by a note herewith sent you may perceive. We pray you all therefore in general to take them into your care; and more especially we recommend them to you Master Pountis, that at their first landing they may be housed, lodged and provided for of diet till they be married, for such was the haste of sending them away, as that straitened with time we had no means to put provisions aboard, which defect shall be supplied by the magazine ship. And in case they cannot be presently married, we desire they may be put to several householders that have wives till they can be provided of husbands. There are near fifty more which are shortly to come, are sent by our most honorable Lord and Treasurer the Earl of Southampton and certain worthy gentlemen, who taking into their consideration that the Plantation can never flourish till families be planted and the respect of wives and children fix the people on the soil, therefore have given this fair beginning, for the reimbursing of whose charges it is ordered that every man that marries them give 120 lbs. weight of the best leaf tobacco for each of them, and in case any of them die, that proportion must be advanced to make it up upon those that survive ... And though we are desirous that marriage be free according to the law of nature, yet would we not have these maids deceived and married to servants, but only to freemen or tenants as have means to maintain them. We pray you therefore to be fathers to them in this business, not enforcing them to marry against their wills; neither send we them to be servants, save in case of extremity, for we would have their condition so much bettered as multitudes may be allured thereby to come unto you.

And you may assure such men as marry those women that the first servants sent over by the Company shall be consigned to them, it being our intent to preserve families and to prefer married men before single persons.

Questions

1. What advantages does the Virginia Company see in the promotion of family life in the colony?

2. Why does the company prefer that the women marry landowning men rather than servants?

---

9. Maryland Act Concerning Religion (1644)

Source: William H. Browne et al., eds., Archives of Maryland, *Vol. 1 (1883), pp. 244–46.*

Religious liberty in a modern sense existed in very few parts of the Atlantic world of the seventeenth century. Most nations and colonies had established churches, supported by public funds, and outlawed various religious groups that rulers deemed dangerous or disruptive. Among the early English colonies in North America, Maryland stood out as an exception. It was established in 1632 as a grant of land and government authority to Cecilius Calvert, a Catholic who hoped to demonstrate that Protestants and Catholics could live in a harmony unknown in Europe. Protestants made up a majority of the settlers, but the early colonists included a number of Catholic gentlemen and priests, and Calvert appointed many Catholics to public office.

With the religious-political battles of the English Civil War echoing in the colony, Maryland in the 1640s verged on total anarchy. To help reestablish order, Maryland in 1649 adopted an Act Concerning Religion, which institutionalized the principle of toleration that had prevailed from the colony's beginning. It provided punishment for anyone who "troubled or molested" a Christian for religious reasons. Repealed and reenacted several times in the decades that followed the act was a milestone in the early history of religious freedom in America.

———

FORASMUCH AS IN a well governed and Christian Commonwealth matters concerning religion and the honor of God ought in the first place to be taken into serious consideration and endeavored to be settled, be it therefore ordered and enacted . . .

That whatsoever person or persons within the Province . . . shall from henceforth blaspheme God, that is curse Him, or deny our Savior Jesus Christ to be the son of God, or shall deny the Holy Trinity, the father, son, and Holy Ghost, or the Godhead of any of the said three persons of the Trinity or the unity of the Godhead, or shall use or utter any reproachful speeches, words, or language concerning the same Holy Trinity, or any of the said three persons thereof, shall be punished with death and confiscation or forfeiture of all his or her lands and goods to the Lord Proprietary and his heirs. . . .

And whereas the enforcing of the conscience in matters of religion has frequently fallen out to be of dangerous consequence in those commonwealths where it has been practiced, and for the more quiet and peaceable government of this Province, and the better to preserve mutual love and amity among the inhabitants thereof. Be it therefore . . . enacted (except as in this present Act is before declared and set forth) that no person or persons whatever in the Province . . . professing to believe in Jesus Christ, shall from henceforth be any ways troubled, molested, or discountenanced for or in respect of his or her religion nor in the free exercise thereof within the Province . . . nor any way compelled to the belief or exercise of any other religion against his or her consent, so [long] as they be not unfaithful to the Lord Proprietary, or molest or conspire against the civil government established or to be established in this Province under him or his heirs.

And that all and every person and persons that shall presume contrary to this Act and the true intent and meaning thereof directly or indirectly either in person or estate willfully to wrong, disturb, trouble, or molest any person whatsoever within this Province professing to believe in Jesus Christ for or in respect of his or her religion or the free exercise thereof within this Province other than is provided for in this Act, that such person or persons so offending shall be compelled to pay triple damages to the party so wronged or molested, and for every such offense shall also forfeit £20 sterling in money or the value thereof, half thereof for the use of the Lord Proprietary ... and the other half for the use of the party so wronged or molested as aforesaid. Or, if the party so offending as aforesaid shall refuse or be unable to recompense the party so wronged, or to satisfy such fine or forfeiture, then such offender shall be severely punished by public whipping and imprisonment.

Questions

1. Members of which religious groups would be excluded from toleration under the Maryland law?

2. What does the law refer to as the major reasons for instituting religious toleration?

10. John Winthrop, Speech to the Massachusetts General Court (1645)

Source: John Winthrop, Speech to the General Court of Massachusetts, July 3, 1645, in James Savage, The History of New England from 1630 to 1649 by John Winthrop *(Boston, 1825–26), Vol. 2, pp. 279–82.*

The early settlers of New England were mainly Puritans, English Protestants who believed that the Church of England in the early seventeenth century retained too many elements of Catholicism. Like other emigrants to America, Puritans came in search of liberty, especially the right to worship and govern themselves in what they deemed a Christian manner. Freedom for Puritans had nothing to do with either religious toleration or unrestrained individual behavior. In a 1645 speech to the Massachusetts legislature explaining the Puritan conception of freedom, Governor John Winthrop distinguished sharply between two kinds of liberty. "Natural" liberty, or acting without restraint, suggested "a liberty to [do] evil." "Moral" liberty meant "a liberty to do only what is good." It meant obedience to religious and governmental authority— following God's law and the law of rulers like Winthrop himself.

Winthrop's distinction between "moral" and "natural" liberty has been invoked many times by religious groups who feared that Americans were becoming selfish and immoral and who tried to impose their moral standards on society as a whole.

• • •

THE GREAT QUESTIONS that have troubled the country, are about the authority of the magistrates and the liberty of the people. It is yourselves who have called us to this office, and being called by you, we have our authority from God, in way of an ordinance, such as hath the image of God eminently stamped upon it, the contempt and violation whereof hath been vindicated with examples of divine vengeance. I entreat you to consider, that when you choose magistrates, you take them from among yourselves, men subject to like passions as you are. Therefore when you see infirmities in us, you should reflect upon your own, and that would make you bear the more with us, and not be severe censurers of the failings of your magistrates, when you have continual experience of the like infirmities in yourselves and others. We account him a good servant, who breaks not his covenant. The covenant between you and us is the oath you have taken of us, which is to this purpose, that we shall govern you and judge your causes by the rules of God's laws and our own, according to our best skill. When you agree with a workman to build you a ship or house, etc., he undertakes as well for his skill as for his faithfulness, for it is his profession, and you pay him for both. But when you call one to be a magistrate, he doth not profess nor undertake to have sufficient skill for that office, nor can you furnish him with gifts, etc., therefore you must run the hazard of his skill and ability. But if he fail in faithfulness, which by his oath he is bound unto, that he must answer for. If it fall out that the case be clear to common apprehension, and the rule clear also, if he transgress here, the error is not in the skill, but in the evil of the will: it must be required of him. But if the case be doubtful, or the rule doubtful, to men of such understanding and parts as your magistrates are, if your magistrates should err here, yourselves must bear it.

For the other point concerning liberty, I observe a great mistake in the country about that. There is a twofold liberty, natural (I mean as our nature is now corrupt) and civil or federal. The first is common to man with beasts and other creatures. By this, man, as he stands in relation to man simply, hath liberty to do what he lists; it is a liberty to evil as well as to good. This liberty is incompatible and inconsistent with authority, and cannot endure the least restraint of the most just authority. The exercise and maintaining of this liberty makes men grow more evil, and in time to be worse than brute beasts. . . . This is that great enemy of truth and peace, that wild beast, which all the ordinances of God are bent against, to restrain and subdue it. The other kind of liberty I call civil or federal, it may also be termed moral, in reference to the covenant between God and man, in the moral law, and the politic covenants and constitutions, amongst men themselves. This liberty is the proper end and object of authority, and cannot subsist without it; and it is a liberty to that only which is good, just, and honest. This liberty you are to stand for, with the hazard (not only of your goods, but) of your lives, if need be. Whatsoever crosseth this, is not authority, but a distemper thereof. This liberty is maintained and exercised in a way of subjection to authority; it is of the same kind of liberty wherewith Christ hath made us free. The woman's own choice makes such a man her husband; yet being so chosen, he is her lord, and she is to be subject to him, yet in a way of liberty, not of bondage; and a true wife accounts her subjection her honor and freedom, and would not think her condition safe and free, but in her subjection to her husband's authority. Such is the liberty of the church under the authority of Christ, her king and husband; his yoke is so easy and sweet to her as a bride's ornaments; and if through forwardness or wantonness, etc., she shake it off, at any time, she is at no rest in her spirit, until she take it up again; and whether her lord smiles upon her, and embraceth her in his arms, or whether he frowns, or rebukes, or smites her, she apprehends the sweetness of his love in all, and is refreshed, supported, and instructed by every such dispensation of his authority over her. On the other side, ye know who they are that complain of this yoke and say, let us break their bands, etc., we will not have this man to rule over us. Even so, brethren, it will be between you and your magistrates. If you stand for your natural corrupt liberties, and will do what is good in your own eyes, you will not endure the least weight of authority, but will murmur, and oppose, and be always striving to shake off that yoke; but if you will be satisfied to enjoy such civil and lawful liberties, such as Christ allows you, then will you quietly and cheerfully submit unto that authority which is set over you, in all the administrations of it, for your good. Wherein, if we fail at anytime, we hope we shall be willing (by God's assistance) to hearken to good advice from any of you, or in any other way of God; so shall your liberties be preserved, in upholding the honor and power of authority amongst you.

Questions

1. Why does Winthrop use an analogy to the status of women within the family to explain his understanding of liberty?

2. Why does Winthrop consider "natural" liberty dangerous?

---

11. The Trial of Anne Hutchinson (1637)

Source: Reprinted by permission of the publisher from Thomas Hutchinson, **The History of the Colony and Province of Massachusetts Bay,** *Vol. II,* *edited by Lawrence Shaw Mayo, pp. 366–91, Cambridge, Mass.: Harvard University Press, Copyright © 1963 by the President and Fellows of Harvard College.*

A midwife and the daughter of a clergyman, Anne Hutchinson arrived in Massachusetts with her husband in 1634. She began holding meetings in her home where she led discussions of religious issues. Hutchinson charged that most of the ministers in Massachusetts were guilty of faulty preaching by distinguishing "saints" predestined to go to Heaven from the damned through activities such as church attendance and moral behavior rather than by an inner state of grace.

   In 1637, Hutchinson was placed on trial before a civil court for sedition (expressing opinions dangerous to authority). Hutchinson's examination by John Winthrop and deputy governor Thomas Dudley, excerpted in the following, is a classic example of the collision between established power and individual conscience. For a time, Hutchinson more than held her own. But when she spoke of divine revelations, of God speaking to her directly rather than through ministers or the Bible, she violated Puritan doctrine and sealed her own fate. Hutchinson and a number of her followers were banished.

TRIAL AT THE COURT AT NEWTON. 1637

GOV. JOHN WINTHROP: Mrs. Hutchinson, you are called here as one of those that have troubled the peace of the commonwealth and the churches here; you are known to be a woman that hath had a great share in the promoting and divulging of those opinions that are the cause of this trouble, and to be nearly joined not only in affinity and affection with some of those the court had taken notice of and passed censure upon, but you have spoken divers things, as we have been informed, very prejudicial to the honour of the churches and ministers thereof, and you have maintained a meeting and an assembly in your house that hath been condemned by the general assembly as a thing not tolerable nor comely in the sight of God nor fitting for your sex, and notwithstanding that was cried down you have continued the same. Therefore we have thought good to send for you to understand how things are, that if you be in an erroneous way we may reduce you that so you may become a profitable member here among us. Otherwise if you be obstinate in your course that then the court may take such course that you may trouble us no further. Therefore I would intreat you to express whether you do assent and hold in practice to those opinions and factions that have been handled in court already, that is to say, whether you do not justify Mr. Wheelwright's sermon and the petition.

MRS. ANNE HUTCHINSON: I am called here to answer before you but I hear no things laid to my charge.

GOV. JOHN WINTHROP: I have told you some already and more I can tell you.

MRS. ANNE HUTCHINSON: Name one, Sir.

GOV. JOHN WINTHROP: Have I not named some already?

MRS. ANNE HUTCHINSON: What have I said or done?

GOV. JOHN WINTHROP: Why for your doings, this you did harbor and countenance those that are parties in this faction that you have heard of.

MRS. ANNE HUTCHINSON: That's matter of conscience, Sir.

GOV. JOHN WINTHROP: Your conscience you must keep, or it must be kept for you.

MRS. ANNE HUTCHINSON: Must not I then entertain the saints because I must keep my conscience.

GOV. JOHN WINTHROP: Say that one brother should commit felony or treason and come to his brother's house, if he knows him guilty and conceals him he is guilty of the same. It is his conscience to entertain him, but if his conscience comes into act in giving countenance and entertainment to him that hath broken the law he is guilty too. So if you do countenance those that are transgressors of the law you are in the same fact.

MRS. ANNE HUTCHINSON: What law do they transgress?

GOV. JOHN WINTHROP: The law of God and of the state.

MRS. ANNE HUTCHINSON: In what particular?

GOV. JOHN WINTHROP: Why in this among the rest, whereas the Lord doth say honour thy father and thy mother.

MRS. ANNE HUTCHINSON: Ey Sir in the Lord.

GOV. JOHN WINTHROP: This honour you have broke in giving countenance to them.

MRS. ANNE HUTCHINSON: In entertaining those did I entertain them against any act (for there is the thing) or what God has appointed?

GOV. JOHN WINTHROP: You knew that Mr. Wheelwright did preach this sermon and those that countenance him in this do break a law.

MRS. ANNE HUTCHINSON: What law have I broken?

GOV. JOHN WINTHROP: Why the fifth commandment.

MRS. ANNE HUTCHINSON: I deny that for he (Mr. Wheelwright) saith in the Lord.

GOV. JOHN WINTHROP: You have joined with them in the faction.

MRS. ANNE HUTCHINSON: In what faction have I joined with them?

GOV. JOHN WINTHROP: In presenting the petition.

MRS. ANNE HUTCHINSON: Suppose I had set my hand to the petition. What then?

GOV. JOHN WINTHROP: You saw that case tried before.

MRS. ANNE HUTCHINSON: But I had not my hand to (not signed) the petition.

GOV. JOHN WINTHROP: You have councelled them.

MRS. ANNE HUTCHINSON: Wherein?

GOV. JOHN WINTHROP: Why in entertaining them.

MRS. ANNE HUTCHINSON: What breach of law is that, Sir?

GOV. JOHN WINTHROP: Why dishonouring the commonwealth, Mrs. Hutchinson.

MRS. ANNE HUTCHINSON: But put the case, Sir, that I do fear the Lord and my parents. May not I entertain them that fear the Lord because my parents will not give me leave?

GOV. JOHN WINTHROP: If they be the fathers of the commonwealth, and they of another religion, if you entertain them then you dishonour your parents and are justly punishable.

MRS. ANNE HUTCHINSON: If I entertain them, as they have dishonoured their parents I do.

GOV. JOHN WINTHROP: No but you by countenancing them above others put honor upon them.

MRS. ANNE HUTCHINSON: I may put honor upon them as the children of God and as they do honor the Lord.

GOV. JOHN WINTHROP: We do not mean to discourse with those of your sex but only this: you so adhere unto them and do endeavor to set forward this faction and so you do dishonour us.

MRS. ANNE HUTCHINSON: I do acknowledge no such thing. Neither do I think that I ever put any dishonour upon you.

• • •

GOV. JOHN WINTHROP: Your course is not to be suffered for. Besides that we find such a course as this to be greatly prejudicial to the state. Besides the occasion that it is to seduce many honest persons that are called to those meetings and your opinions and your opinions being known to be different from the word of God may seduce many simple souls that resort unto you. Besides that the occasion which hath come of late hath come from none but such as have frequented your meetings, so that now they are flown off from magistrates and ministers and since they have come to you. And besides that it will not well stand with the commonwealth that families should be neglected for so many neighbors and dames and so much time spent. We see no rule of God for this. We see no that any should have authority to set up any other exercises besides what authority hath already set up and so what hurt comes of this you will be guilty of and we for suffering you.

MRS. ANNE HUTCHINSON: Sir, I do not believe that to be so.

GOV. JOHN WINTHROP: Well, we see how it is. We must therefore put it away from you or restrain you from maintaining this course.

MRS. ANNE HUTCHINSON: If you have a rule for it from God's word you may.

GOV. JOHN WINTHROP: We are your judges, and not you ours and we must compel you to it.

MRS. ANNE HUTCHINSON: If it please you by authority to put it down I will freely let you for I am subject to your authority. . . .

• • •

DEPUTY GOV. THOMAS DUDLEY: I would go a little higher with Mrs. Hutchinson. About three years ago we were all in peace. Mrs. Hutchinson, from that time she came hath made a disturbance, and some that came over with her in the ship did inform me what she was as soon as she was landed. I being then in place dealt with the pastor and teacher of Boston and desired them to enquire of her, and then I was satisfied that she held nothing different from us. But within half a year after, she had vented divers of her strange opinions and had made parties in the country, and at length it comes that Mr. Cotton and Mr. Vane were of her judgment, but Mr. Cotton had cleared himself that he was not of that mind.

• • •

But now it appears by this woman's meeting that Mrs. Hutchinson hath so forestalled the minds of many by their resort to her meeting that now she hath a potent party in the country. Now if all these things have endangered us as from that foundation and if she in particular hath disparaged all our ministers in the land that they have preached a covenant of works, and only Mr. Cotton a covenant of grace, why this is not to be suffered, and therefore being driven to the foundation and it being found that Mrs. Hutchinson is she that hath depraved all the ministers and hath been the cause of what is fallen out, why we must take away the foundation and the building will fall.

MRS. ANNE HUTCHINSON: I pray, Sir, prove it that I said they preached nothing but a covenant of works.

DEP. GOV. THOMAS DUDLEY: Nothing but a covenant of works. Why a Jesuit may preach truth sometimes.

MRS. ANNE HUTCHINSON: Did I ever say they preached a covenant of works then?

DEP. GOV. THOMAS DUDLEY: If they do not preach a covenant of grace clearly, then they preach a covenant of works.

MRS. ANNE HUTCHINSON: No, Sir. One may preach a covenant of grace more clearly than another, so I said. . . .

DEP. GOV. THOMAS DUDLEY: When they do preach a covenant of works do they preach truth?

MRS. ANNE HUTCHINSON: Yes, Sir. But when they preach a covenant of works for salvation, that is not truth.

DEP. GOV. THOMAS DUDLEY: Ask you this: when the ministers do preach a covenant of works do they preach a way of salvation?

MRS. ANNE HUTCHINSON: I did not come hither to answer questions of that sort.

DEP. GOV. THOMAS DUDLEY: Because you will deny the thing.

MRS. ANNE HUTCHINSON: Ey, but that is to be proved first.

DEP. GOV. THOMAS DUDLEY: I will make it plain that you did say that the ministers did preach a covenant of works.

MRS. ANNE HUTCHINSON: I deny that.

DEP. GOV. THOMAS DUDLEY: And that you said they were not able ministers of the New Testament, but Mr. Cotton only.

MRS. ANNE HUTCHINSON: If ever I spake that I proved it by God's word.

• • •

MRS. ANNE HUTCHINSON: If you please to give me leave I shall give round of what I know to be true. Being much troubled to see the falseness of the constitution of the Church of England, I had like to have turned Separatist. Whereupon I kept a day of solemn humiliation and pondering of the thing; this scripture was brought unto me—he that denies Jesus Christ to be come in the flesh is antichrist. This I considered of and in considering found that the papists did not deny him to be come in the flesh, nor we did not deny him—who then was antichrist? Was the Turk antichrist only? The Lord knows that I could not open scripture; he must by his prophetical office open it unto me. So after that being unsatisfied in the thing, the Lord was pleased to bring this scripture out of the Hebrews. He that denies the testament denies the testator, and in this did open unto me and give me to see that those which did not teach the new covenant had the spirit of antichrist, and upon this he did discover the ministry unto me; and ever since, I bless the Lord, he hath let me see which was the clear ministry and which the wrong.

Since that time I confess I have been more choice and he hath left me to distinguish between the voice of my beloved and the voice of Moses, the voice of John the Baptist and the voice of antichrist, for all those voices are spoken of in scripture. Now if you do condemn me for speaking what in my conscience I know to be truth I must commit myself unto the Lord.

MR. NOWEL (ASSISTANT TO THE COURT): How do you know that was the spirit?

MRS. ANNE HUTCHINSON: How did Abraham know that it was God that bid him offer his son, being a breach of the sixth commandment?

DEP. GOV. THOMAS DUDLEY: By an immediate voice.

MRS. ANNE HUTCHINSON: So to me by an immediate revelation.

DEP. GOV. THOMAS DUDLEY: How! an immediate revelation.

• • •

GOV. JOHN WINTHROP: Mrs. Hutchinson, the sentence of the court you hear is that you are banished from out of our jurisdiction as being a woman not fit for our society, and are to be imprisoned till the court shall send you away.

Questions

1. What seem to be the major charges against Anne Hutchinson?

2. What does the Hutchinson case tell us about how Puritan authorities understood the idea of religious freedom?

━━━━━━━━

12. The Levellers, The Agreement of the People Presented to the Council of the Army (1647)

Source: **The Agreement of the People Presented to the Council of the Army** *(London, 1647).*

During the 1640s, the battle for political supremacy in England between the Stuart monarchs James I and Charles I and Parliament culminated in civil war, the temporary overthrow of the monarchy, and, in 1649, the execution of Charles I. This struggle produced an intense public debate over the concept of English freedom. In 1647, the Levellers, history's first democratic political movement, proposed a written constitution, The Agreement of the People, which began by proclaiming "at how high a rate we value our just freedom." At a time when "democracy" was still widely seen as the equivalent of anarchy and disorder, the document proposed to abolish the monarchy and House of Lords and greatly expand the right to vote. It called for religious freedom and equality before the law for all Englishmen.

The Levellers were soon suppressed. But The Agreement of the People offered a glimpse of the modern, democratic definition of freedom as a universal entitlement in a society based on equal rights, rather than the traditional idea of "liberties" as a collection of limited rights defined by social class, with some groups enjoying far more than others.

AN AGREEMENT OF the People for a firm and present peace upon grounds of common right.

Having by our late labors and hazards made it appear to the world at how high a rate we value our just freedom, and God having so far owned our cause as to deliver the enemies thereof into our hands, we do now hold ourselves bound in mutual duty to each other to take the best care we can for the future to avoid both the danger of returning into a slavish condition and the chargeable remedy of another war; for, as it cannot be imagined that so many of our countrymen would have opposed us in this quarrel if they had understood their own good, so may we safely promise to ourselves that, when our common rights and liberties shall be cleared, their endeavors will be disappointed that seek to make themselves our masters. Since, therefore, our former oppressions and scarce-yet-ended troubles have been occasioned, either by want of frequent national meetings in Council, or by rendering those meetings ineffectual, we are fully agreed and resolved to provide that hereafter our representatives be neither left to an uncertainty for the time nor made useless to the ends for which they are intended. In order whereunto we declare:

I

That the people of England, being at this day very unequally distributed by Counties, Cities and Boroughs for the election of their deputies in Parliament, ought to be more indifferently proportioned, according to the number of the inhabitants; the circumstances whereof for number, place, and manner are to be set down before the end of this present Parliament.

II

That, to prevent the many inconveniences apparently arising from the long continuance of the same persons in authority, this present Parliament be dissolved upon the last day of September which shall be in the year of our Lord 1648.

III

That the people do, of course, choose themselves a Parliament once in two years, viz. upon the first Thursday in every second March, after the manner as shall be prescribed before the end of this Parliament, to begin to sit upon the first Thursday in April following, at Westminster or such other place as shall be appointed from time to time by the preceding Representatives, and to continue till the last day of September then next ensuing, and no longer.

IV

That the power of this, and all future Representatives of this Nation, is inferior only to theirs who choose them, and doth extend, without the consent or concurrence of any other person or persons, to the enacting, altering, and repealing of laws; to the erecting and abolishing of offices and courts; to the appointing, removing, and calling to account magistrates and officers of all degrees; to the making war and peace; to the treating with foreign states; and, generally, to whatsoever is not expressly or impliedly reserved by the represented to themselves:

Which are as followeth,

1. That matters of religion and the ways of God's worship are not at all entrusted by us to any human power, because therein we cannot remit or exceed a title of what our consciences dictate to be the mind of God, without wilful sin; nevertheless the public way of instructing the nation (so it be not compulsive) is referred to their discretion.

2. That the matter of impressing and constraining any of us to serve in the wars is against our freedom; and therefore we do not allow it in our Representatives; the rather, because money (the sinews of war), being always at their disposal, they can never want numbers of men apt enough to engage in any just cause.

3. That after the dissolution of this present Parliament, no person be at any time questioned for anything said or done in reference to the late public differences, otherwise than in execution of the judgments of the present Representatives, or House of Commons.

4. That in all laws made or to be made every person may be bound alike, and that no tenure, estate, charter, degree, birth, or place do confer any exemption from the ordinary course of legal proceedings whereunto others are subjected.

5. That as the laws ought to be equal, so they must be good, and not evidently destructive to the safety and well-being of the people.

These things we declare to be our native rights, and therefore are agreed and resolved to maintain them with our utmost possibilities against all opposition whatsoever; being compelled thereunto not only by the examples of our ancestors, whose blood was often spent in vain for the recovery of their freedoms, suffering themselves through fraudulent accommodations to be still deluded of the fruit of their victories, but also by our own woeful experience, who, having long expected and dearly earned the establishment of these certain rules of government, are yet made to depend for the settlement of our peace and freedom upon him that intended our bondage and brought a cruel war upon us.

Questions

1. What are the Levellers criticizing when they propose that "in all laws made or to be made every person may be bound alike"?

2. What are the main rights that the Levellers are aiming to protect?

━━━━━━━

13. Henry Care, English Liberties, or the Free-Born Subject's Inheritance (1680)

Source: Henry Care, English Liberties: or, the Free-born Subject's Inheritance (London, 1680), pp. 1–5.

The political battles of the seventeenth century ended with England enjoying a "mixed" or "balanced" constitutional system in which the king continued to rule but his power was restrained by that of Parliament and the rule of law. In 1680, in his book, *English Liberties: or, the Free-Born Subject's Inheritance*, the writer Henry Care contrasted the government of England with democracy, on the one hand, and unrestrained monarchy, on the other, as represented by France and other European countries. He described it as "qualified monarchy" and called it the best political structure in the world. Care claimed that the English were more free and happy than any other people. The belief in freedom as the common heritage of all Englishmen and their empire as the world's guardian of liberty would help to legitimize English colonization in the Western Hemisphere and to cast its imperial wars against Catholic France and Spain as struggles between freedom and tyranny.

THE CONSTITUTION OF our English government (the best in the world) is no arbitrary tyranny like the Turkish Grand Seignior's, or the French King's, whose wills (or rather lusts) dispose of the lives and fortunes of their unhappy subjects; nor an Oligarchy where the great ones (like fish in the ocean) prey upon, and live by devouring the lesser at their pleasure. Nor yet a Democracy or popular state, much less an Anarchy, where all confusedly are hail fellows well met. But a most excellently mixed or qualified Monarchy, where the King is vested with large prerogatives sufficient to support majesty; and restrained only from power of doing himself and his people harm, which would be contrary to the end of all government . . . the nobility adorned with privileges to be a screen to majesty, and a refreshing shade to their inferiors, and the commonality, too, so guarded in their persons and properties by the fence of law, [which] renders them Freemen, not Slaves.

In France and other nations the mere will of the prince is law, his word takes off any man's head, imposes taxes, or seizes any man's estate, when, how, and as often as he [wishes], and if one be accused or but so much suspected of any crime, he may either presently execute him, or banish or imprison him at pleasure. . . . Nay if there be no witnesses, yet he may be put to the rack, the tortures whereof make an innocent person confess himself guilty.

• • •

But in England, the law is both the measure and the bond of every subject's duty and allegiance, each man having a fixed fundamental right born with him as to the freedom of his person and property in his estate, which he cannot be deprived of, but either by his consent, or some crime for which the law has imposed such a penalty as forfeiture.

• • •

This original happy frame of government is truly and properly called an Englishman's liberty, a privilege not to [be] exempt from the law, but to be freed in person and estate, from arbitrary violence and oppression.... And this birthright of Englishmen shines most conspicuously in two things: Parliaments [and] juries.

By the first, the subject has a share by his chosen representatives in the legislative (or law-making) power, for no new laws bind the people of England, but such as are by common consent agreed on in that great council.

By the second, he has a share in the executive part of the law, no causes being tried, nor any man adjudged to lose life ... or estate but upon the verdict of his peers (or equals).... These two grand pillars of English liberty, are the fundamental vital privileges, whereby we have been and are preserved more free and happy than any other people in the world.

• • •

Questions

1. Why does Henry Care consider the English system of government "the best in the world"?

2. How does Care define "an Englishman's liberty"?

CHAPTER 3

Creating Anglo-America, 1660–1750

14. New York Charter of Liberties and Privileges (1683)

Source: Charles Z. Lincoln, ed., The Colonial Laws of New York from the Year 1664 to the Revolution *(Albany, 1894), Vol. 1, pp. 111–16.*

Originally established as an outpost of the Dutch empire in the early seventeenth century, New Netherlands was seized by England in 1664. There had been no representative assembly under the Dutch, and governors appointed by the British proprietor, the duke of York, at first ruled without one. Colonists complained that they were being denied "the rights of Englishmen." In 1683, the duke agreed to call an elected assembly, whose first act was to draft a Charter of Liberties and Privileges.

The charter required that elections be held every three years among "freeholders" (male property owners) and the freemen of New York City (residents who paid a fee to obtain that status). It reaffirmed traditional English rights, such as trial by jury and security of property, as well as religious toleration for all Christians. In part, the charter reflected an effort by English colonists to assert dominance over earlier Dutch settlers by establishing the principle that the "liberties" to which New Yorkers were entitled were those enjoyed by Englishmen at home.

THE CHARTER OF Liberties and privileges granted by his Royal Highness to the inhabitants of New York. . . .

For better establishing the government of this province of New York and that justice and right may be equally done to all persons within the same,

Be it enacted by the governor, council, and representatives now in General Assembly met and assembled and by the authority of the same.

1. That the supreme legislative authority under his Majesty and Royal Highness James Duke of York . . . shall forever be and reside in a Governor, Council, and the people met in General Assembly.

• • •

4. That according to the usage, custom, and practice of the realm of England a session of the General Assembly be held in this province once in three years at least.

5. That every freeholder within this province and freemen in any corporation shall have his free choice and vote in the electing of the Representatives without any manner of constraint or imposition. And that in all elections the majority of voices shall carry it and by freeholders is understood every one who is so understood according to the laws of England.

• • •

8. That the said Representatives may appoint their own times of meeting during their sessions and may adjourn their house from time to time as to them shall seem . . . convenient.

9. That the said Representatives are the sole judges of the qualifications of their own members, and likewise of all undue elections and may from time to time purge their house as they shall see [fit].

• • •

11. That all bills agreed upon by the said Representatives or the major part of them shall be presented to the Governor and his Council for their approbation and consent, all and every which said bills so approved or consented to by the Governor and his Council shall be esteemed and accounted the laws of the province,

which said laws shall continue and remain in force until they shall be repealed by the authority foresaid, that is to say the Governor, Council, and Representatives in General Assembly by and with the approbation of his Royal Highness, or expire by their own limitations.

· · ·

13. That no freeman shall be taken and imprisoned ... or be outlawed or exiled or in any other ways destroyed nor shall be passed upon adjudged or condemned but by the lawful judgment of his peers and by the law of this province. Justice nor right shall be neither sold, denied, or deferred to any man within this province.

14. That no aid, tax, tallage, assessment, custom, loan, benevolence, or imposition whatsoever shall be laid, assessed, imposed, or levied on any of his Majesty's subjects within this province or their estates ... but by the act and consent of the Governor, Council, and Representatives of the people in General Assembly met and assembled.

15. That no man of what estate or condition soever shall be put out of his lands or tenements, nor taken, nor imprisoned, nor disinherited, nor banished, nor any ways destroyed without being brought to answer by due course of law.

· · ·

17. All trials shall be by the verdict of twelve men, and as near as may be peers or equals and of the neighborhood and in the county ... where the fact shall arise or grow whether the same be by indictment, information, declaration, or otherwise against the person, offender, or defendant.

18. That in all cases capital or criminal there shall be a grand inquest who shall first present the offence and then twelve men of the neighborhood to try the offender who after his plea to the indictment shall be allowed his reasonable challenge.

· · ·

20. That no freeman shall be compelled to receive any mariners or soldiers into his house and there suffer them to sojourn, against

their wills, provided always that it be not in time of actual war
within this province.

• • •

24. That no estate of a feme covert [married woman] shall be sold
or conveyed but by deed acknowledged by her in some court of
record, the woman being secretly examined if she does it freely without threats or compulsion of her husband.

• • •

26. That a widow after the death of her husband shall have her
dower and shall and may tarry in the chief house of her husband
forty days after the death of her husband within which forty days her
dower shall be assigned her. And for her dower shall be assigned
unto her the third part of all the lands of her husband.

• • •

28. That no person or persons which profess faith in God by Jesus
Christ shall at any time be any ways molested, punished, disquieted,
or called into question for any difference in opinion or matter of religious concernment, who do not actually disturb the civil peace of
the province, but that all and every such person or persons may from
time to time and at all times freely have and fully enjoy his or their
judgments or consciences in matters of religion throughout all the
province, they behaving themselves peaceably and quietly and not
using this liberty to licentiousness nor to the civil injury or outward
disturbance of others.

• • •

Be it hereby enacted that [all] Christian Churches [in New York] be
hereby confirmed therein and that they and every of them shall from
henceforth forever be held and reputed as privileged churches and
enjoy all their former freedoms of their religion in divine worship
and church discipline * * * [and] that all Christian churches that
shall hereafter come and settle within this province shall have the
same privileges.

Questions

1. What are the major liberties protected in the charter?

2. Why does the document refer to "the usage, custom, and practice of . . . England"?

━━━━━

15. William Penn on Religious Liberty, from *England's Present Interests Discovered* (1675)

Source: *William Penn,* England's Present Interests Discovered *(London, 1675), pp. 1–5, 38–47.*

The last English colony to be established in the seventeenth century was Pennsylvania, founded in 1680 by William Penn. A devout member of the Society of Friends, or Quakers, Penn envisioned the colony as a place where those facing religious persecution in Europe could enjoy spiritual freedom. Quakers held that the spirit of God dwelled within all persons, not just the elect, and that this "inner light," rather than the Bible or teachings of the clergy, offered the surest guidance in spiritual matters. Thus, the government had no right to enforce any particular form of religious worship.

In a pamphlet published in 1675, excerpted here, Penn condemned attempts to enforce "religious Uniformity" and offered many practical reasons for religious freedom. Penn did not object to the government promoting "general religion"—that is, moral conduct—as opposed to particular forms of belief and worship. Not religious uniformity but a virtuous citizenry would be the foundation of Penn's social order.

━━━━━

• • •

CERTAIN IT IS, that there are few kingdoms in the world more divided within themselves, and whose religious interests lie more seemingly [in opposition to] all accommodation, than that we live in, which makes a magistrate's task hard, and gives him a difficulty some think insurmountable.

Your endeavors for a [religious] uniformity have been many; your acts not a few to enforce it, but the consequence, whether you intended it or not, through the barbarous practices of those that have had their execution, has been the spoiling of several thousands of the free inhabitants of this kingdom of their unforfeited rights. Persons have been flung into jails, gates and trunks broke open, goods destroyed, till a stool is not been left to sit down on, flocks of cattle driven, whole barns full of corn seized, parents left without children, children without their parents, both without subsistence.

• • •

Finding then by sad experience, and a long tract of time, that the very remedies applied to cure dissension increase it, and that the more vigorously a uniformity is coercively prosecuted, the wider breaches grow, the more inflamed persons are, and fixed in their resolutions to stand by their principles; which, besides all other inconveniences to those that give them trouble, their very sufferings beget that compassion in the multitude . . . and makes a preparation for not a few [converts].

• • •

The Question. What is most fit, easy, and safe at this juncture of affairs to be done, for composing, at least quieting differences, for allaying the heat of contrary interests, and making them subservient to the interest of the government, and consistent with the prosperity of the kingdom?

The Answer.

1. An inviolable and impartial maintenance of equal rights.

2. Our superiors governing themselves upon a balance, as near may be, towards the several religious interests.

3. A sincere promotion of general and practical religion.

• • •

I shall not at this time make it my business to manifest the inconsistency that there is between the Christian religion, and a forced uniformity, not only because it has been so often and excellently done by the men of wit, learning, and conscience, and that I have elsewhere largely delivered my sense about it, but because every free and impartial temper has of a long time observed that such barbarous attempts were so far from being indulged, that they were most severely prohibited by Christ himself, who instructed his disciples to love their enemies, not to persecute their friends for every difference in opinion.

• • •

It cannot be ... where a kingdom is of many minds, [that] one party have the wisdom, wealth, number, sober life, industry, and resolution on its side, which I am sure is not to be found in England.

• • •

Instead of peace, love, and good neighborhood, behold animosity and contest! One neighbor watches another, ... this divides them, their family and acquaintance.

• • •

Nor is this severity only injurious to the affairs of England, but the whole Protestant world, for besides that it calls the sincerity of their proceedings against the Papists into question, it furnishes them with this sort of unanswerable [question]: "The Protestants exclaim against us for persecutors, and are they not the very men themselves? Was severity an instance of weakness in our religion, and is it become a valid argument in theirs? Are not our actions (once void of all excuse with them) now defended by their own practice?"

• • •

Such procedure is a great reflection upon the justice of the government, in that it enacts penalties inadequate to the fault committed: That I should lose my liberty and property, natural endowments, and confirmed civil privileges, for some error in judgment about matters of religion, as if I must not be a man, because I am not such a sort of religious man as the government would have me, but must lose my claim to all natural benefits, though I harmonize with them in civil affairs.

• • •

But there are ... objections that some make against what I have urged, not unfit to be considered. The first is this: If the liberty desired be granted, what know we but Dissenters may employ their meetings to insinuate against the government, inflame the people into a dislike of their superiors, and thereby prepare them for mischief? Answer. * * * What Dissenter can be so destitute of reason and love to common safety, as to expose himself and family, by plotting against a government that is kind to him, and gives him the liberty he desires?

• • •

Questions

1. Who does Penn seem to be addressing in this pamphlet?

2. What are the main benefits he claims will follow from religious toleration?

▬▬▬▬▬▬▬▬

16. Nathaniel Bacon on Bacon's Rebellion (1676)

Source: Virginia Magazine of History and Biography, *Vol. 1 (1894), pp. 55–61.*

The largest popular revolt in the early English colonies was Bacon's Rebellion, which occurred in Virginia in 1676. For thirty years, Governor William Berkeley had run a corrupt regime in alliance with an inner circle of tobacco planters, while heavy taxes reduced the prospects of small farmers. His refusal to allow white settlement in areas reserved for Indians angered colonists who saw land ownership as central to freedom.

After a minor confrontation between Indians and settlers on Virginia's western frontier, settlers demanded that the governor authorize the extermination or removal of the colony's Indians to open more land for whites.

Berkeley refused. An uprising began that quickly grew into a full-fledged rebellion. The leader, Nathaniel Bacon, was himself a wealthy and ambitious planter. But his call for the removal of all Indians from the colony, a reduction of taxes, and an end to rule by "grandees," rapidly gained support from small farmers, landless men, indentured servants, and even some slaves. Bacon's "manifesto," which follows, outlined the rebel's complaints against the governor and the colony's "protected and darling Indians." The uprising failed. But the frightened authorities reduced taxes and adopted a more aggressive Indian policy, opening western areas to small farmers. They also accelerated the shift from indentured white labor to African slaves.

If virtue be a sin, if piety be guilt, all the principles of morality, goodness and justice be perverted, we must confess that those who are now called rebels may be in danger of those high imputations. Those loud and several bulls would affright innocents and render the defence of our brethren and the inquiry into our sad and heavy oppressions, treason. But if there be, as sure there is, a just God to appeal to; if religion and justice be a sanctuary here; if to plead the cause of the oppressed; if sincerely to aim at his Majesty's honour and the public good without any reservation or by interest; if to stand in the gap after so much blood of our dear brethren bought and sold; if after the loss of a great part of his Majesty's colony deserted and dispeopled, freely with our lives and estates to endeavour to save the remainders be treason; God Almighty judge and let guilty die. But since we cannot in our hearts find one single spot of rebellion or treason, or that we have in any manner aimed at the subverting the settled government or attempting of the person of any either magistrate or private man, notwithstanding the several reproaches and threats of some who for sinister ends were disaffected to us and censured our innocent and honest designs, and since all people in all places where we have yet been can attest our civil, quiet, peaceable behaviour far different from that of rebellion and tumultuous persons, let truth be bold and all the world know the real foundations of pretended guilt.

We appeal to the country itself what and of what nature their oppressions have been, or by what cabal and mystery the designs of many of those whom we call great men have been transacted and carried on; but let us trace these men in authority and favour to whose hands the dispensation of the country's wealth has been committed. Let us observe the sudden rise of their estates [compared] with the quality in which they first entered this country, or the reputation they have held here amongst wise and discerning men. And let us see whether their extractions and education have not been vile, and by what pretence of learning and virtue they could so soon [come] into employments of so great trust and consequence. Let us consider their sudden advancement and let us also consider whether any public work for our safety and defence or for the advancement and propagation of trade, liberal arts, or sciences is here extant in any way adequate to our vast charge. Now let us compare these things together and see what sponges have sucked up the public treasure, and whether it has not been privately contrived away by unworthy favourites and juggling parasites whose tottering fortunes have been repaired and supported at the public charge. Now if it be so, judge what greater guilt can be than to offer to pry into these and to unriddle the mysterious wiles of a powerful cabal; let all people judge what can be of more dangerous import than to suspect the so long safe proceedings of some of our grandees, and whether people may with safety open their eyes in so nice a concern.

Another main article of our guilt is our open and manifest aversion of all, not only the foreign but the protected and darling Indians. This, we are informed, is rebellion of a deep dye for that both the governor and council are ... bound to defend the queen and the Appamatocks with their blood. Now, whereas we do declare and can prove that they have been for these many years enemies to the king and country, robbers and thieves and invaders of his Majesty's right and our interest and estates, but yet have by persons in authority been defended and protected even against his Majesty's loyal subjects, and that in so high a nature that even the complaints and oaths of his Majesty's most loyal subjects in a lawful manner proffered by them against those barbarous outlaws, have been by the right honourable governor rejected and the delinquents from his presence dismissed, not only with pardon and indemnity, but with all encouragement and favour; their firearms so destructful to us and by our laws prohibited, commanded to be restored them, and open declaration before witness made that they must have ammunition, although directly contrary to our law. Now what greater guilt can be than to oppose and endeavour the destruction of these honest, quiet neighbours of ours?

Another main article of our guilt is our design not only to ruin and extirpate all Indians in general, but all manner of trade and commerce with them. Judge who can be innocent that strike at this tender eye of interest: since the right honourable the governor hath been pleased by his commission to warrant this trade, who dare oppose it, or opposing it can be innocent? Although plantations be deserted, the blood of our dear brethren spilled; on all sides our complaints; continually murder upon murder renewed upon us; who may or dare think of the general subversion of all manner of trade and commerce with our enemies who can or dare impeach any of . . . traders at the heads of the rivers, if contrary to the wholesome provision made by laws for the country's safety; they dare continue their illegal practises and dare asperse the right honourable governor's wisdom and justice so highly to pretend to have his warrant to break that law which himself made; who dare say that these men at the heads of the rivers buy and sell our blood, and do still, notwithstanding the late act made to the contrary, admit Indians painted and continue to commerce; although these things can be proved, yet who dare be so guilty as to do it? . . .

• • •

THE DECLARATION OF THE PEOPLE

For having upon specious pretences of public works, raised unjust taxes upon the commonalty for the advancement of private favourites and other sinister ends, but no visible effects in any measure adequate.

For not having during the long time of his government in any measure advanced this hopeful colony, either by fortification, towns or trade.

For having abused and rendered contemptible the majesty of justice, of advancing to places of judicature scandalous and ignorant favourites.

For having wronged his Majesty's prerogative and interest by assuming the monopoly of the beaver trade.

By having in that unjust gain bartered and sold his Majesty's country and the lives of his loyal subjects to the barbarous heathen.

For having protected, favoured and emboldened the Indians against his Majesty's most loyal subjects, never contriving, requiring, or appointing any due or proper means of satisfaction for their many invasions, murders, and robberies committed upon us.

• • •

For having the second time attempted the same thereby calling down our forces from the defence of the frontiers, and most weak exposed places, for the prevention of civil mischief and ruin amongst ourselves, whilst the barbarous enemy in all places did invade, murder, and spoil us, his Majesty's most faithful subjects.

Of these, the aforesaid articles, we accuse Sir William Berkeley, as guilty of each and every one of the same, and as one who has traitorously attempted, violated and injured his Majesty's interest here, by the loss of a great part of his colony, and many of his faithful and loyal subjects by him betrayed, and in a barbarous and shameful manner exposed to the incursions and murders of the heathen.

And we do further demand, that the said Sir William Berkeley ... be forthwith delivered up ... within four days after the notice hereof, or otherwise we declare as followeth: that in whatsoever house, place, or ship [he] shall reside, be hid, or protected, we do declare that the owners, masters, or inhabitants of the said places, to be confederates and traitors to the people, and the estates of them, as also of all the aforesaid persons, to be confiscated. This we, the commons of Virginia, do declare desiring a prime union amongst ourselves, that we may jointly, and with one accord defend ourselves against the common enemy.

NATH BACON, Gen'l.
By the Consent of the People.

Questions

1. What are the rebels' main complaints against the government of Virginia?

2. Do Bacon and his followers envision any place for Indians in Virginia society?

17. Letter by an Immigrant to Pennsylvania (1769)

Source: Johannes Hänner: Letter by an Immigrant to Pennsylvania, 1769, Unpublished Documents on Emigration from the Archives of Switzerland, Albert B. Faust, Deutsch-Amerikanische Geschichtsblätter, Vols. 18–19, pp. 37–39. Translation by Volker Berghahn. Reprinted by permission of Volker Berghahn.

Germans, 110,000 in all, formed the largest group of newcomers to the British colonies in the eighteenth century. The desire for religious freedom inspired many migrants, but the primary motivation for emigration was economic. German areas of Europe were plagued by persistent agricultural crises. Families found it increasingly difficult to acquire land.

Most German newcomers settled in frontier areas—rural New York, western Pennsylvania, and the southern backcountry—where they formed tightly knit farming communities in which German for many years remained the dominant language. The letter below, by a German-speaking emigrant from Switzerland to Pennsylvania, illustrates the response of many immigrants to life in America. "We have a free country," he wrote to his relatives at home, singling out ample employment opportunities, low taxes, plentiful food, and abundant land as reasons for coming to America.

⸻

Lebanon, August 23, 1769

Dearest Father, Brother, and Sister and Brother-in-law, . . .

To begin with, we are all, thank God, fresh and healthy as long as the Lord wills, and if at last you are also in good health, this would delight my heart. What I must tell you first of all is that I have been dreaming one day after Johannis and that it seemed to me that my beloved brother-in-law in Bubendorff had died. This would pain me a lot, and the Lord will protect him of this.

I have told you quite fully about the trip, and I will tell you what will not surprise you—that we have a free country. Of the sundry craftsmen, one may do whatever one wants. Nor does the land require payment of tithes [taxes requiring payment of a portion of a farmer's produce to a local landlord, typical in Europe]. . . . By the way, wheat is grown most frequently, rye, oats, . . . apples are plentiful. . . . The land is very big from Canada to the east of us to Carolina in the south and to the Spanish border in the west. . . . Except for Carolina [there are] many large and small rivers. One can settle wherever one wants without asking anyone when he buys or leases something. . . .

I have always enough to do and we have no shortage of food. Bread is plentiful. If I work for two days I earn more bread than in eight days [at home]. . . . Also I can buy many things so reasonably [for example] a pair of shoes for [roughly] seven Pennsylvania shillings. . . . I think that with God's help I will obtain land. I am not pushing for it until I am in a better position. I would like for my brother to come . . . and it will then be even nicer in the country. . . . I assume that the land has been described to you sufficiently by various people and it is not surprising that the immigrant agents [demand payment]. For the journey is long and it costs much to stay away for one year.... And at this point I finally greet you all with all good friends and acquaintances very cordially, and I command all of you to the care of the Lord so that you may be well in soul and body.

Johannes Hänner

Questions

1. What does Johannes Hänner seem to mean when he calls America a "free country"?

2. How does it appear that people in Europe learn about conditions in America?

---

18. Gottlieb Mittelberger on the Trade in Indentured Servants (1750)

Source: Gottlieb Mittelberger, Gottlieb Mittelberger's Journey to Pennsylvania in the Year 1750 and Return to Germany in the Year 1754, *trans. Carl Theo Eben (Philadelphia, 1898), pp. 28–38.*

During the eighteenth century, most emigrants to British North America arrived either as slaves or indentured servants. Gottlieb Mittelberger, a German schoolteacher and organ player, traveled to Pennsylvania in 1750 and returned to Germany four years later. The passage that follows is taken from his diary, in which he vividly described conditions on the ship carrying indentured servants and the trying situation many of them faced when they landed in Philadelphia. The German men and women he describes had borrowed money to pay for their passage and had no choice but to sign long-term labor contracts in America to pay off their debt. Although indentured servants were not held for life, as slaves were, they were bought and sold and their families could easily be broken up. Mittelberger's account offers a different perspective on immigration to the American colonies from the previous document.

———

DURING THE VOYAGE there is on board these ships terrible misery, stench, fumes, horror, vomiting, many kinds of seasickness, fever, dysentery, headache, heat, constipation, boils, scurvy, cancer, mouth rot, and the like, all of which come from old and sharply-salted food and meat, also from very bad and foul water, so that many die miserably.

Add to this want of provisions, hunger, thirst, frost, heat, dampness, anxiety, want, afflictions and lamentations, together with other trouble, as e.g., the lice abound so frightfully, especially on sick people, that they can be scraped off the body. The misery reaches a climax when a gale rages for two or three nights and days, so that every one believes that the ship will go to the bottom with all human beings on board. In such a visitation the people cry and pray most piteously. . . .

No one can have an idea of the sufferings which women in confinement have to bear with their innocent children on board these ships. Few of this class escape with their lives; many a mother is cast into the water with her child as soon as she is dead. One day, just as we had a heavy gale, a woman in our ship, who was to give birth and could not give birth under the circumstances, was pushed through a loophole (porthole) in the ship and dropped into the sea, because she was far in the rear of the ship and could not be brought forward.

Children from one to seven years rarely survive the voyage; and many a time parents are compelled to see their children miserably suffer and die from hunger, thirst, and sickness, and then to see them cast into the water. I witnessed such misery in no less than thirty-two children in our ship, all of whom were thrown into the sea. The parents grieve all the more since their children find no resting place in the earth, but are devoured by the monsters of the sea. It is a notable fact that children who have not yet had the measles or smallpox generally get them on board the ship, and mostly die of them. . . .

When the ships have landed at Philadelphia after their long voyage, no one is permitted to leave them except those who pay for their passage or can give good security; the others, who cannot pay, must remain on board the ships till they are purchased and are released from the ships by their purchasers. The sick always fare the worst, for the healthy are naturally preferred and purchased first; and so the sick and wretched must often remain on board in front of the city for two or three weeks, and frequently die, whereas many a one, if he could pay his debt and were permitted to leave the ship immediately, might recover and remain alive. . . .

The sale of human beings in the market on board the ship is carried on thus: Every day Englishmen, Dutchmen, and High German people come from the city of Philadelphia and other places, in part from a great distance, say twenty, thirty, or forty hours away, and go on board the newly-arrived ship that has brought and offers for sale passengers from Europe, and select among the healthy persons such as they deem suitable for their business, and bargain with them how long they will serve for their passage money, which most of them are still in debt for. When they have come to an agreement, it happens that adult persons bind themselves in writing to serve three, four, five, or six years for the amount due by them, according to their age and strength. But very young people, from ten to fifteen years, must serve till they are twenty-one years old.

Many parents must sell and trade away their children like so many head of cattle, for if their children take the debt upon themselves, the parents can leave the ship free and unrestrained; but as the parents often do not know where and to what people their children are going, it often happens that such parents and children, after leaving the ship, do not see each other again for many years, perhaps no more in all their lives. . . .

It often happens that whole families, husband, wife, and children, are separated by being sold to different purchasers, especially when they have not paid any part of their passage money.

When a husband or wife has died at sea, when the ship has made more than half of her trip, the survivor must pay or serve not only for himself or herself, but also for the deceased. When both parents have died over halfway at sea, their children, especially when they are young and have nothing to pawn or to pay, must stand for their own and their parents' passage, and serve till they are twenty-one years old. When one has served his or her term, he or she is entitled to a new suit of clothes at parting; and if it has been so stipulated, a man gets in addition a horse, a woman, a cow.

Questions

1. Which aspects of the situation of the German immigrants seem most offensive to Mittelberger?

2. How public and regular does the trade in indentured servants appear to be from his account?

---

19. Complaint of an Indentured Servant (1756)

Source: Elizabeth Sprigs letter to John Spyer, September 22, 1756, Colonial Captivities, Marches, and Journeys, *1935, Isabel M. Calder, pp. 151–52.*

The letter that follows was written to her father in England by Elizabeth Sprigs, an indentured servant in mid-eighteenth century Maryland. It expresses complaints voiced by many servants from the beginning of settlement. Sprigs, who had clearly had some kind of falling out with her father, described constant labor, poor food and living conditions, and physical abuse. "Many Negroes are better used," she added.

Unlike slaves, servants could look forward to a release from bondage after their period of labor was over, and to receiving a payment known as "freedom dues." Many, however, died before the end of their terms and freedom dues were sometimes so meager that they did not enable recipients to acquire land.

Maryland September 22, 1756

Honored Father,

My being forever banished from your sight, will I hope pardon the boldness I now take of troubling you with these. My long silence has been purely owing to my undutifulness to you, and well knowing I had offended in the highest degree, put a tie to my tongue and pen, for fear I should be extinct from your good graces and add a further trouble to you. But too well knowing your care and tenderness for me so long as I retained my duty to you, induced me once again to endeavor, if possible, to kindle up that flame again.

O Dear father, believe what I am going to relate the words of truth and sincerity, and balance my former bad conduct [to] my sufferings here, and then I am sure you'll pity your distressed daughter. What we unfortunate English people suffer here is beyond the probability of you in England to conceive. Let it suffice that I am one of the unhappy number, am toiling almost day and night, and very often in the horse's drudgery, with only this comfort that you bitch you do not half enough, and then tied up and whipped to that degree that you now serve an animal. Scarce any thing but Indian corn and salt to eat and that even begrudged nay many Negroes are better used, almost naked no shoes nor stockings to wear, and the comfort after slaving during master's pleasure, what rest we can get is to wrap ourselves up in a blanket and lie upon the ground. This is the deplorable condition your poor Betty endures, and now I beg if you have any bowels of compassion left show it by sending me some relief. Clothing is the principal thing wanting, which if you should condescend to, may easily send them to me by any of the ships bound to Balti-more town, Patapsco River, Maryland. And give me leave to conclude in duty to you and uncles and aunts, and respect to all friends.

Honored Father
Your undutiful and disobedient child
Elizabeth Sprigs

Questions

1. What are Elizabeth Springs's main complaints about her treatment?

2. Why does she compare her condition unfavorably to that of blacks?

20. Women in the Household Economy (1709)

John Lawson, A New Voyage to Carolina *(London, 1709), pp. 84–85.*

In the household economy of eighteenth-century America, the family was the center of economic life. Most work revolved around the home, and all members—men, women, and children—contributed to the family's liveli-hood. John Lawson, an English naturalist, came to Carolina in 1700 and traveled over a thousand miles, studying the natural environment and trad-ing with Indians. His *New Voyage to Carolina* offered a very favorable de-scription of life in the colony. Lawson's account vividly described the lives of free Carolina women and the numerous kinds of labor they performed. The work of farmers' wives and daughters often spelled the difference be-tween a family's self-sufficiency and poverty. Lawson was captured and killed during an Indian uprising in 1711.

THE WOMEN ARE the most industrious sex in that place, and, by their good houswifery, make a great deal of cloth of their own cotton, wool and flax; some of them keeping their families (though large) very decently appareled, both with linens and woolens, so that they have no occasion to run into the merchant's debt, or lay their money out on stores for clothing. . . .

They marry very young; some at thirteen or fourteen; and she that stays till twenty, is reckoned a stale maid; which is a very indifferent character in that warm country. The women are very fruitful; most houses being full of little ones. It has been observed, that women long married, and without children, in other places, have removed to Carolina, and become joyful mothers. They have very easy travail in their child-bearing, in which they are so happy, as seldom to miscarry. . . .

Many of the women are very handy in canoes, and will manage them with great dexterity and skill, which they become accustomed to in this watery country. They are ready to help their husbands in any servile work, as planting, when the season of the weather requires expedition; pride seldom banishing good houswifery. The girls are not bred up to the [spinning] wheel and sewing only; but the dairy and affairs of the house they are very well acquainted withal; so that you shall see them, whilst very young, manage their business with a great deal of conduct and alacrity. The children of both sexes are very docile, and learn any thing with a great deal of Ease and Method; and those that have the advantages of education, write good hands, and prove good accountants, which is most coveted, and indeed most necessary in these parts.

Questions

1. What are the most important kinds of work done by Carolina women, according to Lawson?

2. How strict do gender roles appear to have been in early Carolina?

CHAPTER 4

Slavery, Freedom, and the Struggle for Empire, to 1763

21. Olaudah Equiano on Slavery (1789)

Source: The Interesting Narrative of the Life of Olaudah Equiano, or Gustavas Vassa, the African, Written by Himself *(London, 1789), Vol. 1, pp. 46–49, 69–72, 83–88.*

Of the estimated 7.7 million Africans transported to the New World between 1492 and 1820, over half arrived between 1700 and 1800. Every European empire utilized slave labor and battled for control of this profitable trade. A series of triangular trading routes crisscrossed the Atlantic, carrying British goods to Africa and the colonies, colonial slave-grown products like tobacco, sugar, and rice to Europe, and slaves from Africa to the New World.

The era's most popular account of the slave experience was written by Olaudah Equiano, the son of a West African village chief, kidnaped by slave traders in the 1750s. In the passages that follow, Equiano describes his capture, encounter with other African peoples with whom he had no previous contact, passage to the New World, and sale in the West Indies. Equiano went on the purchase his freedom. His life underscored the greatest contradiction in the history of the eighteenth century—the simultaneous expansion of freedom and slavery.

My FATHER, BESIDES many slaves, had a numerous family, of which seven lived to grow up, including myself and a sister, who was the only daughter. As I was the youngest of the sons, I became, of course, the greatest favourite with my mother, and was always with her; and she used to take particular pains to form my mind. I was trained up from my earliest years in the arts of agriculture and war: my daily exercise was shooting and throwing javelins; and my mother adorned me with emblems, after the manner of our greatest warriors. In this way I grew up till I was turned the age of eleven, when an end was put to my happiness in the following manner:— Generally, when the grown people in the neighbourhood were gone far in the fields to labour, the children assembled together in some of the neighbours' premises to play; and commonly some of us used to get up a tree to look out for any assailant, or kidnapper, that might come upon us; for they sometimes took those opportunities of our parents' absence, to attack and carry off as many as they could seize. One day, as I was watching at the top of a tree in our yard, I saw one of those people come into the yard of our next neighbour but one, to kidnap, there being many stout young people in it. Immediately, on this, I gave the alarm of the rogue, and he was surrounded by the stoutest of them, who entangled him with cords, so that he could not escape till some of the grown people came and secured him. But, alas! ere long it was my fate to be thus attacked, and to be carried off, when none of the grown people were nigh. One day, when all our people were gone out to their works as usual, and only I and my dear sister were left to mind the house, two men and a woman got over our walls, and in a moment seized us both; and, without giving us time to cry out, or make resistance, they stopped our mouths, tied our hands, and ran off with us into the nearest wood: and continued to carry us as far as they could, till night came on, when we reached a small house, where the robbers halted for refreshment, and spent the night. We were then unbound, but were unable to take any food; and, being quite overpowered by fatigue and grief, our only relief was some sleep, which allayed our misfortune for a short time. The next morning we left the house, and continued travelling all the day. . . .

• • •

I continued to travel, sometimes by land, sometimes by water, through different countries, and various nations, till, at the end of six or seven months after I had been kidnapped, I arrived at the sea coast. It would be tedious and uninteresting to relate all the incidents which befel me during this journey, and which I have not yet forgotten, of the various hands I passed through, and the manners and customs of all the different people among whom I lived: I shall therefore only observe, that, in all the places where I was, the soil was exceedingly rich; the pomkins, eadas, plantains, yams, &c. &c. were in great abundance, and of incredible size. There were also vast quantities of different gums, though not used for any purpose; and every where a great deal of tobacco. The cotton even grew quite wild; and there was plenty of red wood. I saw no mechanics whatever in all the way, except such as I have mentioned. The chief employment in all these countries was agriculture, and both the males and females, as with us, were brought up to it, and trained in the arts of war.

The first object which saluted my eyes when I arrived on the coast was the sea, and a slave-ship, which was then riding at anchor, and waiting for its cargo. These filled me with astonishment, which was soon converted into terror, which I am yet at a loss to describe, nor the then feelings of my mind. When I was carried on board I was immediately handled, and tossed up, to see if I were sound, by some of the crew; and I was now persuaded that I had gotten into a world of bad spirits, and that they were going to kill me. Their complexions too differing so much from ours, their long hair, and the language they spoke, which was very different from any I had ever heard, united to confirm me in this belief. Indeed, such were the horrors of my views and fears at the moment, that, if ten thousand worlds had been my own, I would have freely parted with them all to have exchanged my condition with that of the meanest slave in my own country. When I looked round the ship too, and saw a large furnace of copper boiling, and a multitude of black people of every description chained together, every one of their countenances expressing dejection and sorrow, I no longer doubted of my fate, and, quite overpowered with horror and anguish, I fell motionless on the deck and fainted. When I recovered a little, I found some black people about me, who I believed were some of those who brought me on board, and had been receiving their pay; they talked to me in order to cheer me, but all in vain. I asked them if we were not to be eaten by those white men with horrible looks, red faces, and long hair? They told me I was not; and one of the crew brought me a small portion of spirituous liquor in a wine glass; but, being afraid of him, I would not take it out of his hand . . .

• • •

At last we came in sight of the island of Barbadoes, at which the whites on board gave a great shout, and made many signs of joy to us. We did not know what to think of this; but as the vessel drew nearer we plainly saw the harbour, and other ships of different kinds and sizes: and we soon anchored amongst them off Bridge Town. Many merchants and planters now came on board, though it was in the evening. They put us in separate parcels, and examined us attentively. They also made us jump, and pointed to the land, signifying we were to go there. We thought by this we should be eaten by these ugly men, as they appeared to us; and, when soon after we were all put down under the deck again, there was much dread and trembling among us, and nothing but bitter cries to be heard all the night from these apprehensions, insomuch that at last the white people got some old slaves from the land to pacify us. They told us we were not to be eaten, but to work, and were soon to go on land, where we should see many of our country people. This report eased us much; and sure enough, soon after we were landed, there came to us Africans of all languages. We were conducted immediately to the merchant's yard, where we were all pent up together like so many sheep in a fold, without regard to sex or age. As every object was new to me, every thing I saw filled me with surprise. What struck me first was, that the houses were built with bricks, in stories, and in every other respect different from those I have seen in Africa: but I was still more astonished on seeing people on horseback. I did not know what this could mean; and indeed I thought these people were full of nothing but magical arts. . . .

• • •

We were not many days in the merchant's custody before we were sold after their usual manner, which is this:—On a signal given, (as the beat of a drum), the buyers rush at once into the yard where the slaves are confined, and make choice of that parcel they like best. The noise and clamour with which this is attended, and the eagerness visible in the countenances of the buyers, serve not a little to increase the apprehensions of the terrified Africans, who may well be supposed to consider them as the ministers of that destruction to which they think themselves devoted. In this manner, without scruple, are relations and friends separated, most of them never to see each other again. I remember in the vessel in which I was brought over, in the men's apartment, there were several brothers, who, in the sale, were sold in different lots; and it was very moving on this occasion to see and hear their cries at parting. O, ye nominal Christians! might not an African ask you, learned you this from your God? who says unto you, Do unto all men as you would men should do unto you? Is it not enough that we are torn from our country and friends to toil for your luxury and lust of gain? Must every tender feeling be likewise sacrificed to your avarice? Are the dearest friends and relations, now rendered more dear by their separation from their kindred, still to be parted from each other, and thus prevented from cheering the gloom of slavery with the small comfort of being together and mingling their sufferings and sorrows? Why are parents to lose their children, brothers their sisters, or husbands their wives? Surely this is a new refinement in cruelty, which, while it has no advantage to atone for it, thus aggravates distress, and adds fresh horrors even to the wretchedness of slavery.

Questions

1. What picture of life in Africa does Equiano present?

2. What elements of slavery does he seem to think will most outrage his readers?

---

22. Slave Conspiracy in Virginia (1709)

Source: Proceedings of the Council of Virginia, March 21, 1709, in H. R. McIlwaine, ed., Executive Journals of the Council of Colonial Virginia, *(Richmond, 1925–66), Vol. 3, pp. 234–35, 573–74. Courtesy of the Library of Virginia.*

By 1700, slavery had become a presence in every colony, and the foundation of the economy in Virginia. Recognizing the growing importance of slavery, the House of Burgesses in 1705 enacted a new slave code, bringing together the scattered legislation of the previous century. Slaves were property, subject to the will of their masters and of the white community. But although legal avenues to liberty receded, the desire for freedom did not. The document that follows details the Virginia government's reaction to a "dangerous conspiracy" among the colony's slaves in 1709. The president of the Virginia Council issued a proclamation demanding that owners strictly enforce laws regulating their slave's conduct and detailing the punishment if they failed to do so. As the proclamation made clear, the existence of slavery shaped the legal obligations of whites as well as blacks.

WHEREAS THERE HAS been lately discovered a dangerous conspiracy formed and carried on by great numbers of Negroes and other slaves for making their escape by force from the service of their masters and for the destroying and calling off such of her majesty's subjects as should oppose their design. And whereas diverse of the chief conspirators and their accomplices have been apprehended in the counties of Surry and Isle of Wight and are now in custody, this board being desirous to bring to . . . speedy punishment such as have been concerned in their pernicious design according to the nature and quality of their respective faults . . . it is hereby ordered that the justices of said counties . . . do as soon as may be meet and take in writing the examination of all the Negroes committed or that shall be committed for the offenses aforesaid. And where they shall find reason to believe that any of the said Negroes have been ignorantly drawn into the said conspiracy or have been only so far concerned therein as barely to consent . . . that the said justices do then and there cause to be inflicted on the said slaves such correction as they judge the nature of their offense may deserve. But where they shall find any of the said slaves to have been engaged as the principal contrivers or otherwise remarkable in promoting the aforesaid conspiracy, it is ordered that they cause such slaves to be secured in the public jail of their respective counties, there to remain till further order.

• • •

Ordered that a Proclamation issue enjoining the strict observance and execution of the Act of Assembly concerning Servants and Slaves and a Proclamation was prepared accordingly:

A Proclamation

Whereas I have received intelligence of several illegal, unusual, and unwarrantable concourses, meetings, and assemblings together of Negro, Mulatto, and Indian slaves at quarters where there are no white or freemen overseers and more particularly of a notorious insurrection intended and contrived at such meetings by several slaves in this her majesty's colony and dominion and having caused several of them to be apprehended (who have confessed the fact) the prosecution and punishment of whom I speedily intend, and finding the toleration and permission of the masters, mistresses, or overseers of the said slaves of going abroad and remaining absent longer time than the law allows has been the occasion of such dangerous and unlawful concourses, meetings, and assemblings together and has given the opportunity of forming of such pernicious designs and considering the fatal consequences of such illegal toleration—

I, Edmund Jennings Esq., president of the Council of State of this her majesty's Colony and Dominion of Virginia, do by and with the advice and consent of her majesty's said Council strictly charge and require all her majesty's . . . subjects punctually to observe and keep all the articles and clauses in one Act of Assembly of this Colony entitled an Act Concerning Servants and Slaves but more especially the following clauses in the said act:

That no master, mistress, or overseer of a family shall knowingly permit any slave not belonging to him or her to be and remain upon his or her plantation above four hours at any one time without the leave of such slave's master, mistress, or overseer on penalty of one hundred and fifty pounds of tobacco to the informer . . . and also of this other following clause, that no slave go armed with gun, sword, club, staff, or other weapon nor go off the plantation and seat of land where such slave shall be appointed to live without a certificate of leave in writing for so doing from his master, mistress, or overseer. . . . And I do also command and require that this proclamation be published in all churches, chapels, and courthouses within this colony.

• • •

Questions

1. In what ways did the law of slavery limit the freedom of whites as well as blacks?

2. How closely does slavery seem to have been linked to race in early eighteenth-century Virginia?

23. *The Independent Reflector* on Limited Monarchy and Liberty (1752)

Source: The Independent Reflector *(New York), December 21, 1752.*

During the eighteenth century, the idea of the "freeborn Englishman" became powerfully entrenched in the outlook of both colonists and Britons. More than any other principle, liberty was seen as what made the British empire distinct. The passage that follows, from the New York monthly magazine *The Independent Reflector,* founded in 1752, offers an example of the era's many paeans to the "inexpressible charm" of liberty and England's role as liberty's "defender." The author, probably the magazine's editor, Edward Livingston, contrasts the national prosperity and personal happiness enjoyed by citizens of a "free state" (defined as a limited monarchy in which freedom of speech and religion were protected), with the sorry condition of subjects of absolute monarchies. Until the 1770s, most colonists believed themselves to be part of the freest political system humankind had ever known.

WHEN ONE CONSIDERS the Difference between an absolute, and a limited Monarchy, it seems unaccountable, that any Person in his Senses, should prefer the former to the latter. . . .

In *limited* Monarchies, the Pride and Ambition of Princes, and their natural Lust for Dominion, are check'd and restrained. . . .

Liberty gives an inexpressible Charm to all our Enjoyments. It imparts a Relish to the most indifferent Pleasure, and renders the highest Gratification the more consummately delightful. It is the Refinement of Life; it sooths and alleviates our Toils; smooths the rugged Brow of Adversity, and endears and enhances every Acquisition. The Subjects of a free State, have something open and generous in their Carriage; something of Grandeur and Sublimity in their Appearance, resulting from their Freedom and Independence, that is never to be met with in those dreary Abodes, where the embittering Circumstance of a precarious Property, mars the Relish of every Gratification, and

damps the most magnanimous Spirits. They can think for themselves; publish their Sentiments, and animadvert on Religion and
Government, secure and unmolested.

• • •

But in *absolute* Monarchies, the whole Country is overspread with
a dismal Gloom. *Slavery* is stamp'd on the Looks of the Inhabitants;
and *Penury* engraved on their Visages, in strong and legible Characters. To prevent Complaints, the Press is prohibited; and a Vindication of the natural Rights of Mankind, is Treason. Every generous
Spirit is broke and depressed: Human Nature is degraded, insulted,
spurn'd, and outrag'd: The lovely Image of GOD, is defaced and dis-
figur'd, and the Lord of the Creation treated like the bestial Herd. The
liberal Sciences languish: The politer Arts droop their Heads: Merit is
banished to Cells and Deserts; and Virtue frowned into Dungeons, or
dispatched to the Gallies: Iniquity is exalted: Goodness trod under
Foot: Truth perverted; and the barbarous Outrages of Tyranny, sanc-
tified and adored. The Fields lie waste and uncultivated: Commerce
is incumbered with supernumerary Duties: The Tyrant riots in the
Spoils of his People; and drains their Purses, to replenish his insatiate
Treasury. He wages War against his own Subjects. . . .

Does any one think the above Representation, the Result of a rov-
ing Fancy, or figur'd beyond the Life; let him take a Survey of *Rome*;
e'er-while the Nurse of Heroes, and the Terror of the World; but now
the obscene Haunt of sequestred Bigots, and effeminate Slaves.
Where are now her *Scipios*, and *Tullys*, her *Brutuses*, and her *Catos*,
with other Names of equal Lustre, who plann'd her Laws, and fought
her Battles, during her Freedom and Independence? Alas! they are
succeeded by cloistered Monks and castrated Musicians, in Subjection to a filthy old Harlot, that pretends to a Power of devouring her
Mediator, and claims a Right to eat up her People. Let him survey all
Italy, once the Seat of Arts and Arms, and every Thing great and valuable; now the joyless Theatre of Oppression and Tyranny, Superstition and Ignorance. Let him behold all this; and when he has
finished his Survey, then let him *believe and tremble.*

But far otherwise, is the Condition of a free People. Under the mild
and gentle Administration of a *limited* Prince, every Thing looks cheerful and happy, smiling and serene. Agriculture is encouraged, and
proves the annual Source of immense Riches to the Kingdom: The
Earth opens her fertile Bosom to the Plough-share, and luxuriant Harvests diffuse Wealth and Plenty thro' the Land: The Fields stand thick
with Corn: The Pastures smile with Herbage: The Hills and Vallies are
cover'd with Flocks and Herds: Manufactures flourish; and unprecari-
ous Plenty recompenses the Artificer's Toil: In a Word, Nothing is seen
but universal Joy and Festivity. Such is the Happiness of the People, under the blissful Reign of a good King. But do they get a Prince, whose
Heart is poison'd with Regard to regal Authority, and who vainly imag-
ines; that the Grandeur of Princes consists in making themselves
feared; and accordingly plays the Devil in the Name of the Lord: They
boldly assert their Rights, and call aloud for Justice; They cannot, they
will not be enslaved. Sooner shall the royal Sinner have the Honour of
Martyrdom, and the *Lord's Anointed* perish for his Iniquity, than the
whole Frame of the Government be unhinged and dissolved. . . .

• • •

How signal is our Happiness, in being blessed with a Prince, form'd
for the Friend of the Nation, and the Defender of the Liberties of *Europe!* A Prince, who despises the Thought of placing his Grandeur in
the Violation of the Laws; but is nobly ambitious of reigning in the
Hearts of his People: A Prince, who invariably exerts his native Greatness of Soul, and all his inherent and hereditary Virtues, in the Support of Truth, Religion and Liberty: A Prince, in fine, unemulous of
arbitrary Sway; but ardently aspiring after those brighter Trophies,
that are earn'd in the Paths of Virtue and heroic Deeds; in relieving
the Injured, protecting the Oppressed, and by a diffusive Benevolence, promoting the Happiness of Mankind. Long, oh long may he
still adorn the Throne of his Ancestors! and when the Sovereign Dis-
poser of Events, shall at last, to the keen and universal Affliction of
his People, translate him to the Possession of a Crown, eternal and in-
corruptible; we may presage, (which will be the only Consideration

capable of alleviating our Sorrow,) the greatest Glory, and the brightest Triumphs, from his Royal Highness's eminent Virtues; whose future Reign promises the most distinguished Prosperity to the Nation; and will exhibit to *Britain,* a Monarch, from his benevolent Disposition, and princely Education, the Father of his People, as well as a shining Ornament to that illustrious Family, of which we have already seen two Heroes on the *British Throne;* the Scourges of Tyrants, and the Assertors of Liberty.

Questions

1. What does the author mean by a "free state"?

2. Does the author think that the institution of monarchy is incompatible with freedom?

––––––––––––

24. The Trial of John Peter Zenger (1735)

Source: The Trial of John Peter Zenger *(London, 1765), pp. 19–46.*

Under British and colonial law, the government could not censor newspapers, books, and pamphlets before they appeared in print, but authors and publishers could be prosecuted for "seditious libel"—a crime that included defaming government officials—or punished for contempt of public authority. In colonial America, dozens of publishers were hauled before assemblies and forced to apologize for comments regarding one or another member. If they refused, they were jailed.

The most famous colonial court case involving freedom of the press occurred in 1735. This was the trial of John Peter Zenger, a German-born printer, whose newspaper, the *Weekly Journal,* lambasted New York's governor for corruption and "tyranny." Zenger was arrested and put on trial for seditious libel. The judge instructed the jurors to consider only whether Zenger had in fact published the offending words. But Zenger's attorney,

Andrew Hamilton, told the jury that the "cause of liberty" itself was at stake. If Zenger's charges were correct, he went on, they should acquit him and, "every man who prefers freedom to a life of slavery will bless you." Zenger was found not guilty. The outcome demonstrated that the idea of free expression was becoming ingrained in the popular imagination.

MR. ATTORNEY. The case before the court is whether Mr. Zenger is guilty of libeling His Excellency the Governor of New York, and indeed the whole administration of the government. Mr. Hamilton has confessed the printing and publishing, and I think nothing is plainer than that the words in the information [indictment] are scandalous, and tend to sedition, and to disquiet the minds of the people of this province. And if such papers are not libels, I think it may be said there can be no such thing as a libel.

MR. HAMILTON. May it please Your Honor, I cannot agree with Mr. Attorney. For though I freely acknowledge that there are such things as libels, yet I must insist, at the same time, that what my client is charged with is not a libel. And I observed just now that Mr. Attorney, in defining a libel, made use of the words "scandalous, seditious, and tend to disquiet the people." But (whether with design or not I will not say) he omitted the word "false."

MR. ATTORNEY. I think I did not omit the word "false." But it has been said already that it may be a libel, notwithstanding it may be true.

MR. HAMILTON. In this I must still differ with Mr. Attorney; for I depend upon it, we are to be tried upon this information now before the court and jury, and to which we have pleaded not guilty, and by it we are charged with printing and publishing a certain false, malicious, seditious, and scandalous libel. This word "false" must have some meaning, or else how came it there? . . .

• • •

MR. CHIEF JUSTICE. You cannot be admitted, Mr. Hamilton, to give the truth of a libel in evidence. A libel is not to be justified; for it is nevertheless a libel that it is true. . . .

MR. HAMILTON. I thank Your Honor. Then, gentlemen of the jury, it is to you we must now appeal, for witnesses, to the truth of the facts we have offered, and are denied the liberty to prove. And let it not seem strange that I apply myself to you in this manner. I am warranted so to do both by law and reason.

The law supposes you to be summoned out of the neighborhood where the fact [crime] is alleged to be committed; and the reason of your being taken out of the neighborhood is because you are supposed to have the best knowledge of the fact that is to be tried. And were you to find a verdict against my client, you must take upon you to say the papers referred to in the information, and which we acknowledge we printed and published, are false, scandalous, and seditious. But of this I can have no apprehension. You are citizens of New York; you are really what the law supposes you to be, honest and lawful men. And, according to my brief, the facts which we offer to prove were not committed in a corner; they are notoriously known to be true; and therefore in your justice lies our safety. And as we are denied the liberty of giving evidence to prove the truth of what we have published, I will beg leave to lay it down, as a standing rule in such cases, that the suppressing of evidence ought always to be taken for the strongest evidence; and I hope it will have weight with you . . .

• • •

I hope to be pardoned, sir, for my zeal upon this occasion. It is an old and wise caution that when our neighbor's house is on fire, we ought to take care of our own. For though, blessed be God, I live in a government [Pennsylvania] where liberty is well understood, and freely enjoyed, yet experience has shown us all (I'm sure it has to me) that a bad precedent in one government is soon set up for an authority in another. And therefore I cannot but think it mine, and every honest man's duty; that (while we pay all due obedience to men in authority) we ought at the same time to be upon our guard against power, wherever we apprehend that it may affect ourselves or our fellow subjects.

I am truly very unequal to such an undertaking on many accounts. And you see I labor under the weight of many years, and am borne down with great infirmities of body. Yet old and weak as I am, I should think it my duty, if required, to go to the utmost part of the land, where my service could be of any use, in assist—to quench the flame of prosecutions upon informations, set on foot by the government, to deprive a people of the right of remonstrating (and complaining too) of the arbitrary attempts of men in power. Men who injure and oppress the people under their administration provoke them to cry out and complain; and then make that very complaint the foundation for new oppressions and prosecutions. I wish I could say there were no instances of this kind.

But to conclude. The question before the court and you, gentlemen of the jury, is not of small nor private concern. It is not the cause of a poor printer, nor of New York alone, which you are now trying. No! It may, in its consequence, affect every freeman that lives under a British government on the main [land] of America. It is the best cause. It is the cause of liberty. And I make no doubt but your upright conduct, this day, will not only entitle you to the love and esteem of your fellow citizens; but every man who prefers freedom to a life of slavery will bless and honor you, as men who have baffled the attempt of tyranny, and, by an impartial and uncorrupt verdict, have laid a noble foundation for securing to ourselves, our posterity, and our neighbors, that to which nature and the laws of our country have given us a right—the liberty both of exposing and opposing arbitrary power (in these parts of the world, at least) by speaking and writing truth.

• • •

Questions

1. Why does Hamilton equate Zenger's defense with "the cause of liberty"?

2. What does Hamilton seem to think is the greatest threat to liberty?

25. A Defense of George Whitefield (1739)

Source: The American Weekly Mercury *(New York), November 22–29, 1739.*

A series of religious revivals known as the Great Awakening swept through the colonies beginning in the 1730s. The revivals were united by a commitment to a "religion of the heart," a more emotional and personal Christianity than that offered by existing churches. More than any other individual, the English minister George Whitefield, who declared "the whole world his parish," sparked the Great Awakening. For two years after his arrival in America in 1739, Whitefield brought his highly emotional brand of preaching to colonies from Georgia to New England. God, Whitefield proclaimed, was merciful. Rather than being predestined for damnation, men and women could save themselves by repenting of their sins. Whitefield appealed to the passions of his listeners, powerfully sketching the boundless joy of salvation and the horrors of damnation. Whitefield's sermons were widely reported in the American press, which also published criticisms of him for encouraging disrespect for established churches and ministers. In New York City, Jonathan Arnold, a local minister, published an attack on Whitefield, and was answered by a writer under the name of Magnus Falconar, who identified himself as a sailor. Since writers often took fictional names and occupations for publication it is impossible to know who Falconar actually was, but his choice of identity illustrates how the Awakening encouraged ordinary Americans to call into question aspects of established authority.

———

Mr. Arnold's Letter against the Reverend Mr. George Whitefield, Answered, by Magnus Falconar, Mariner.

To the Inhabitants of New York.

Your seemingly zealous brother Jonathan Arnold, out of a regard (as he says) for the good of your soul, cautions you to beware of the false doctrine, the Rev. Mr. Whitefield preaches, and charges him as being a deceiver. Yet I am hopeful the good Christians amongst you who heard him, will be very far from charging him with the least appearance of deceit or false doctrine. And unless you are indeed under a dreadful delusion, you may plainly enough perceive that this Arnold is the deceiver and preacher of false doctrine, who in the very beginning of his epistle strives to impose upon the world two abominable lies.

1st, That the Rev. Mr. Whitefield exclaims against all the bishops and clergymen of the Church of England, 2nd, That he passes unwarrantable sentences upon men as if he was the Supreme Judge.

As to the first, he is so far from exclaiming against all the clergy of the Church, that in his public sermons preached here, he not only sticks to true church principles, but has likewise named several worthy ministers of that Church; and surely if your brother Arnold was of that number he would not take upon him to exclaim against those that are . . .

And as to his second aspersion, of passing condemnatory sentences upon men as if he was the Supreme Judge, this is likewise as false. He condemns none, but invites the worst of sinners to come to Christ for salvation, and to accept of him in the terms of the Gospel, not trusting in their own righteousness, but by a steady faith rely entirely, solely and without reserve upon the righteousness of our Lord Jesus Christ and even his only. Surely they who preach any other doctrine than this, read their Bible backward. . . .

As to his charge against the Rev. Mr. Whitefield for ignorance, surely Mr. Arnold appears by his writings to be possessed with the grossest of ignorance. . . . His prayers and wishes are abomination unto the Lord, and his lies proceed from the Father of Lies, the Devil.

Questions

1. Which ideas of Whitefield seem most offensive to the Rev. Arnold?

2. Does the tone of the letter by Magnus Falconer suggest why many persons were alarmed by the Great Awakening?

26. Pontiac, Two Speeches (1762 and 1763)

Source: Alexander Henry, Travels and Adventures In Canada and the Indian Territories Between the Years *1760* and *1776 [1809], (Toronto, 1901), p. 44; and Francis Parkman,* The Conspiracy of Pontiac and the Indian Wars after the Conquest of Canada *(6th ed., Boston, 1874), Vol. 1, pp. 204–07.*

Victory in the Seven Years War, confirmed in the Treaty of Paris of 1763, established British preeminence in North America east of the Mississippi River. To Indians, it was clear that the abrupt departure of the French from Canada and the Mississippi and Ohio Valleys, and the continued expansion of the British settler population, posed a dire threat.

In 1763, Indians of the Ohio Valley and Great Lakes launched a revolt against British rule. Although known as Pontiac's rebellion, after an Ottawa war leader, the rebellion owed much to the teachings of Neolin, a Delaware religious prophet. Neolin and Pontiac promoted a pan-Indian identity among members of different tribes, urging all Indians in fight to regain their lost independence. In 1763, Indians seized several British forts and killed hundreds of white settlers who had intruded onto Indian lands. British forces soon launched a counterattack and one by one the tribes made peace. But the uprising lay the groundwork for future resistance.

———

ENGLISHMAN, ALTHOUGH YOU have conquered the French, you have not yet conquered us! We are not your slaves. These lakes, these woods and mountains, were left to us by our ancestors. They are our inheritance; and we will part with them to none. Your nation supposes that we, like the white people, cannot live without bread—and pork—and beef! But, you ought to know, that He, the Great Spirit and Master of Life, has provided food for us, in these spacious lakes, and on these woody mountains . . .

• • •

"A Delaware Indian [Neolin]," said Pontiac, "conceived an eager desire to learn wisdom from the Master of Life; but, being ignorant where to find him, he had recourse to fasting, dreaming, and magical incantations. By these means it was revealed to him, that, by moving forward in a straight, undeviating course, he would reach the abode of the Great Spirit. He told his purpose to no one, and having provided the equipments of a hunter,—gun, powder-horn, ammunition, and a kettle for preparing his food,—he set out on his errand. For some time he journeyed on in high hope and confidence. On the evening of the eighth day, he stopped by the side of a brook at the edge of a meadow, where he began to make ready his evening meal, when, looking up, he saw three large openings in the woods before him, and three well-beaten paths which entered them. He was much surprised; but his wonder increased, when, after it had grown dark, the three paths were more clearly visible than ever. Remembering the important object of his journey, he could neither rest nor sleep; and, leaving his fire, he crossed the meadow, and entered the largest of the three openings. He had advanced but a short distance into the forest, when a bright flame sprang out of the ground before him, and arrested his steps. In great amazement, he turned back, and entered the second path, where the same wonderful phenomenon again encountered him; and now, in terror and bewilderment, yet still resolved to persevere, he took the last of the three paths. On this he journeyed a whole day without interruption, when at length, emerging from the forest, he saw before him a vast mountain, of dazzling whiteness. So precipitous was the ascent, that the Indian thought it hopeless to go farther, and looked around him in despair: at that moment, he saw, seated at some distance above, the figure of a beautiful woman arrayed in white, who arose as he looked upon her, and thus accosted him: 'How can you hope, encumbered as you are, to succeed in your design? Go down to the foot of the mountain, throw away your gun, your ammunition, your provisions, and your clothing; wash yourself in the stream which flows there, and you will then be prepared to stand before the Master of Life.' The Indian obeyed, and again began to ascend among the rocks, while the woman, seeing him still discouraged, laughed at his faintness of heart, and told him that, if he wished for success, he must climb by the aid of one hand and one foot only. After great toil and suffering, he at length found himself at the summit. The woman had disappeared, and he was left alone. A rich and beautiful plain lay before him, and at a little distance he saw three great villages, far superior to the squalid wigwams of the Delawares. As he approached the largest, and stood hesitating whether he should enter, a man gorgeously attired stepped forth, and, taking him by the hand, welcomed him to the celestial abode. He then conducted him into the presence of the Great Spirit, where the Indian stood confounded at the unspeakable splendor which surrounded him. The Great Spirit bade him be seated, and thus addressed him:—

" 'I am the Maker of heaven and earth, the trees, lakes, rivers, and all things else. I am the Maker of mankind; and because I love you, you must do my will. The land on which you live I have made for you, and not for others. Why do you suffer the white men to dwell among you? My children, you have forgotten the customs and traditions of your forefathers. Why do you not clothe yourselves in skins, as they did, and use the bows and arrows, and the stonepointed lances, which they used? You have bought guns, knives, kettles, and blankets, from the white men, until you can no longer do without them; and, what is worse, you have drunk the poison fire-water, which turns you into fools. Fling all these things away; live as your wise forefathers lived before you. And as for these English,—these dogs dressed in red, who have come to rob you of your hunting-grounds, and drive away the game,—you must lift the hatchet against them. Wipe them from the face of the earth, and then you will win my favor back again, and once more be happy and prosperous.

Questions

1. How does Pontiac seem to understand the meaning of freedom?

2. What elements of Indian life does Neolin criticize most strongly?

CHAPTER 5

The American Revolution, 1763–1783

27. Virginia Resolutions on the Stamp Act (1765)

Source: John Pendleton Kennedy, ed., Journals of the House of Burgesses of Virginia 1761–1765 *(Richmond, 1907), pp. lxvi–lxvii, 360.*

The passage of the Stamp Act by Parliament in 1765 inspired the first major split between colonists and Great Britain. Pressed for funds because of the enormous expense it had incurred in fighting the Seven Years' War, Parliament for the first time attempted to raise money from direct taxes in the colonies rather than through the regulation of trade. The act required that all sorts of printed material produced in the colonies carry a stamp purchased from authorities.

By imposing the stamp tax without colonial consent, Parliament directly challenged the authority of local elites who, through the assemblies they controlled, had established their power over the raising and spending of money. They were ready to defend this authority in the name of liberty. Virginia's House of Burgesses approved four resolutions offered by the fiery orator Patrick Henry. The Burgesses rejected as too radical the last three resolutions that follow, including one calling for outright resistance to unlawful taxation.

WHEREAS, THE HONOURABLE House of Commons in England, have of late draw[n] into question how far the General Assembly of this colony hath power to enact laws for laying of taxes and imposing duties payable by the people of this, his Majesty's most ancient colony; for settling and ascertaining the same to all future times, the House of Burgesses of this present General Assembly have come to the following resolves.

Resolved, that the first adventurers, settlers of this his Majesty's colony and dominion of Virginia, brought with them and transmitted to their posterity, and all other his Majesty's subjects since inhabiting in this his Majesty's colony, all the privileges and immunities that have at any time been held, enjoyed, and possessed by the people of Great Britain.

Resolved, that by two royal charters granted by King James the first, the colonists aforesaid are declared and entitled to all privileges and immunities of natural born subjects, to all intents and purposes as if they had been abiding and born within the realm of England.

Resolved, that the taxation of the people by themselves, or by persons chosen by themselves to represent them, who can only know what taxes the people are able to bear, or the easiest method of raising them, and must themselves be affected by every tax laid on the people, is the only security against a burdensome taxation, and the distinguishing characteristic of British freedom, without which the ancient constitution cannot exist.

Resolved, that his Majesty's liege people of this ancient colony have enjoyed the right of being thus governed by their own Assembly in the article of taxes and internal police, and that the same have never been forfeited, or any other way yielded up, but have been constantly recognized by the king and people of Great Britain.

Resolved, therefore, that the General Assembly of this colony, together with his Majesty or his substitutes, have in their representatives capacity, the only exclusive right and power to lay taxes and imposts upon the inhabitants of this colony; and that every attempt to vest such power in any other person or persons whatever than the General Assembly aforesaid, is illegal, unconstitutional, and unjust, and has a manifest tendency to destroy British as well as American liberty.

Resolved, that his Majesty's liege people, the inhabitants of this colony, are not bound to yield obedience to any law or ordinance whatever, designed to impose any taxation whatsoever upon them, other than the laws or ordinances of the General Assembly aforesaid.

Resolved, that any person who shall, by speaking or writing, assert or maintain that any person or persons other than the General Assembly of this colony, have any right or power to impose or lay any taxation on the people here, shall be deemed an enemy to his Majesty's colony.

Questions

1. Why do you think the Virginia House of Burgesses adopted the first four resolutions but rejected the final three?

2. What would be the difference between resting the resolutions' arguments on "British freedom" and appealing to a more universal concept of liberty?

---

28. Petition of North Carolina Regulators (1769)

Source: William L. Saunders, ed., The Colonial Records of North Carolina *(Raleigh, 1886–90), Vol. 8, pp. 75–78.*

Even as the dispute between Britain and America over taxation grew deeper during the 1760s, several colonies experienced internal social divisions. Rural areas had a long tradition of resistance by settlers and small farmers against the claims of land speculators and large proprietors. One

such group, in North Carolina, were known as the Regulators. They mobi-
lized small farmers, who refused to pay taxes, kidnaped local officials, as-
saulted the homes of land speculators, merchants, and lawyers, and
disrupted court proceedings. A petition to the colonial assembly by the
Regulators of Anson county outlines their grievances. Demanding the
democratization of local government, the Regulators condemned the
colony's elite who used their political authority to prosper at the expense
of poor industrious farmers. At their peak, the Regulators numbered
around 8,000 armed farmers. The region remained in turmoil until 1771
when, in the "battle of Alamance," the farmers were suppressed by the
colony's militia.

HUMBLY SHEWETH

That the Province in general labour under general grievances, and
the Western part thereof under particular ones; which we not only
see, but very sensibly feel, being crouch'd beneath our sufferings: and
notwithstanding our sacred privileges, have too long yielded ourselves slaves to remorseless oppression.—Permit us to conceive it to
be our inviolable right to make known our grievances, and to petition for redress; as appears in the Bill of Rights pass'd in the reign of
King Charles the first, as well as the act of Settlement of the Crown of
the Revolution. We therefore beg leave to lay before you a specimen
thereof that your compassionate endeavours may tend to the relief
of your injured Constituents, whose distressed condition calls aloud
for aid. The alarming cries of the oppressed possibly may reach your
Ears; but without your zeal how shall they ascend the throne—how
relentless is the breast without sympathy, the heart that cannot
bleed on a View of our calamity; to see tenderness removed, cruelty
stepping in; and all our liberties and priviledges invaded and abridg'd
(by as it were) domesticks: who are conscious of their guilt and void
of remorse.—O how daring! how relentless! whilst impending Judgments loudly threaten and gaze upon them, with every emblem of
merited destruction.

A few of the many grievances are as follows, (Viz.)

1. That the poor Inhabitants in general are much oppress'd by reason of disproportionate Taxes, and those of the western Counties in particular; as they are generally in mean circumstances.

2. That no method is prescribed by Law for the payment of the Taxes of the Western Counties in produce (in lieu of a Currency) as is in other Counties within this Province; to the Peoples great oppression.

3. That Lawyers, Clerks, and other pentioners; in place of being obsequious Servants for the Country's use, are become a nuisance, as the business of the people is often transacted without the least degree of fairness, the intention of the law evaded, exorbitant fees extorted, and the sufferers left to mourn under their oppressions.

4. That an Attorney should have it in his power, either for the sake of ease or interest, or to gratify their malevolence and spite, to commence suits to what Courts he pleases, however inconvenient it may be to the Defendant: is a very great oppression.

5. That all unlawful fees taken on Indictment, where the Defendant is acquitted by his Country (however customary it may be) is an oppression.

6. That Lawyers, Clerks, and others, extorting more fees than is intended by law; is also an oppression.

7. That the violation of the King's Instructions to his delegates, their artfulness in concealing the same from him; and the great Injury the People thereby sustains: is a manifest oppression.

And for remedy whereof, we take the freedom to recommend the following mode of redress, not doubting audience and acceptance; which will not only tend to our relief, but command prayers as a duty from your humble Petitioners.

1. That at all elections each suffrage be given by Ticket & Ballot.

2. That the mode of Taxation be altered, and each person to pay in proportion to the profits arising from his Estate.

3. That no future tax be laid in Money, until a currency is made.

4. That there may be established a Western as well as a Northern and Southern District, and a Treasurer for the same.

5. That when a currency is made it may be let out by a Loan office (on Land security) and not to be call'd in by a Tax.

6. That all debts above 40s. and under £10 be tried and determined without Lawyers, by a jury of six freeholders, impanneled by a Justice, and that their verdict be enter'd by the said Justice, and be a final judgment.

7. That the Chief Justice have no perquisites, but a Salary only.

8. That Clerks be restricted in respect to fees, costs, and other things within the course of their office.

9. That Lawyers be effectually Barr'd from exacting and extorting fees.

10. That all doubts may be removed in respect to the payment of fees and costs on Indictments where the Defendant is not found guilty by the jury, and therefore acquitted.

11. That the Assembly make known by Remonstrance to the King, the conduct of the cruel and oppressive Receiver of the Quit Rents, for omitting the customary easie and effectual method of collecting by distress, and pursuing the expensive mode of commencing suits in the most distant Courts.

12. That the Assembly in like manner make known that the governor and Council do frequently grant Lands to as many as they think proper without regard to Head Rights, notwithstanding the contrariety of His Majesties Instructions; by which means immense sums has been collected, and numerous Patents granted, for much of the most fertile lands in this Province, that is yet uninhabited and uncultivated, environed by great numbers of poor people who are necessitated to toil in the cultivation of bad Lands whereon they hardly can subsist, who are thereby deprived of His Majesties liberality and Bounty: nor is there the least regard paid to the cultivation clause in said Patent mentioned, as many of the said Council as well as their friends and favorites enjoy large Quantities of Lands under the above-mentioned circumstances.

13. That the Assembly communicates in like manner the Violation of His Majesties Instructions respecting the Land Office by the Governor and Council, and of their own rules, customs and orders, if it be sufficiently proved, that after they had granted Warrants for many Tracts of Land, and that the same was in due time survey'd and return'd, and the Patent fees timely paid into the said office; and that if a private Council was called on purpose to avoid spectators, and peremptory orders made that Patents should not be granted; and Warrants by their orders arbitrarily to have Issued in the names of other Persons for the same Lands, and if when intreated by a solicitor they refus'd to render so much as a reason for their so doing, or to refund any part of the money by them extorted.

• • •

Questions

1. What are the main precedents to which the petitioners refer in claiming their "inviolable rights"?

2. In what ways do the authors claim that their "liberties" have been violated?

29. Association of the New York Sons of Liberty (1773)

Source: Hezekiah Niles, **Principles and Acts of the Revolution in America** *(Baltimore, 1822), pp. 169–70.*

The Sons of Liberty of New York City was one of many such groups that sprang up during the Stamp Act crisis of 1765. It was led by talented and ambitious lesser merchants who enjoyed no standing among the colony's wealthy but commanded a broad following among the city's craftsmen, laborers, and sailors. The Sons took the lead in enforcing the boycott of British imports that led to Parliament's repeal of the act and a second boycott directed against the Townshend Duties of 1767.

In 1773, when Parliament passed the Tea Act, another taxation measure, the Sons again organized resistance. On December 15, the Sons of Liberty announced an agreement or association to resist the Tea Act. Signed by "a great number of the principal gentlemen of the city, merchants, lawyers, and other inhabitants of all ranks," the agreement forthrightly accused Britain of trampling on the freedom of the colonists and threatening to reduce them to "slavery."

THE FOLLOWING ASSOCIATION is signed by a great number of the principal gentlemen of the city, merchants, lawyers, and other inhabitants of all ranks, and it is still carried about the city to give an opportunity to those who have not yet signed, to unite with their fellow citizens, to testify their abhorrence to the diabolical project of enslaving America.

THE ASSOCIATION OF THE SONS OF LIBERTY OF NEW YORK

It is essential to the freedom and security of a free people, that no taxes be imposed upon them but by their own consent, or their representatives. For "What property have they in that which another may, by right, take when he pleases to himself?" The former is the undoubted right of Englishmen, to secure which they expended millions and sacrificed the lives of thousands. And yet, to the astonishment of all the world, and the grief of America, the Commons of Great Britain, after the repeal of the memorable and detestable Stamp Act, reassumed the power of imposing taxes on the American colonies; and insisting on it as a necessary badge of parliamentary supremacy, passed a bill, in the seventh year of his present Majesty's reign, imposing duties on all glass, painters' colours, paper, and teas, that should, after the 20th of November, 1767, be "imported from Great Britain into any colony or plantation in America". This bill, after the concurrence of the Lords, obtained the royal assent. And thus they who, from time immemorial, have exercised the right of giving to, or withholding from the crown, their aids and subsidies, according to their *own free will and pleasure*, signified by their representatives in Parliament, do, by the Act in question, deny us, their brethren in America, the enjoyment of the same right. As this denial, and the execution of that Act, involves our slavery, and would sap the foundation of our freedom, whereby we should become slaves to our brethren and fellow subjects, born to no greater stock of freedom than the Americans—the merchants and inhabitants of this city, in conjunction with the merchants and inhabitants of the ancient American colonies, entered into an agreement to decline a part of their commerce with Great Britain, until the above mentioned Act should be totally repealed.

This agreement operated so powerfully to the disadvantage of the manufacturers of England that many of them were unemployed. To appease their clamours, and to provide the subsistence for them, which the non-importation had deprived them of, the Parliament, in 1770, repealed so much of the Revenue Act as imposed a duty on glass, painters' colours, and paper, and left the duty on tea, as *a test of the parliamentary right to tax us.* The merchants of the cities of New York and Philadelphia, having strictly adhered to the agreement, so far as it is related to the importation of articles subject to an American duty, have convinced the ministry, that some other measures must be adopted to execute parliamentary supremacy over this country, and to remove the distress brought on the East India Company, by the ill policy of that Act. Accordingly, to increase the temptation to the shippers of tea from England, an Act of Parliament passed the last session, which gives the whole duty on tea, the company were subject to pay, upon the importation of it into England, to the purchasers and exporters; and when the company have ten millions of pounds of tea in their warehouses exclusive of the quantity they may want to ship, they are allowed to export tea, discharged from the payment of that duty with which they were before chargeable.

In hopes of aid in the execution of this project, by the influence of the owners of the American ships, application was made by the company to the captains of those ships to take the tea on freight; but they virtuously rejected it. Still determined on the scheme, they have chartered ships to bring the tea to this country, which may be hourly expected, to make an important trial of our virtue. If they succeed in the sale of that tea, we shall have no property that we can call our own, and then we may bid adieu to American liberty. Therefore, to prevent a calamity which, of all others, is the most to be dreaded—slavery and its terrible concomitants—we, the subscribers, being influenced from a regard to liberty, and disposed to use all lawful endeavours in our power, to defeat the pernicious project, and to transmit to our posterity those blessings of freedom which our ancestors have handed down to us; and to contribute to the support of the common liberties of America, which are in danger to be subverted, *do*, for those important purposes, agree to associate together, under the name and style of the *sons of New York*, and engage our honour to, and with each other faithfully to observe and perform the following resolutions, viz.

1st. Resolved, that whoever shall aid or abet, or in any manner assist, in the introduction of tea from any place whatsoever, into this colony, while it is subject, by a British Act of Parliament, to the payment of a duty, for the purpose of raising a revenue in America, he shall be deemed an enemy to the liberties of America.

2d. Resolved, that whoever shall be aiding, or assisting, in the landing, or carting of such tea, from any ship, or vessel, or shall hire any house, storehouse, or cellar or any place whatsoever, to deposit the tea, subject to a duty as aforesaid, he shall be deemed an enemy to the liberties of America.

3d. Resolved, that whoever shall sell, or buy, or in any manner contribute to the sale, or purchase of tea, subject to a duty as aforesaid, or shall aid, or abet, in transporting such tea, by land or water, from this city, until the 7th George III, chap. 46, commonly called the Revenue Act, shall be totally and clearly repealed, he shall be deemed an enemy to the liberties of America.

4th. Resolved, that whether the duties on tea, imposed by this Act, be paid in Great Britain or in America, our liberties are equally affected.

5th. Resolved, that whoever shall transgress any of these resolutions, we will not deal with, or employ, or have any connection with him.

Questions

1. How do the Sons of Liberty explain Britain's motivations for passing the Tea Act?

2. What do they consider the relationship between property and liberty?

30. Farmington, Connecticut, Resolutions on the Intolerable Acts (1774)

*Source: Peter Force, **American Archives** (Washington, D. C., 1837–1853), Series 4, Vol. 1, p. 336.*

Parliament responded to the Boston Tea Party by passing a series of coercive laws. These closed the port of Boston to all trade until the tea had been paid for, radically altered the Massachusetts Charter of 1691 by curtailing town meetings and authorizing the governor to appoint previously elected members of the council, and empowered military commanders to lodge soldiers in private homes. These measures, called the Intolerable Acts by Americans, destroyed the legitimacy of the imperial government in the eyes of many colonists. Opposition now spread to small towns and rural areas that had not participated actively in previous resistance. A gathering of 1,000 residents of Farmington, Connecticut, in May 1774 erected a liberty pole and adopted resolutions that proclaimed that they were "the sons of freedom," who "scorn the chains of slavery" Britain had fashioned for America. The Farmington resolutions accused the British ministry of being "instigated by the devil." Especially in New England, the cause of liberty had become the cause of God.

PROCEEDINGS OF FARMINGTON, Connecticut, on the Boston Port Act, May 19, 1774.

Early in the morning was found the following handbill, posted up in various parts of the town, viz:

> To pass through the fire at six o'clock this evening, in honour to the immortal goddess of Liberty, the late infamous Act of the British Parliament for farther distressing the American Colonies; the place of execution will be the public parade, where all Sons of Liberty are desired to attend.

Accordingly, a very numerous and respectable body were assembled of near one thousand people, when a huge pole, just forty-five feet high, was erected and consecrated to the shrine of liberty; after which the Act of Parliament for blocking up the Boston harbour was read aloud, sentenced to the flames and executed by the hands of the common hangman; then the following resolves were passed, *nem. con.*:

1st. That it is the greatest dignity, interest and happiness of every American to be united with our parent State, while our liberties are duly secured, maintained and supported by our rightful Sovereign, whose person we greatly revere; whose government, while duly administered, we are ready with our lives and properties to support.

2d. That the present ministry, being instigated by the devil and led on by their wicked and corrupt hearts, have a design to take away our liberties and properties and to enslave us *forever*.

3d. That the late Act which their malice hath caused to be passed in Parliament, for blocking up the port of Boston, is unjust, illegal and oppressive; and that we and every American are sharers in the insults offered to the town of Boston.

4th. That those pimps and parasites who dared to advise their master to such detestable measures be held in utter abhorrence by us and every American, and their names loaded with the curses of all succeeding generations.

5th. That we scorn the chains of slavery; we despise every attempt to rivet them upon us; we are the sons of freedom and resolved that, till time shall be no more, godlike virtue shall blazon our hemisphere.

Questions

1. In what way does the language of the resolutions suggest that feelings toward Great Britain have hardened in the colonies?

2. How do the resolutions qualify or limit Americans' sense of loyalty to the British government?

---

31. Thomas Paine, *Common Sense* (1776)

Source: Thomas Paine, Common Sense (2nd ed.: Philadelphia, 1776), pp. 1, 6–12, 15–30.

Ironically, a recent emigrant from England offered the most persuasive argument for American independence. Thomas Paine arrived in Philadelphia late in 1774 and quickly became associated with a group of advocates of the American cause. His pamphlet, *Common Sense*, appeared in January 1776. It began not with a recital of colonial grievances but with an attack on the principles of hereditary rule and monarchial government. Paine then drew on the colonists' experiences to make his case for independence. Within the British empire, America's prospects were limited; trading freely with the entire world, its future prosperity was certain. With independence, moreover, the colonies could for the first time insulate themselves from involvement in the endless imperial wars of Europe. But more than such practical considerations, Paine outlined a stirring vision of the historical importance of the American Revolution. The new nation would become the home of freedom, "an asylum for mankind."

Previous political writings had generally been directed toward the educated elite. Paine pioneered a new style of political writing, one designed to expand dramatically the public sphere where political discussion took place. *Common Sense* quickly became one of the most successful and influential pamphlets in the history of political writing.

<hr/>

INTRODUCTION

Perhaps the sentiments contained in the following pages, are not *yet* sufficiently fashionable to procure them general Favor; a long Habit of not thinking a Thing *wrong*, gives it a superficial appearance of being *right*, and raises at first a formidable outcry in defence of Custom. But the Tumult soon subsides. Time makes more Converts than Reason.

As a long and violent abuse of power is generally the means of calling the right of it in question, (and in matters too which might never have been thought of, had not the sufferers been aggravated into the inquiry,) and as the King of England hath undertaken in his *own right*, to support the Parliament in what he calls *Theirs*, and as the good People of this Country are grievously oppressed by the Combination, they have an undoubted privilege to enquire into the Pretensions of both, and equally to reject the Usurpation of *either*.

In the following Sheets, the Author hath studiously avoided every thing which is personal among ourselves. Compliments as well as censure to individuals make no part thereof. The wise and the worthy need not the triumph of a Pamphlet; and those whose sentiments are injudicious or unfriendly will cease of themselves, unless too much pain is bestowed upon their conversions.

The cause of America is in a great measure the cause of all mankind. Many circumstances have, and will arise, which are not local, but universal, and through which the principles of all lovers of mankind are affected, and in the event of which their affections are interested. The laying a country desolate with fire and sword, declaring war against the natural rights of all mankind, and extirpating the defenders thereof from the face of the earth, is the concern of every man to whom nature hath given the power of feeling.

• • •

Of Monarchy and Hereditary Succession

Mankind being originally equals in the order of creation, the equality could only be destroyed by some subsequent circumstance; the distinctions of rich, and poor, may in a great measure be accounted for, and that without having recourse to the harsh ill sounding names of oppression and avarice. Oppression is often the *consequence*, but seldom or never the *means* of riches; and though avarice will preserve a man from being necessitously poor, it generally makes him too timorous to be wealthy.

But there is another and greater distinction for which no truly natural or religious reason can be assigned, and that is, the distinction of men into KINGS and SUBJECTS. Male and female are the distinctions of nature, good and bad the distinctions of heaven; but how a race of men came into the world so exalted above the rest, and distinguished like some new species, is worth enquiring into, and whether they are the means of happiness or of misery to mankind.

• • •

All men being originally equals, no *one* by *birth* could have a right to set up his own family in perpetual preference to all others for ever, and though himself might deserve *some* decent degree of honors of his contemporaries, yet his descendants might be far too unworthy to inherit them. One of the strongest *natural* proofs of the folly of hereditary right in kings, is, that nature disapproves it, otherwise she would not so frequently turn it into ridicule by giving mankind an *ass for a lion.*

As to usurpation, no man will be so hardy as to defend it; and that William the Conqueror was an usurper is a fact not to be contradicted.

The plain truth is, that the antiquity of English monarchy will not bear looking into.

. . .

THOUGHTS ON THE PRESENT STATE OF AMERICAN AFFAIRS

In the following pages I offer nothing more than simple facts, plain arguments, and common sense: and have no other preliminaries to settle with the reader, than that he will divest himself of prejudice and prepossession, and suffer his reason and his feelings to determine for themselves: that he will put on, or rather that he will not put off, the true character of a man, and generously enlarge his views beyond the present day.

Volumes have been written on the subject of the struggle between England and America. Men of all ranks have embarked in the controversy, from different motives, and with various designs; but all have been ineffectual, and the period of debate is closed. Arms as the last resource decide the contest; the appeal was the choice of the King, and the Continent has accepted the challenge.

. . .

The Sun never shined on a cause of greater worth. 'Tis not the affair of a City, a County, a Province, or a Kingdom; but of a Continent—of at least one eighth part of the habitable Globe. 'Tis not the concern of a day, a year, or an age; posterity are virtually involved in the contest, and will be more or less affected even to the end of time, by the proceedings now. Now is the seed-time of Continental union, faith and honour. The least fracture now will be like a name engraved with the point of a pin on the tender rind of a young oak; the wound would enlarge with the tree, and posterity read it in full grown character.

. . .

As much hath been said of the advantages of reconciliation, which, like an agreeable dream, hath passed away and left us as we were, it is but right that we should examine the contrary side of the argument, and enquire into some of the many material injuries which these Colonies sustain, and always will sustain, by being connected with and dependent on Great-Britain. To examine that connection and dependence, on the principles of nature and common sense, to see what we have to trust to, if separated, and what we are to expect, if dependant.

I have heard it asserted by some, that as America has flourished under her former connection with Great-Britain, the same connection is necessary towards her future happiness, and will always have the same effect. Nothing can be more fallacious than this kind of argument. We may as well assert that because a child has thrived upon milk, that it is never to have meat, or that the first twenty years of our lives is to become a precedent for the next twenty. But even this is admitting more than is true; for I answer roundly, that America would have flourished as much, and probably much more, had no European power taken any notice of her. The commerce by which she hath enriched herself are the necessaries of life, and will always have a market while eating is the custom of Europe.

But she has protected us, say some. That she hath engrossed us is true, and defended the Continent at our expense as well as her own, is admitted; and she would have defended Turkey from the same motive, *viz.* for the sake of trade and dominion.

Alas! we have been long led away by ancient prejudices and made large sacrifices to superstition. We have boasted the protection of Great Britain, without considering, that her motive was *interest* not *attachment*; and that she did not protect us from *our enemies* on *our account*; but from *her enemies* on *her own account*, from those who had no quarrel with us on any *other account*, and who will always be our enemies on the *same account*. Let Britain waive her pretensions to the Continent, or the Continent throw off the dependence, and we should be at peace with France and Spain, were they at war with Britain.

• • •

But Britain is the parent country, say some. Then the more shame upon her conduct. Even brutes do not devour their young, nor savages make war upon their families; Wherefore, the assertion, if true, turns to her reproach; but it happens not to be true, or only partly so, and the phrase *parent* or *mother country* hath been jesuitically adopted by the King and his parasites, with a low papistical design of gaining an unfair bias on the credulous weakness of our minds. Europe, and not England, is the parent country of America. This new World hath been the asylum for the persecuted lovers of civil and religious liberty from *every part* of Europe. Hither have they fled, not from the tender embraces of the mother, but from the cruelty of the monster; and it is so far true of England, that the same tyranny which drove the first emigrants from home, pursues their descendants still.

• • •

Our plan is commerce, and that, well attended to, will secure us the peace and friendship of all Europe; because it is the interest of all Europe to have America a free port. Her trade will always be a protection, and her barrenness of gold and silver secure her from invaders.

I challenge the warmest advocate for reconciliation to show a single advantage that this continent can reap by being connected with Great Britain. I repeat the challenge; not a single advantage is derived. Our corn will fetch its price in any market in Europe, and our imported goods must be paid for by them where we will.

But the injuries and disadvantages which we sustain by that connection, are without number; and our duty to mankind at large, as well as to ourselves, instruct us to renounce the alliance: because, any submission to, or dependence on, Great Britain, tends directly to involve this Continent in European wars and quarrels, and set us at variance with nations who would otherwise seek our friendship, and against whom we have neither anger nor complaint. As Europe is our market for trade, we ought to form no partial connection with any part of it. It is the true interest of America to steer clear of European contentions, which she never can do, while, by her dependence on Britain, she is made the makeweight in the scale of British politics.

• • •

'Tis repugnant to reason, to the universal order of things, to all examples from former ages, to suppose that this Continent can long remain subject to any external power. The most sanguine in Britain doth not think so. The utmost stretch of human wisdom cannot, at this time, compass a plan, short of separation, which can promise the continent even a year's security. Reconciliation is *now* a fallacious dream. Nature hath deserted the connection, and art cannot supply her place. For, as Milton wisely expresses, "never can true reconcilement grow where wounds of deadly hate have pierced so deep."

A government of our own is our natural right: and when a man seriously reflects on the precariousness of human affairs, he will become convinced, that it is infinitely wiser and safer, to form a constitution of our own in a cool deliberate manner, while we have it in our power, than to trust such an interesting event to time and chance.

• • •

O! ye that love mankind! Ye that dare oppose not only the tyranny but the tyrant, stand forth! Every spot of the old world is overrun with oppression. Freedom hath been hunted round the Globe. Asia and Africa have long expelled her. Europe regards her like a stranger, and England hath given her warning to depart. O! receive the fugitive, and prepare in time an asylum for mankind.

Questions

1. Why does Paine begin his argument for independence with an attack on the principle of monarchy and hereditary succession?

2. What passages illustrate Paine's effort to write in a language ordinary readers can understand?

32. James Chalmers, *Plain Truth* (1776)

Source: *James Chalmers,* Plain Truth: Addressed to the Inhabitants of America *(Philadelphia, 1776), pp. 1–3, 28, 33, 63–66.*

Common Sense inspired a wide-ranging debate about whether American freedom would be more secure inside or outside the British empire. James Chalmers, a Maryland plantation owner, made the case for the Loyalists, as those who opposed American independence were called. In *Plain Truth, Addressed to the Inhabitants of America*, published in March 1776, he defended the British system of government against Paine's attack, related the many benefits he believed the colonists received from their association with Great Britain, and predicted that independence would unleash continuous strife within the new nation. Chalmers appealed to men of property, warning that the democratic government Paine proposed would allow the poor to pass laws interfering with the collection of debts. Chalmers went on to serve in the British army during the War of Independence

IF INDIGNANT AT the doctrine contained in the pamphlet entitled Common Sense I have expressed myself in the following observations with some ardor...[it is because] I adore my country. Passionately devoted to true liberty, I glow with the purest flame of patriotism [and have an] abhorrence of Independency, which if effected, would inevitably plunge our once preeminently envied country into ruin, horror, and desolation....

Our Political Quack [attempts] to cajole the people into the most abject slavery under the delusive name of independence. His first indecent attack is against the English constitution; which with all its imperfections is, and ever will be the pride and envy of mankind....

Can a reasonable being for a moment believe that Great Britain, whose political existence depends on our constitutional obedience, who but yesterday made such prodigious efforts to save us from France, will not exert herself as powerfully to preserve us from our frantic schemes of Independency.... We remember with unfeigned gratitude, the many benefits derived through our connections with Great Britain, by whom but yesterday we were emancipated from slavery and death . . . We venerate the constitution, which with all its imperfections (too often exaggerated) we apprehend almost approaches as near to perfection as human kind can bear. . . .

His scheme of independency would soon, very soon give way to a government imposed on us, by some Cromwell of our armies. . . . A failure of commerce [would] preclude the numerous tribe of planters, farmers and others, from paying their debts . . . A war will ensure between the creditors and their debtors, which will eventually end in a general abolition of debts. . . .

Volumes were insufficient to describe the horror, misery and desolation, awaiting the people at large in the form of American independence. In short, I affirm that it would be most excellent policy in those who wish for True Liberty to submit by an advantageous reconciliation to the authority of Great Britain. . . . Independence and Slavery are synonymous terms.

Questions

1. Why does Chalmers equate independence with slavery?

2. Which Americans would be most likely to be persuaded by Chalmers's arguments?

CHAPTER 6

The Revolution Within

33. Abigail and John Adams on Women and the American Revolution (1776)

Source: Charles F. Adams, ed., Familiar Letters of John Adams and His Wife Abigail Adams During the Revolution *(New York, 1876), pp. 148–50, 155.*

Abigail Adams was one of the revolutionary era's most important women. During the War of Independence, she peppered her husband, John Adams, with questions about the progress of the struggle, kept him informed of events in Massachusetts and offered opinions on political matters. When Adams served as president during the 1790s, he relied on her advice more than on members of his cabinet. In March 1776, Abigail Adams wrote her best-known letter to her husband. She urged Congress, when it drew up a new "Code of Laws," to "remember the ladies." All men, she warned, "would be tyrants if they could."

At a time when many Americans—slaves, servants, women, Indians, apprentices, propertyless men—were denied full freedom, the struggle against Britain inspired challenges to all sorts of inequalities. As John Adams's reply demonstrates, not all American leaders welcomed this upheaval. To him, it was an affront to the natural order of things. To others, it formed the essence of the American Revolution.

Abigail Adams to John Adams

Braintree [Mass.], March 31, 1776

I wish you would ever write me a letter half as long as I write you, and tell me if you may where your fleet are gone? What sort of defense Virginia can make against our common enemy? Whether it is so situated as to make an able defense? Are not the gentry lords and the common people vassals, are they not like the uncivilized natives Britain represents us to be? I hope their riflemen who have shown themselves very savage and even blood-thirsty, are not a specimen of the generality of the people.

. . .

I have sometimes been ready to think that the passion for Liberty cannot be equally strong in the breasts of those who have been accustomed to deprive their fellow creatures of theirs. Of this I am certain, that it is not founded upon that generous and Christian principle of doing to others as we would that others should do unto us.

. . .

I feel very differently at the approach of spring to what I did a month ago. We knew not then whether we could plant or sow with safety, whether when we had toiled we could reap the fruits of our own industry, whether we could rest in our own cottages, or whether we should not be driven from the sea coasts to seek shelter in the wilderness. But now we feel as if we might sit under our own vine and eat the good of the land. . . . I think the sun looks brighter, the birds sing more melodiously, and nature puts on a more cheerful countenance. We feel a temporary peace, and the poor fugitives are returning to their deserted habitations.

Though we felicitate ourselves, we sympathize with those who are trembling lest the lot of Boston should be theirs. But they cannot be in similar circumstances unless . . . cowardice should take possession of them. They have time and warning given them to see the evil and shun it.

I long to hear that you have declared an independency, and by the way in the new Code of Laws which I suppose it will be necessary for you to make I desire you would Remember the Ladies, and be more generous and favorable to them than your ancestors. Do not put such unlimited power into the hands of the husbands. Remember all men would be tyrants if they could. If particular care and attention is not paid to the Ladies we are determined to foment a Rebellion, and will not hold ourselves bound by any laws in which we have no voice, or representation.

That your sex are naturally tyrannical is a truth so thoroughly established as to admit of no dispute, but such of you as wish to be happy willingly give up the harsh title of Master for the more tender and endearing one of Friend. Why then, not put it out of the power of the vicious and the lawless to use us with cruelty and indignity with impunity? Men of sense in all ages abhor those customs which treat us only as the vassals of your sex. Regard us then as beings placed by providence under your protection and in imitation of the Supreme Being make use of that power only for our happiness.

John Adams to Abigail Adams

Philadelphia, April 14, 1776

As to Declarations of Independency, be patient.... As to your extraordinary Code of Laws, I cannot but laugh. We have been told that our struggle has loosened the bands of government everywhere. That children and apprentices were disobedient, that schools and colleges were grown turbulent, that Indians slighted their guardians and Negroes grew insolent to their masters. But your letter was the first intimation that another tribe more numerous and powerful than all the rest were grown discontented. This is rather too coarse a compliment but you are so saucy, I won't blot it out.

Depend on it. We know better than to repeal our masculine systems. Although they are in full force, you know they are little more than theory. We dare not exert our power in its full latitude. We are obligated to go fair, and softly, and in practice you know we are the subjects. We have only the names of Masters, and rather than give this up, which would completely subject us to the despotism of the petticoat, I hope General Washington, and all our brave heroes, would fight. I am sure every good politician would plot, as long as he would against despotism, empire, monarchy, aristocracy, oligarchy, or ochlocracy [mob rule]. A fine story indeed.

Questions

1. What do you think Abigail Adams has in mind when she writes of the "unlimited power" husbands exercise over their wives?

2. Why did the struggle for independence "loosen the bands of government everywhere," as John Adams remarks?

34. The Right of "Free Suffrage" (1776)

Source: Letter by "Watchman," Maryland Gazette (Annapolis), August 15, 1776.

Among the dramatic changes in American life inspired by the War of Independence was the expansion of the right to vote. As ordinary Americans engaged in public debates, enlisted in state militias, and took part in legal and extralegal committees that enforced the orders of Congress, they demanded an end to property qualifications for voting.

The essay that follows, which appeared in a Maryland newspaper in 1776, illustrates the democratic upsurge that accompanied independence. The writer challenged the decision of the colony's leaders to restrict voting to those with property. The essay also shows how equality—"an equal claim to all the privileges, liberties, and immunities" of citizens, including the right to vote—had become linked to many Americans' understanding of freedom. By the 1780s, with the exceptions of Virginia, Maryland, and New York, a large majority of the adult white male population could meet voting requirements.

WHEN DESPOTISM REARED her head, and regal power was straining every nerve to ruin and enslave this country, opposition became expedient, opposition became absolutely necessary. The old government, ever treacherous and oppressive, could not be trusted, [and] the mode of government by convention was therefore instituted. But such mode of government proving extremely imperfect, attended with many inconveniences, and not competent to the exigencies of affairs, and the honorable Congress having recommended that a government be formed, in each colony, under the "authority of the people," of such colony only, ... the last convention resolved, that a convention be elected for the express purpose of forming a new government, by the authority of the people only, and enacting and ordering all things for the preservation, safety, and general weal of this colony.

Unfortunately, in the same sitting, they passed a resolve restricting the right of voting, thereby excluding nearly half of the members of this state [from] the enjoyment of their inherent right of free suffrage.... Is it not an insult to common sense to say that a government can be formed by the authority of the people only, when near half of them are excluded from any share in the election of the convention which is to form the government? This inequality of representation, contained in the resolve, cannot be justified on any principle. Every freeman must stand amazed at it. It struck at the grandest right of a freeman.... The ultimate end of all freedom is the enjoyment of a free suffrage. A constitution formed without this important right of free voting being preserved to the people, would be despotic.... For a people governed contrary to their inclination, or by persons to whom they have given no commission for that purpose, are, in the properest sense of the phrase, an *enslaved people*, if ever there was an enslaved people. That a *part* of the people should engross the power of electing legislators for the *whole* community is the grossest injustice that can be imagined....

• • •

Every poor man has a life, a personal liberty, and a right to his earnings, and is in danger of being injured by government in a variety of ways; therefore it is necessary that these people should enjoy the right of voting for representatives, to be protectors of their lives, personal liberty, and their little property which, though small, is yet, upon the whole, a very great object to them. It would be unjust and oppressive in the extreme to shut out the poor in having a share in declaring who shall be the lawmakers of their country, and yet bear a very heavy share in the support of government. Would not the rich complain grievously if they had no power of electing representatives? . . . Every member of this state, who lends his aid to the support of it, has an equal claim to all the privileges, liberties, and immunities with every [one] of his fellow countrymen; circumstances which are essential to the existence of a free state, and inseparable from the exercise and operation of a free people. . . . No power in the state can legally diminish this *equal right,* either by reducing the number of those privileges to which the whole community is justly entitled, or by imparting to men, or particular societies of men, such degrees of power and privilege that shall, in fact, render the other members less free or more subservient to the purposes of others, than the equal right of freedom can allow. If these be not the innate rights and privileges of the people, they are *not* free. . . .

Let, therefore, all hateful distinctions cease, and elections [be] made open and by the free suffrage of the people stand good and valid. . . . And let a government be established, where equal liberty can be enjoyed, the interest of the people promoted, and the cause of America maintained.

Questions

1. How does the writer define freedom and slavery?

2. What are his arguments for allowing men without property to vote?

35. Thomas Jefferson, An Act for Establishing Religious Freedom (1785)

Source: W. W. Hening, ed., Statutes at Large of Virginia *(Richmond, 1823), pp. 84–86.*

As remarkable as the expansion of political freedom was the Revolution's impact on American religion. During the Revolution, religious toleration came to be seen as an essential element of freedom by many Americans. Throughout the new nation, states disestablished their established churches, that is, deprived them of public funding and special legal privileges. Catholics gained the right to worship without persecution.

In Virginia, Thomas Jefferson drew up a Bill for Establishing Religious Freedom, introduced in the House of Burgesses in 1779 and adopted, after considerable controversy, in 1786. Jefferson's bill, whose preamble declared that God "hath created the mind free," eliminated religious requirements for voting and officeholding and government financial support for churches, and barred the state from "forcing" individuals to adopt one or another religious outlook. Late in life, Jefferson would list this measure, along with the Declaration of Independence and the founding of the University of Virginia, as the three accomplishments (leaving out his two terms as president) for which he wished to be remembered.

I. Whereas Almighty God hath created the mind free; that all attempts to influence it by temporal punishments or burthens, or by civil incapacitations, tend only to beget habits of hypocrisy and meanness, and are a departure from the plan of the Holy author of our religion, who being Lord both of body and mind, yet chose not to propagate it by coercions on either, as was in his Almighty power to do; that the impious presumption of legislators and rulers, civil as well as ecclesiastical, who being themselves but fallible and uninspired men, have assumed dominion over the faith of others, setting up their own opinions and modes of thinking as the only true and infallible, and as such endeavouring to impose them on others, hath established and maintained false religions over the greatest part of

the world, and through all time; that to compel a man to furnish contributions of money for the propagation of opinions which he disbe-
lieves, is sinful and tyrannical; that even the forcing him to support
this or that teacher of his own religious persuasion, is depriving him
of the comfortable liberty of giving his contributions to the particular pastor whose morals he would make his pattern, and whose powers he feels most persuasive to righteousness, and is withdrawing
from the ministry those temporary rewards, which proceeding from
an approbation of their personal conduct, are an additional incite-
ment to earnest and unremitting labours for the instruction of
mankind; that our civil rights have no dependence on our religious
opinions, any more than our opinions in physics or geometry; that
therefore the proscribing any citizen as unworthy the public confidence by laying upon him an incapacity of being called to offices of
trust and emolument, unless he profess or renounce this or that religious opinion, is depriving him injuriously of those privileges and
advantages to which in common with his fellow-citizens he has a
natural right; that it tends only to corrupt the principles of that religion it is meant to encourage, by bribing with a monopoly of worldly
honours and emoluments, those who will externally profess and
conform to it; that though indeed these are criminal who do not
withstand such temptation, yet neither are those innocent who lay
the bait in their way; that to suffer the civil magistrate to intrude his
powers into the field of opinion, and to restrain the profession or
propagation of principles on supposition of their ill tendency, is a
dangerous fallacy, which at once destroys all religious liberty, because he being of course judge of that tendency will make his opinions the rule of judgment, and approve or condemn the sentiments
of others only as they shall square with or differ from his own; that it
is time enough for the rightful purposes of civil government, for its
officers to interfere when principles break out into overt acts against
peace and good order; and finally, that truth is great and will prevail
if left to herself, that she is the proper and sufficient antagonist to
error, and has nothing to fear from the conflict, unless by human

interposition disarmed of her natural weapons, free argument and debate, errors ceasing to be dangerous when it is permitted freely to contradict them.

II. Be it enacted by the General Assembly, that no man shall be compelled to frequent or support any religious worship, place or ministry whatsoever, nor shall be enforced, restrained, molested, or burthened in his body or goods, nor shall otherwise suffer on account of his religious opinions or belief; but that all men shall be free to profess, and by argument to maintain their opinion in matters of religion, and that the same shall in no wise diminish, enlarge or affect their civil capacities.

III. And though we well know that this Assembly, elected by the people for the ordinary purposes of legislation only, have no power to restrain the acts of succeeding Assemblies, constituted with powers equal to our own, and that therefore to declare this Act to be irrevocable would be of no effect in law; yet as we are free to declare, and do declare, that the rights hereby asserted are of the natural rights of mankind, and that if any Act shall hereafter be passed to repeal the present, or to narrow its operation, such Act will be an infringement of natural right.

Questions

1. Why does Jefferson consider religious liberty one of the "natural rights of mankind"?

2. What is the bill's main argument for religious freedom?

---

36. Noah Webster on Equality (1787)

Source: Noah Webster, **An Examination into the Leading Principles of the Federal Constitution** *(Philadelphia, 1787), pp. 46–47.*

Americans of the revolutionary generation were preoccupied with the social conditions of freedom. Could a republic survive with a sizable dependent class of citizens? In the excerpt that follows, from a pamphlet published in 1787, the educator and political writer Noah Webster identified equality as essential for the stability of republican government. Citing and amending the teachings of the French political theorist Montesquieu, Webster proclaimed, "A general and tolerably equal distribution of landed property is the whole basis of national freedom." "Equality," he added, was "the very soul of a republic."

To most free Americans, "equality" meant equal opportunity, rather than equality of condition. Many leaders of the Revolution nevertheless assumed that in the exceptional circumstances of the New World, with its vast areas of available land and large population of independent farmers and artisans, the natural workings of society would enable all free Americans to acquire land and achieve, if not complete equality, at least the economic independence necessary for political "virtue."

———

IN AMERICA, WE begin our empire with more popular privileges than the Romans ever enjoyed. We have not to struggle against a monarch or an aristocracy—power is lodged in the mass of the people.

On reviewing the English history, we observe a progress similar to that in Rome—an incessant struggle for liberty from the date of Magna Charta, in John's reign, to the revolution. The struggle has been successful, by abridging the enormous power of the nobility. But we observe that the power of the people has increased in an exact proportion to their acquisitions of property. Wherever the right of primogeniture is established, property must accumulate and remain in families. Thus the landed property in England will never be sufficiently distributed, to give the powers of government wholly into the hands of the people. But to assist the struggle for liberty, commerce has interposed, and in conjunction with manufacturers, thrown a vast weight of property into the democratic scale. Wherever we cast our eyes, we see this truth, that *property* is the basis of *power;* and this, being established as a cardinal point, directs us to the means of preserving our freedom. Make laws, irrevocable laws in every state, destroying and barring entailments; leave real estates to revolve from hand to hand, as time and accident may direct; and no family influence can be acquired and established for a series of generations—no man can obtain dominion over a large territory—the laborious and saving, who are generally the best citizens, will possess each his share of property and power, and thus the balance of wealth and power will continue where it is, in the *body of the people.*

A general and tolerably equal distribution of landed property is the whole basis of national freedom: The system of the great Montesquieu will ever be erroneous, till the words *property or lands in fee simple* are substituted for *virtue,* throughout his *Spirit of Laws.*

Virtue, patriotism, or love of country, never was and never will be, till mens' natures are changed, a fixed, permanent principle and support of government. But in an agricultural country, a general possession of land in fee simple, may be rendered perpetual, and the inequalities introduced by commerce, are too fluctuating to endanger government. An equality of property, with a necessity of alienation, constantly operating to destroy combinations of powerful families, is the very *soul of a republic*—While this continues, the people will inevitably possess both *power* and *freedom;* when this is lost, power departs, liberty expires, and a commonwealth will inevitably assume some other form.

The liberty of the press, trial by jury, the Habeas Corpus writ, even Magna Charta itself, although justly deemed the palladia of freedom, are all inferior considerations, when compared with a general distribution of real property among every class of people. The power of entailing estates is more dangerous to liberty and republican government, than all the constitutions that can be written on paper, or even than a standing army. Let the people have property, and they *will* have power—a power that will for ever be exerted to prevent a restriction of the press, and abolition of trial by jury, or the abridgement of any other privilege. The liberties of America, therefore, and her forms of government, stand on the broadest basis. Removed from the fears of a foreign invasion and conquest, they are not exposed to the convulsions that shake other governments; and the principles of freedom are so general and energetic, as to exclude the possibility of a change in our republican constitutions.

Questions

1. Why does Webster consider an equal distribution of landed property more important to freedom than liberty of the press, trial by jury, and other rights?

2. Why does Webster believe the republican institutions of the United States will survive indefinitely?

37. Liberating Indentured Servants (1784)

Source: **New York Independent Journal,** *January 24, 1784.*

The upsurge of demands for equality during the Revolution brought into question many forms of inequality. In 1784, a group of "respectable" New Yorkers proposed to "liberate" a newly arrived shipload of indentured servants on the grounds that their status was "contrary to . . . the idea of liberty this country has so happily established." The incident was one small contribution to the rapid decline of indentured servitude, which by 1800 had all but disappeared from the United States. This development sharpened the distinction between freedom and slavery, and between a northern economy relying on what would come to be called "free labor" (that is, working for wages or owning a farm or shop) and a South ever more heavily dependent on the labor of slaves.

WHEREAS THE TRAFFIC of *White people*, heretofore countenanced by this State while under the arbitrary control of the British Government, is contrary to the feelings of a number of respectable Citizens, and to the idea of *liberty* this country has so happily established.

And whereas it is necessary to encourage emigration to this country, upon the most liberal plan, and for that purpose, a number of Citizens of this State, have proposed to *liberate* a cargo of Servants just arrived, by paying their passage, and repaying themselves by a small rateable deduction out of the wages of such Servants, Such of the Citizens of this State as wish to encourage so laudable an undertaking, and if necessary, to petition the Legislature for a completion of their humane intentions, are requested to meet at the Hyderally Tavern, the lower end of King Street, *this Evening*, at Six of the Clock.

Questions

1. What practical reason does the notice give for eliminating indentured servitude?

2. Why do you think the notice singles out the sale of "White people" as contrary to liberty?

---

38. Petition of Slaves to the Massachusetts Legislature (1777)

Source: Collections of the Massachusetts Historical Society, *Series 5, Vol. 3 (1877), pp. 434–37.*

The revolutionary generation's emphasis on liberty inevitably raised questions about the future of slavery in the new republic. The first concrete steps toward emancipation were "freedom petitions"—arguments for liberty presented to New England's courts and legislatures in the 1770s by enslaved African-Americans. As the petition that follows indicates, the slaves used the language of the Declaration of Independence—unalienable rights, the laws of nature, etc.—in the cause of abolition. Many slaves did gain their freedom during the era of the Revolution. The northern states enacted laws modeled on the one proposed by these petitioners (freeing the children of slaves after they reached adulthood). Far more slaves became free by running away to British lines. But the stark fact is that slavery survived the Revolution and, because of the natural increase of the slave population, continued to grow. The first national census, in 1790, revealed that despite all those who had become free through state laws, voluntary emancipation, and escape, the number of slaves in the United States was 700,000—200,000 more than in 1776.

To the Honorable Council and House of Representatives for the State of Massachusetts Bay in General Court assembled, January 13, 1777
The petition of a great number of blacks detained in a state of slavery in the bowels of a free and Christian country.... Your petitioners apprehend that they have in common with all other men a natural and unalienable right to that freedom which the Great Parent of the Universe has bestowed equally on all mankind and which they have never forfeited by any compact or agreement whatever, but ... were unjustly dragged by the hand of cruel power from their dearest friends and some of them even torn from the embraces of their tender parents, from a populous, pleasant, and plentiful country and in violation of laws of nature and of nations and in defiance of all the tender feelings of humanity brought here either to be sold like beasts of burden and like them condemned to slavery for life, among a people professing the mild religion of Jesus, a people not insensible of the secrets of rational being nor without spirit to resent the unjust endeavors of others to reduce them to a state of bondage and subjection. Your honors need not to be informed that a life of slavery like that of your petitioners, deprived of every social privilege, of everything requisite to render life tolerable is far worse than nonexistence.

In imitation of the laudable example of the good people of these states your petitioners have long and patiently waited the event of petition after petition by them presented to the legislative body of this state. . . . They cannot but express their astonishment that it has never been considered that every principle from which America has acted in the course of their unhappy difficulties with Great Britain pleads stronger than a thousand arguments in favor of your petitioners. They therefore humbly beseech your honors to give this petition its due weight and consideration and cause an act of the legislature to be passed whereby they may be restored to the enjoyments of that which is the natural right of all men—and their children who were born in this land of liberty may not be held as slaves after they arrive at the age of twenty-one years. So may the inhabitants of this state no longer [be] chargeable with the inconsistency of acting themselves the part which they condemn and oppose in others. . . .

Questions

1. What specifically do the petitioners mean when they say that "every principle" Americans have invoked against Britain offers an argument in their favor?

2. How do the slaves use the language of the white revolutionaries to argue for an end to slavery?

―――――――

39. Pennsylvania Act for the Gradual Abolition of Slavery (1780)

Source: William H. Egle, History of the Counties of Dauphin and Lebanon in the Commonwealth of Pennsylvania *(Philadelphia, 1883), p. 50.*

What one historian calls the "contagion of liberty" unleashed by the Revolution for a time threatened the existence of slavery. Between 1777 (when Vermont drew up a constitution that banned slavery) and 1804 (when New Jersey acted), every state north of Maryland took steps toward emancipation, the first time in recorded history that legislative power had been invoked to eradicate slavery. Pennsylvania's law of 1780 is excerpted here. But even in the North, where slavery was peripheral to the economy, abolition laws did not free living slaves. Instead, they provided for the liberty of any child born in the future to a slave mother, and only after he or she had served the mother's master until adulthood. Abolition in the North was a slow, drawn-out process. In 1860, eighteen elderly slaves still resided in New Jersey.

An Act for the Gradual Abolition of Slavery.

Section 1. When we contemplate our abhorrence of that condition to which the arms and tyranny of Great Britain were exerted to reduce us; when we look back on the variety of dangers to which we have been exposed, and how miraculously our wants in many instances have been supplied, and our deliverances wrought, when even hope and human fortitude have become unequal to the conflict; we are unavoidably led to a serious and grateful sense of the manifold blessings which we have undeservedly received from the hand of that Being from whom every good and perfect gift cometh. Impressed with these ideas, we conceive that it is our duty, and we rejoice that it is in our power to extend a portion of that freedom to others, which hath been extended to us; and a release from that state of thraldom to which we ourselves were tyrannically doomed, and from which we have now every prospect of being delivered. It is not for us to enquire why, in the creation of mankind, the inhabitants of the several parts of the earth were distinguished by a difference in feature or complexion. It is sufficient to know that all are the work of an Almighty Hand. We find in the distribution of the human species, that the most fertile as well as the most barren parts of the earth are inhabited by men of complexions different from ours, and from each other; from whence we may reasonably, as well as religiously, infer, that He who placed them in their various situations, hath extended equally his care and protection to all, and that it becometh not us to

The petition, of us the subscribers now residing on the western side of the Ohio, humbly show our grateful acknowledgments to those patriots of our country who under Divine Providence so wisely directed and steered the helm of government in that great and unparalleled conflict for liberty, bringing to a happy period the troubles of the states, laying the foundation . . . of the most glorious form of government any people on earth could ever yet boast of.

• • •

Notwithstanding when the joyful sound of peace had reached our ears, we had scarce enough left us to support the crying distresses of our families occasioned wholly by being exposed to the ravages of a cruel and savage enemy, on an open frontier where the most of us had the misfortune to reside through the whole continuance of the war, where the only recourse was to sit confined in forts for the preservation of our lives, by which we were reduced almost to the lowest ebb of poverty, the greatest part of us having no property in lands, our stocks reduced almost to nothing, our case seemed desperate.

But viewing as it appeared to us an advantage offering of vacant lands which the alarming necessities we were under joined with the future prospect of bettering our circumstances, invited us to enter on those lands fully determined to comply with every requisition of the legislature. . . . With hopes of future happiness we sat content in the enjoyment of our scanty morsel, thinking ourself safe under the protection of government, when on the fifth of this instant we were visited by a command of men sent by the commandant at Fort McIntosh, with orders from government . . . to dispossess us and to destroy our dwellings . . . by which order it now appears our conduct in settling here is considered by the legislature to be prejudicial to the common good, of which we had not the least conception until now. We are greatly distressed in our present circumstances, and humbly pray if you in your wisdom think proper to grant us liberty, to rest where we are and to grant us the preference to our actual settlements when the land is to be settled by order of the government.

• • •

Questions

1. Who do the authors of the petition seem to feel are the greatest enemies of their liberty?

2. Who do the authors claim ought to have preference when western land is distributed?

41. James Madison, *The Federalist*, No. 51 (1787)

Source: E. H. Scott, ed., The Federalist and Other Constitutional Papers (2 Vols.: Chicago, 1894), Vol. 1, pp. 285–90. Scott attributes this essay to Alexander Hamilton, but modern scholars have determined that James Madison was the author.

The question of ratifying the new national Constitution produced a fierce public debate. Hundreds of pamphlets and newspaper articles discussed the pros and cons of the new frame of government. To generate support for the Constitution, Alexander Hamilton, James Madison, and John Jay composed a series of eighty-five essays that appeared in newspapers under the pen name Publius and were gathered as a book, *The Federalist*, in 1788.

Again and again, the authors of *The Federalist* repeated that, rather than posing a danger to Americans' liberties, as critics charged, the Constitution in fact protected them. Madison's essays, including *Federalist* number 51, excerpted here, insisted that the security for liberty lay in the way power balanced power in the structure of government and in the nation's size and diversity. Previously, republics had existed only in small territories—the Dutch republic or Italian city-states of the Renaissance. But, Madison insisted, the larger the republic, the more distinct interests would exist, and no single one would ever be able to take over the government and oppress the rest.

• • •

To WHAT EXPEDIENT, then, shall we finally resort, for maintaining in practice the necessary partition of power among the several departments, as laid down in the Constitution? ... It is ... evident that the members of each department should be as little dependent as possible on those of the others, for the emoluments annexed to their offices ...

• • •

But the great security against a gradual concentration of those several powers in the same department consists in giving to those who administer each department the necessary constitutional and personal motives to resist the encroachments of the others. The provision for defense must in this, as in all other cases, be made commensurate to the danger of the attack. Ambition must be made to counteract ambition. The interest of the man must be connected with the constitutional rights of the place. It may be a reflection on human nature, that such devices should be necessary to control the abuses of government. But what is government itself, but the greatest of all reflections on human nature? If men were angels, no government would be necessary. If angels were to govern men, neither external nor internal controls on government would be necessary. In framing a government which is to be administered by men over men, the great difficulty lies in this: you must first enable the government to control the governed; and in the next place oblige it to control itself. A dependence on the people is, no doubt, the primary control on the government; but experience has taught mankind the necessity of auxiliary precautions.

• • •

There are ... two considerations particularly applicable to the federal system of America, which place that system in a very interesting point of view ...

First. In a single republic all the power surrendered by the people is submitted to the administration of a single government, and the usurpations are guarded against by a division of the government into distinct and separate departments. In the compound republic of America the power surrendered by the people is first divided between two distinct governments [federal and state], and then the portion allotted to each subdivided among distinct and separate departments. Hence a double security arises to the rights of the people. The different governments will control each other, at the same time that each will be controlled by itself.

Second. It is of great importance in a republic not only to guard the society against the oppression of its rulers, but to guard one part of society against the injustice of the other part. Different interests necessarily exist in different classes of citizens. If a majority be united by common interest, the rights of the minority will be insecure. There are but two methods of providing against this evil: the one by creating a will in the community independent of the majority . . . the other by comprehending in the society so many separate descriptions of citizens as will render an unjust combination of a majority of the whole very improbable, if not impracticable. . . . The second method will be exemplified in the federal republic of the United States. Whilst all authority in it will be derived from and dependent on the society, the society itself will be broken into so many parts, interests and classes of citizens, that the rights of individuals, or of the minority, will be in little danger from interested combinations of the majority.

In a free government the security for civil rights might be the same as that for religious rights. It consists in the one case in the multiplicity of interests, and in the other in the multiplicity of sects. The degree of security in both cases will depend on the number of interests and sects; and this may presume to depend on the extent of country and number of people comprehended under the same government.

• • •

Justice is the end of government. It is the end of civil society. It ever has and ever will be pursued until it be obtained, or until liberty is lost in the pursuit. In a society under the forms of which the stronger faction can readily unite and oppress the weaker, anarchy may as truly be said to reign as in a state of nature, where the weaker individual is not secured against the violence of the stronger. . . .

In the extended republic of the United States, and among the great variety of interests, parties, and sects which it embraces, a coalition of a majority of the whole society could seldom take place on any other principles than those of justice and general good. . . . It is no less certain than it is important . . . that the larger the society . . . the more duly capable it will be of self government. And happily for the republican cause. . . .

Questions

1. Why does Madison believe that the example of religious liberty offers a precedent relevant to political rights?

2. How does Madison argue that a large republic is more conducive to liberty than a small one?

———

42. James Winthrop on the Anti-Federalist Argument (1787)

Source: *E. H. Scott, ed.,* **The Federalist and Other Constitutional Papers** *(2 vols.: Chicago, 1894), Vol. 2, pp. 515–16, 554–55.*

Opponents of the ratification of the Constitution, called "Anti-Federalists," insisted that the document shifted the balance between liberty and power too far in the direction of the latter. Anti-Federalists repeatedly predicted that the new government would fall under the sway of merchants, creditors, and others hostile to the interests of ordinary Americans. Popular self-government, they claimed, flourished best in small communities, where rulers and ruled interacted daily.

The excerpt that follows, from one of a series of newspaper articles written by James Winthrop under the pen name Agrippa, illustrates some of the Anti-Federalists' arguments. Unlike Madison, Winthrop insisted that large states inevitably sought to enforce a uniformity that ignored local difference. The new Constitution, he went on, consolidated all power in the new national government. A Bill of Rights, moreover, was essential as a defense against tyranny. The Anti-Federalists' insistence was the primary reason why Congress and the states added the Bill of Rights to the Constitution soon after ratification.

IT IS THE opinion of the ablest writers on the subject, that no extensive empire can be governed upon republican principles, and that such a government will degenerate to a despotism, unless it be made up of a confederacy of smaller states, each having the full powers of internal regulation. This is precisely the principle which has hitherto preserved our freedom. No instance can be found of any free government of considerable extent which has been supported upon any other plan. Large and consolidated empires may indeed dazzle the eyes of a distant spectator with their splendor, but if examined more nearly are always found to be full of misery. The reason is obvious. In large states the same principles of legislation will not apply to all the parts. The inhabitants of warmer climates are more dissolute in their manners, and less industrious, than in colder countries. A degree of severity is, therefore, necessary with one which would cramp the spirit of the other. We accordingly find that the very great empires have always been despotick. They have indeed tried to remedy the inconveniences to which the people were exposed by local regulations; but these contrivances have never answered the end. The laws not being made by the people, who felt the inconveniences, did not suit their circumstances. It is under such tyranny that the Spanish provinces languish, and such would be our misfortune and degradation, if we should submit to have the concerns of the whole empire managed by one legislature. To promote the happiness of the people it is necessary that there should be local laws; and it is necessary that those laws should be made by the representatives of those who are immediately subject to the want of them. By endeavoring to suit both extremes, both are injured.

It is impossible for one code of laws to suit Georgia and Massa-chusetts. They must, therefore, legislate for themselves. Yet there is, I believe, not one point of legislation that is not surrendered in the proposed plan. Questions of every kind respecting property are de-terminable in a continental court, and so are all kinds of criminal causes. The continental legislature has, therefore, a right to make rules in all cases by which their judicial courts shall proceed and de-cide causes. No rights are reserved to the citizens. The laws of Congress are in all cases to be the supreme law of the land, and paramount to the constitutions of the individual states. The Congress may insti-tute what modes of trial they please, and no plea drawn from the constitution of any state can avail. This new system is, therefore, a consolidation of all the states into one large mass, however diverse the parts may be of which it is to be composed. The idea of an un-compounded republick, on an average one thousand miles in length, and eight hundred in breadth, and containing six millions of white inhabitants all reduced to the same standard of morals, of habits, and of laws, is in itself an absurdity, and contrary to the whole experience of mankind. The attempt made by Great Britain to introduce such a system, struck us with horrour, and when it was proposed by some theorist that we should be represented in parlia-ment, we uniformly declared that one legislature could not repre-sent so many different interests for the purposes of legislation and taxation. This was the leading principle of the revolution, and makes an essential article in our creed. All that part, therefore, of the system, which relates to the internal government of the states, ought at once to be rejected.

• • •

It is now generally understood that it is for the security of the people that the powers of the government should be lodged in dif-ferent branches. By this means public business will go on when they all agree, and stop when they disagree. The advantage of checks in government is thus manifested where the concurrence of different branches is necessary to the same act, but the advantage of a division of business is advantageous in other respects. As in every extensive empire, local laws are necessary to suit the different interests, no single legislature is adequate to the business. All human capacities are limited to a narrow space, and as no individual is capable of practising a great variety of trades, no single legislature is capable of managing all the variety of national and state concerns. Even if a legislature was capable of it, the business of the judicial department must, from the same cause, be slovenly done. Hence arises the necessity of a division of the business into national and local. Each department ought to have all the powers necessary for executing its own business, under such limitations as tend to secure us from any inequality in the operations of government. I know it is often asked against whom in a government by representation is a bill of rights to secure us? I answer, that such a government is indeed a government by ourselves; but as a just government protects all alike, it is necessary that the sober and industrious part of the community should be defended from the rapacity and violence of the vicious and idle. A bill of rights, therefore, ought to set forth the purposes for which the compact is made, and serves to secure the minority against the usurpation and tyranny of the majority. It is a just observation of his excellency, Doctor [John] Adams, in his learned defence of the American constitutions that unbridled passions produce the same effect, whether in a king, nobility, or a mob. The experience of all mankind has proved the prevalence of a disposition to use power wantonly. It is therefore as necessary to defend an individual against the majority in a republic as against the king in a monarchy.

• • •

Questions

1. To what provisions of the Constitution does Winthrop refer in arguing that the new government will endanger liberty?

2. Why does Winthrop claim that the "leading principle of the revolution" is violated by the new Constitution?

▬▬▬▬▬▬▬

43. A July Fourth Oration (1800)

Source: American Mercury *(Hartford, Conn.), July 10, 1800.*

From the earliest days of the new nation, July Fourth became a day of public commemoration. In 1800, a speaker whose name was not reported in the press delivered an Independence Day oration at Hartford, Connecticut. He celebrated the "universal principles" of the Declaration of Independence but chastised his fellow citizens for failing to live up to them fully. Like many other Americans, he rejoiced in the revolutions that, beginning in France, had swept parts of Europe, predicted further progress for the Rights of Man in years to come, and identified the American example as the catalyst for the spread of freedom overseas.

On the other hand, the speaker condemned slavery as a flagrant violation of American values and a source of shame for the nation, asking pointedly, "Declaration of Independence! Where art thou now?" He went on to urge that "our daughters" ought to enjoy the same rights as "our sons," an idea that had been put forth by a few writers in the 1790s, but was quite unusual for the time. Overall, the speech offered both an illustration of American nationalism in the aftermath of the Revolution, and a telling commentary on the extent and limits of American freedom at the dawn of the nineteenth century.

▬▬▬▬▬▬▬

• • •

To the principles, the genuine, universal principles of the Declaration of Independence, we consecrate this day. Our festivity is not on account of the achievements of armies, nor merely because the seat of government is removed from London to Philadelphia, but because the American people have calmly and deliberately declared, that "all men are created equal," and in the presence of the supreme God have, in support of this declaration, pledged their lives, their fortunes, and their sacred honor.

• • •

Whatever may be the future fate of America, she has destroyed the Bastille, she has liberated Belgium, her principles have scaled the Alps, and inundated the plains of Italy, they have climbed the walls of Rome.... [Before] long Ireland shall take her harp ... and shake the air with notes of liberty. Greece shall wake from her long slumber, some new Demosthenes shall plead the Rights of Man, while new Homers sing the triumphs of the free.... The Spanish monarchy totters at its base, exhausted by frequent wars, impoverished by a profligate administration. Farther degrees of colonial oppression will be the [attempted cure].... Then will the inward burnings of colonial rage burst into a flame, then will the Rights of Man echo from Florida to Chile, and re-echo from Lima to St. Salvador. The principles of freedom will then be learned from those who now wield the scourge of slavery, the benevolent system of Jesus shall resound from the ruins of the ... Inquisition.

• • •

And thou, sable Ethiop! Suffering brother, let the principles of this day irradiate thy benighted countenance! Already has the voice of thy tears and blood reached heaven! ... St. Domingo [has] seen thy race revenged, and their chains broken on the tyrants' heads.

• • •

Citizens, my soul shrinks from herself, and startles at the name of Africa! Where we have heaped crime upon crime! Where we have excited murders, robberies, and burnings, that we might punish them in our own land with endless, hopeless slavery.... Declaration of Independence! Where art thou now?

• • •

It is pleasing to turn from the contemplation of our inconsistencies, to the purity of our principles. The basis of the Declaration, from which the friend of his species hopes so much, is the Equality of Man. How the idea first got abroad, that men were not equal, is difficult to conceive, unless we refer the claim to the arrogance of power in the dark ages of the world. . . . The Equality of Man is the bond of our union and the constituted law of the land.

• • •

Citizens, you must teach your children the principles of this day, and by the best education in your power to bestow, teach them to understand them. . . . But citizens, in this, as in all other things, if you do not begin well, you will never end well. Those principles of freedom, which embrace only half mankind, are only half systems, and will no more support the burden of humanity, than [a] section of an arch will support a column. Our daughters are the same relations to us as our sons, we owe them the same duties, they . . . are equally competent to their attainments. The contrary idea originated in the same abuse of power, as monarchy and slavery, and owes its little remaining support to the same sophistry.

• • •

What is liberty? Is it a something that men may keep without care and lose without injury? No citizens. Liberty is a tender plant, which wants the constant vigilance of its owner—he must weed and water, and defend it *himself;* hirelings may destroy it by carelessness, by accident, or by design, and once it withers, it is difficult to be restored.

The habits of men who have been [raised] under a monarchy ill comport with the simplicity of republicanism. It is not enough that we have a republican form of government, we must acquire a *republican mind.* We must be frugal, sober, industrious, self-dependent, privately and publicly hospitable. . . . We must eradicate national prejudices. . . . We must always remember that *men,* and not soil, constitute the state.

• • •

Questions

1. How does the speaker seek to persuade his audience of the evils of slavery?

2. What does the speaker identify as the major reasons to celebrate American independence?

---

44. Thomas Jefferson on Race and Slavery (1781)

Source: Thomas Jefferson, Notes on the State of Virginia *(Philadelphia, 1788), pp. 145–53, 172–73.*

No American of the revolutionary generation did more to shape prevailing views on race than Thomas Jefferson. His writings reflected a divided, even tortured mind. In *Notes on the State of Virginia*, written in 1781 and published a few years later, Jefferson ruminated on whether blacks should be considered inferior to whites. Although generally, Jefferson attributed different peoples' varying degrees of civilization to environmental factors, Jefferson concluded that what he considered blacks' inferiority was innate. Jefferson made clear that he understood that slavery violated the principles of the Declaration of Independence he had written. He looked forward to the day when slaves would be emancipated. But, he insisted, once freed, they must be removed from the United States. Blacks, in Jefferson's view, could never become equal members of the American nation.

MANY OF THE laws which were in force during the monarchy being relative merely to that form of government, or inculcating principles inconsistent with republicanism, the first assembly which met after the establishment of the commonwealth appointed a committee to revise the whole code. . . . The following are the most remarkable alterations proposed. . . .

To emancipate all slaves born after passing the act. The bill reported by the revisors does not itself contain this proposition; but an amendment containing it was prepared, to be offered the legislature whenever the bill should be taken up, and further directing, that they should continue with their parents to a certain age, then be brought up, at the public expence, to tillage, arts or sciences, according to their geniusses, till the females should be eighteen, and the males twenty-one years of age, when they should be colonized to such place as the circumstances of the time should render most proper, sending them out with arms, implements of household and of the handicraft arts, seeds, pairs of the useful domestic animals, &c. to declare them a free and independant people, and extend to them our alliance and protection, till they have acquired strength; and to send vessels to the other parts of the world for an equal number of white inhabitants; to induce whom to migrate hither, proper encouragements were to be proposed. It will probably be asked, Why not retain and incorporate the blacks into the state, and thus save the expence of supplying, by importation of white settlers, the vacancies they will leave? Deep rooted prejudices entertained by the whites; ten thousand recollections, by the blacks, of the injuries they have sustained; new provocations; the real distinctions which nature has made; and many other circumstances, will divide us into parties, and produce convulsions which will probably never end but in the extermination of one or the other race.

• • •

—To these objections, which are political, may be added others, which are physical and moral. The first difference which strikes us is that of colour. Whether the black of the negro resides in the reticular membrane between the skin and scarf-skin, or in the scarf-skin itself; whether it proceeds from the colour of the blood, the colour of the bile, or from that of some other secretion, the difference is fixed in nature, and is as real as if its seat and cause were better known to us. And is this difference of no importance? Is it not the foundation of a greater or less share of beauty in the two races? Are not the fine mixtures of red and white, the expressions of every passion by greater or less suffusions of colour in the one, preferable to that eternal monotony, which reigns in the countenances, that immoveable veil of black which covers all the emotions of the other race? . . .

They seem to require less sleep. A black after hard labour through the day, will be induced by the slightest amusements to sit up till midnight, or later though knowing he must be out with the first dawn of the morning. They are at least as brave, and more adventuresome. But this may perhaps proceed from a want of forethought, which prevents their seeing a danger till it be present. When present, they do not go through it with more coolness or steadiness than the whites. They are more ardent after their female: but love seems with them to be more an eager desire, than a tender delicate mixture of sentiment and sensation. Their griefs are transient. Those numberless afflictions, which render it doubtful whether heaven has given life to us in mercy or in wrath, are less felt, and sooner forgotten with them. In general, their existence appears to participate more of sensation than reflection. . . .

—The opinion, that they are inferior in the faculties of reason and imagination, must be hazarded with great diffidence. To justify a general conclusion, requires many observations, even where the subject may be submitted to the anatomical knife, to optical glasses, to analysis by fire, or by solvents. How much more then where it is a faculty, not a substance, we are examining; where it eludes the research of all the senses; where the conditions of its existence are various and variously combined; where the effects of those which are present or absent bid defiance to calculation; let me add too, as a circumstance of great tenderness, where our conclusion would degrade a whole race of men from the rank in the scale of beings which their Creator may perhaps have given them. . . . I advance it therefore as a suspicion only, that the blacks, whether originally a distinct race, or made distinct by time and circumstances, are inferior to the whites in the endowments both of body and mind. . . .

There must doubtless be an unhappy influence on the manners of our people produced by the existence of slavery among us. The whole commerce between master and slave is a perpetual exercise of the most boisterous passions, the most unremitting despotism on the one part, and degrading submissions on the other. Our children see this, and learn to imitate it; for man is an imitative animal. This quality is the germ of all education in him. From his cradle to his grave he is learning to do what he sees others do. If a parent could find no motive either in his philanthropy or his self-love, for restraining the intemperance of passion towards his slave, it would always be a sufficient one that his child is present. But generally it is not sufficient. The parent storms, the child looks on, catches the lineaments of wrath, puts on the same airs in the circle of smaller slaves, gives a loose to his worst of passions, and thus nursed, educated, and daily exercised in tyranny, cannot but be stamped by it with odious peculiarities. The man must be a prodigy who can retain his manners and morals undepraved by such circumstances. And with what execration should the statesman be loaded, who permitting one half the citizens thus to trample on the rights of the other, transforms those into despots, and these into enemies, destroys the morals of the one part, and the amor patriae of the other. For if a slave can have a country in this world, it must be any other in preference to that in which he is born to live and labour for another: in which he must lock up the faculties of his nature, contribute as far as depends on his individual endeavours to the evanishment of the human race, or entail his own miserable condition on the endless generations proceeding from him. With the morals of the people, their industry also is destroyed. For in a warm climate, no man will labour for himself who can make another labour for him. This is so true, that of the proprietors of slaves a very small proportion indeed are ever seen to labour. And can the liberties of a nation be thought secure when we have removed their only firm basis, a conviction in the minds of the people that these liberties are of the gift of God? That they are not to be violated but with his wrath? Indeed I tremble for my country when I reflect that God is just: that his justice cannot sleep for ever.

Questions

1. What reasons does Jefferson offer for colonizing blacks outside the United States in the event of emancipation?

2. How does Jefferson describe the effect of slavery on the morals and behavior of white Virginians?

CHAPTER 8

Securing the Republic, 1790–1815

45. William Manning on the Nature of Free Government (1799)

Source: Reprinted by permission of the publisher from The Key of Liberty: The Life and Democratic Writings of William Manning, *edited by Michael Merrill and Sean Wilentz, pp. 125–26, 130–31, 136–38, Cambridge, Mass.: Harvard University Press, Copyright © 1993 by the President and Fellows of Harvard College.*

The 1790s was a decade of intense political conflict. Two political parties emerged, the Federalists and Republicans, representing radically different visions of how American society ought to be organized. The decade's partisan warfare produced an expansion of the public sphere and, with it, the democratic content of American freedom. More and more citizens attended political meetings and became avid readers of pamphlets and newspapers. Hundreds of "obscure men" wrote pamphlets and newspaper essays and formed political organizations.

This democratic ferment was reflected in writings like *The Key of Liberty* by William Manning, a self-educated Massachusetts farmer who had fought at the battle of Concord that began the War of Independence. Although not published until many years later, Manning's work, addressed to "friends to liberty and free government," reflected the era's popular political thought.

To ALL THE Republicans, Farmers, Mechanics, and Laborers in America. Your candid attention is requested to the sentiments of a Laborer.

Learning and knowledge is essential to the preservation of liberty; and unless we have more of it among us, we cannot support our liberties long....

• • •

I am not a man of learning, for I never had the advantage of six months schooling in my life. I am no traveler, for I never was fifty miles from where I was born. I am no great reader, for though I have a small landed interest, I always followed labor for a living.

But I always thought it my duty to search into and see for myself in all matters that concerned me as a member of society. And when the revolution began in America I was in the prime of life, and highly taken up with the ideas of liberty and a free government. I was in the Concord fight and saw almost the first blood shed in the cause. I thought then and still think that it is a good cause, which we ought to fight for and maintain. I have also been a constant reader of public newspapers and have closely attended to men and measures ever since—through the war, through the operation of paper money, framing constitutions, and making and construing laws. Seeing what little selfish and contracted ideas of interest would twist and turn the best picked men and bodies of men, I have often almost despaired of ever supporting a free government. But firmly believing it to be the best sort, and the only one approved of by heaven, it has been my unwearied study to find out the real cause of the ruin of republics and a remedy....

• • •

A Description of a Free Government

There are many sorts of government, or rather names by which governments have been distinguished—such as despotic, monarchical, and aristocratical. In these the power to govern is in the hands of one or a Few to govern as they please. Consequently they are masters and not servants, so that the government is not free.

There are also sundry names by which free governments are described, such as democratical, republican, elective, and free governments, all of which I take to mean nearly the same thing, or that all those nations who ever adopted them aimed at nearly the same thing; viz., to be governed by known laws in which the whole nation had a voice in making by a full and fair representation, and in which all the officers in every department are (or ought to be) servants and not masters.

• • •

That government is the most free that causes the greatest sum or degree of individual happiness in this world with the least national expense. The happiness of a person consisteth in eating and drinking and enjoying the good of his own labors, and feeling that his life and liberties (both civil and religious) and his property are all safe and secure; and not in the abundance he possesseth, nor in expensive and national grandeur, which have a tendency to make other men miserable.

Economy in expenditures ought to be the first principle of a free government. The people ought to support just so many without labor as is necessary for the public good and no more, and ought to pay them so much salary and fees as would command sufficient abilities and no more. All taxes for the support of government ought to be laid equally according to the property each one has and the advantage he receives from government, and collected in the easiest and least expensive manner. The sole end of government is the protection of the life, liberty, and property of individuals. The poor man's shilling ought to be as much the care of government as the rich man's pound and no more. Every person ought to have justice done to him freely and promptly, without delay. . . .

• • •

From the great varieties of capacities, strength, and abilities of men, there always was and always will be a very unequal distribution of property in the world. Many are so rich that they can live without labor. So, also, can the merchant, physician, lawyer, and divine, the philosopher and schoolmaster, the judicial and executive officers, and many others who can get a living honestly and for the benefit of the community without bodily labors. And as all these professions require a considerable time and expense of property to qualify themselves for them; and as no person after thus qualifying himself and making a pick on a profession by which he means to live can desire to have it dishonorable or unproductive—so they all naturally unite to make these professions as honorable and lucrative as possible . . .

• • •

Here lies the great scuffle between the Few and the Many.

As the interests of the Few—and their incomes—lie chiefly in money at interest, rents, salaries, and fees that are fixed on the nominal value of money, they are interested to have the money scarce and the prices of labor and produce as low as possible. For instance, if the price of labor and produce should fall one-half, it would be just the same to them as if their rents, fees, and salaries were doubled—all of which increase they get of the Many. Besides, the fall of the price of labor and produce, and the scarcity of money, always bring the Many into distress and compel them into a state of dependence on the Few for favors and assistances in a thousand ways.

On the other hand, if the Many could raise the price of labor and produce, and have money circulate freely, they would pay their debts and enjoy the good of their labors without being dependent on the Few for assistance. Also, when prices are high, a prudent and industrious person may presciently lay up something against a time of need. But the person that doth not work and lives high when the prices are up will soon spend all his property.

But the Few cannot bear to be on a level with their fellow creatures, or submit to the determination of a legislature where (as they say) the swinish multitude are fairly represented. They sicken at the idea, and are ever hankering and striving after monarchy or aristocracy, where the people have nothing to do in matters of government but to support the Few in luxury and idleness. For these and many other reasons, a large majority of those that live without labor are ever opposed to a free government. And though the whole of them do not amount to one-eighth part of the people, and not one-half of them are needed in their professions, yet by their arts, combinations, and schemes they have always made out to destroy free government sooner or later.

Questions

1. What does Manning mean by a "free government"?

2. Why does he think that a "scuffle" between the "Few" and the "Many" is inevitable?

46. Address of the Democratic-Republican Society of Pennsylvania (1794)

Source: Excerpt from Minutes of The Democratic Society of Pennsylvania, December 18, 1794. The Historical Society of Pennsylvania (HSP), Collection # Am. 315/3150. Reprinted with permission.

Another example of the spread of public involvement in politics during the 1790s was the emergence in 1793 and 1794 of the Democratic-Republic societies. The societies harshly criticized the policies of George Washington's administration, which they claimed were planting the seeds of aristocracy in the United States.

Federalists saw the societies as an example of how American freedom was getting out of hand. The government, not "self-created societies," declared the president, was the authentic voice of the American people. They also accused the societies of helping to foment the Whiskey Rebellion of 1794, in which farmers in western Pennsylvania resisted paying a new federal tax on distilled liquor. Forced to justify their existence, the societies developed a defense of the right of the people to debate political issues and organize to affect public policy. As a statement adopted by the Democratic-Republican Society of Pennsylvania insisted, "freedom of opinion" was the "bulwark of liberty," a natural right that no government could restrict.

———

The Democratic Society of Pennsylvania, established in Philadelphia, to their Fellow Citizens throughout the United States.

FELLOW CITIZENS,

The principles and proceedings of our Association have lately been caluminated. We should think ourselves unworthy to be ranked as Freemen, if awed by the name of any man, however he may command the public gratitude for past services, we could suffer in silence so sacred a right, so important a principle, as the freedom of opinion to be infringed, by attack on Societies which stand on that constitutional basis.

We shall not imitate our opponents, by resorting to declamation and abuse, instead of calm reasoning, and substituting assertion for proof. They have termed us anarchists; they have accused us of fomenting the unfortunate troubles in the western counties of this State:—yet not a single fact have they been able to adduce in support of the charge,—They have accused us of aiming at the overthrow of the Constitution; and this also rests upon their bare assertion. Neither shall we recriminate; though we might with at least as much plausibility assert, that endeavours to crush the freedom of opinion and of speech, denote liberticide intentions. But we shall content ourselves with a bare examination of the question, which has agitated the public mind; and refute the calumnies heaped on our Institution.

Freedom of thought, and a free communication of opinions by speech or through the medium of the press, are the safeguards of our Liberties. Apathy as to public concerns, too frequent even in Republics, is the reason for usurpation: by the communication or collision of sentiments, knowledge is increased, and truth prevails.

By the freedom of opinion, cannot be meant the right of thinking merely; for of this right the greatest Tyrant cannot deprive his meanest slave; but, it is freedom in the communication of sentiments, [by] speech or through the press. This liberty is an imprescriptable right, independent of any Constitution or social compact: it is as complete a right as that which any man has to the enjoyment of his life. These principles are eternal—they are recognized by our Constitution; and that nation is already enslaved that does not acknowledge their truth.

In the expression of sentiments, speech is the natural organ—the press an artificial one and though the latter, from the services it has rendered, has obtained the just appellation of Bulwark of Liberty; it would not be difficult to show that the former should be more prized because more secure from usurpation.

If freedom of opinion, in the sense we understand it, is the right of every Citizen, by what mode of reasoning can that right be denied to an assemblage of Citizens? A conviction that the exercise of this right collectively could not be questioned, led to the formation of our institution; and in the conduct the Society have held since their first establishment, they trust, no instance can be adduced in which they have overstepped the just bounds of the right, of which they claim the enjoyment. . . .

• • •

The Society are free to declare that they never were more strongly impressed with a sentiment of the importance of associations, on the principles which they hold, than at the present time. The germ of an odious Aristocracy is planted among us—it has taken root,—and has indeed already produced fruit worthy of the parent stock. If it be imprudent to eradicate this baneful exotic, let us at least unite in checking its growth. Let us remain firm in attachment to principles, and with a jealous eye guard our rights against the least infringement. The enlightened state of the public mind in this country, frees us, we trust, of all apprehension from bold and open usurpation; but the gradual approaches of artful ambition, are the source of great danger. Let us especially guard, with firmness, the outposts of our Liberties: and, if we wish to baffle the efforts of the enemies of freedom, whatever garb they may assume, let us be particularly watchful to preserve inviolate the freedom of opinion, assured that it is the most effectual weapon for the protection of our liberty.

Resolved, That the said Address be signed by the President and attested by the Acting Secretary: and that it be published.

Questions

1. How do the member of the Democratic-Republican Society defend their right to form a society that comments on public affairs?

2. What do they mean by writing that "the germ of an odious Aristocracy" has been planted in the United States?

47. Judith Sargent Murray, "On the Equality of the Sexes" (1790)

Source: *Judith Sargent Murray, "On the Equality of the Sexes,"* Massachusetts Magazine, *Vol. 2 (March 1790), pp. 132–35.*

The expansion of the public sphere during the era of the Revolution offered women an opportunity to take part in political discussions, read newspapers, and hear orations even though outside of New Jersey they could not vote. Judith Sargent Murray, one of the era's most accomplished American women, wrote plays, novels, and poetry. She also wrote essays on public issues for the *Massachusetts Magazine* and other journals under the pen name "The Gleaner."

Although Judith Murray could not attend college because of her sex, she studied alongside her brother with a tutor preparing the young man for admission to Harvard. In her essay "On the Equality of the Sexes," written in 1779 and published in 1790, Murray insisted that women had as much right as men to exercise all their talents and should be allowed equal educational opportunities to enable them to do so. Murray forthrightly demanded "equality" for women, and attacked the common idea that women's happiness rested on devoting themselves to their duties within the family.

▬▬▬▬▬▬▬▬▬

• • •

IS IT UPON mature consideration we adopt the idea, that nature is thus partial in her distributions? Is it indeed a fact, that she hath yielded to one half of the human species so unquestionable a mental superiority? I know that to both sexes elevated understandings, and the reverse, are common. But, suffer me to ask, in what the minds of females are so notoriously deficient, or unequal. May not the intellectual powers be ranged under these four heads—imagination, reason, memory and judgment. The province of imagination hath long since been surrendered up to us, and we have been crowned undoubted sovereigns of the regions of fancy. Invention is perhaps the most arduous effort of the mind; this branch of imagination hath been particularly ceded to us, and we have been time out of mind invested with that creative faculty. Observe the variety of fashions (here I bar the contemptuous smile) which distinguish and adorn the female world; how continually are they changing, insomuch that they almost render the wise man's assertion problematical, and we are ready to say, *there is something new under the sun.* Now what a playfulness, what an exuberance of fancy, what strength of inventive imagination, doth this continual variation discover?

Again, it hath been observed, that if the turpitude of the conduct of our sex, hath been ever so enormous, so extremely ready are we, that the very first thought presents us with an apology, so plausible, as to produce our actions even in an amiable light. Another instance of our creative powers, is our talent for slander; how ingenious are we at inventive scandal? what a formidable story can we in a moment fabricate merely from the force of a prolifick imagination? how many reputations, in the fertile brain of a female, have been utterly despoiled? how industrious are we at improving a hint? suspicion how easily do we convert into conviction, and conviction, embellished by the power of eloquence, stalks abroad to the surprise and confusion of unsuspecting innocence. Perhaps it will be asked if I furnish these facts as instances of excellency in our sex. Certainly not; but as proofs of a creative faculty, of a lively imagination. Assuredly great activity of mind is thereby discovered, and was this activity properly directed, what beneficial effects would follow. Is the needle and kitchen sufficient to employ the operations of a soul thus organized? I should conceive not. Nay, it is a truth that those very departments leave the intelligent principle vacant, and at liberty for speculation.

Are we deficient in reason? we can only reason from what we know, and if an opportunity of acquiring knowledge hath been denied us, the inferiority of our sex cannot fairly be deduced from thence. Memory, I believe, will be allowed us in common, since every one's experience must testify, that a loquacious old woman is as frequently met with, as a communicative old man; their subjects are alike drawn from the fund of other times, and the transactions of their youth, or of maturer life, entertain, or perhaps fatigue you, in the evening of their lives. "But our judgment is not so strong—we do not distinguish so well."—Yet it may be questioned, from what doth this superiority, in this determining faculty of the soul, proceed. May we not trace its source in the difference of education, and continued advantages?

Will it be said that the judgment of a male of two years old, is more sage than that of a female's of the same age? I believe the reverse is generally observed to be true. But from that period what partiality! how is the one exalted, and the other depressed, by the contrary modes of education which are adopted! the one is taught to aspire, and the other is early confined and limited. As their years increase, the sister must be wholly domesticated, while the brother is led by the hand through all the flowery paths of science. Grant that their minds are by nature equal, yet who shall wonder at the *apparent* superiority, if indeed custom becomes *second nature*; nay if it taketh place of nature, and that it doth the experience of each day will evince. At length arrived at womanhood, the uncultivated fair one feels a void, which the employments allotted her are by no means capable of filling. What can she do? to books she may not apply; or if she doth, *to those only of the novel kind,* lest she merit the appellation of a *learned lady;* and what ideas have been affixed to this term, the observation of many can testify. Fashion, scandal, and sometimes what is still more reprehensible, are then called in to her relief; and who can say to what lengths the liberties she takes may proceed. Meantime she herself is most unhappy; she feels the want of a cultivated mind. Is she single, she in vain seeks to fill up time from sexual employments or amusements. Is she united to a person whose soul nature made equal to her own, education hath set him so far above her, that in those entertainments which are productive of such rational felicity, she is not qualified to accompany him. She experiences a mortifying consciousness of inferiority, which embitters every enjoyment. Doth the person to whom her adverse fate hath consigned her, possess a mind incapable of improvement, she is equally wretched, in being so closely connected with an individual whom she cannot but despise. Now, was she permitted the same instructors as her brother, (with an eye however to their particular departments) for the employment of a rational mind an ample field would be opened. . . .

Will it be urged that those acquirements would supersede our domestic duties. I answer that every requisite in female economy is easily attained; and, with truth I can add, that when once attained, they require no further *mental attention.* Nay, while we are pursuing the needle, or the superintendency of the family, I repeat, that our minds are at full liberty for reflection; that imagination may exert itself in full vigor; and that if a just foundation is early laid, our ideas will then be worthy of rational beings. If we were industrious we might easily find time to arrange them upon paper, or should avocations press too hard for such an indulgence, the hours allotted for conversation would at least become more refined and rational. Should it still be vociferated, "Your domestic employments are sufficient"—I would calmly ask, is it reasonable, that a candidate for immortality, for the joys of heaven, an intelligent being, who is to spend an eternity in contemplating the works of Deity, should at present be so degraded, as to be allowed no other ideas, than those which are suggested by the mechanism of a pudding, or the sewing the seams of a garment? Pity that all such censurers of female improvement do not go one step further, and deny their future existence; to be consistent they surely ought.

Yes, ye lordly, ye haughty sex, our souls are by nature *equal* to yours; the same breath of God animates, enlivens, and invigorates us; and that we are not fallen lower than yourselves, let those witness who have greatly towered above the various discouragements by which they have been so heavily oppressed. . . . Were we to grant that animal strength proved any thing, taking into consideration the accustomed impartiality of nature, we should be induced to imagine, that she had invested the female mind with superior strength as an equivalent for the bodily powers of man. But waving this however palpable advantage, for *equality only*, we wish to contend.

• • •

Questions

1. Why does Murray refer to the "variety of fashions" among women as an argument for their intellectual capacity?

2. How does she answer the charge that offering educational opportunities to women will lead to neglect of their "domestic duties"?

═══════

48. George Washington, Farewell Address (1796)

Source: James D. Richardson, ed., A Compilation of the Messages and Papers of the Presidents *(Washington, D.C., 1896–1899), Vol. 1, pp. 223–24.*

In 1796, after two terms in office, George Washington announced his intention to retire from public life, in part to establish the precedent that the presidency is not a life office. His Farewell Address (mostly drafted by Alexander Hamilton but carefully reviewed by Washington and published in the newspapers rather than delivered orally), became one of the most often-quoted public pronouncements in American history.

Washington called on Americans to overcome party and regional divisions and unite in "the name of American." He warned against the party spirit, insisting that political parties created ill will and substituted the interests of a portion of the people for the good of the whole. And he advised his countrymen to steer clear of European power politics by avoiding permanent alliances with any other country. While Washington's warning against the formation of political parties would go unheeded, his principle that, as much as possible, the United States should avoid "political connection" with foreign powers would shape American foreign policy for the next century.

THE PERIOD FOR a new election of a citizen to administer the executive government of the United States being not far distant, and the time actually arrived when your thoughts must be employed in designating the person who is to be clothed with that important trust, it appears to me proper, especially as it may conduce to a more distinct expression of the public voice, that I should now apprise you of the resolution I have formed to decline being considered among the number of those out of whom a choice is to be made . . .

• • •

The unity of government which constitutes you one people is also now dear to you. It is justly so, for it is a main pillar in the edifice of your real independence, the support of your tranquility at home, your peace abroad, of your safety, of your prosperity, of that very liberty which you so highly prize. But as it is easy to foresee that from different causes and from different quarters much pains will be taken, many artifices employed, to weaken in your minds the conviction of this truth, as this is the point in your political fortress against which the batteries of internal and external enemies will be most constantly and actively (though often covertly and insidiously) directed, it is of infinite moment that you should properly estimate the immense value of your national union to your collective and individual happiness; that you should cherish a cordial, habitual, and immovable attachment to it; accustoming yourselves to think and speak of it as of the palladium of your political safety and prosperity; watching for its preservation with jealous anxiety; discountenancing whatever may suggest even a suspicion that it can in any event be abandoned, and indignantly frowning upon the first dawning of every attempt to alienate any portion of our country from the rest or to enfeeble the sacred ties which now link together the various parts.

For this you have every inducement of sympathy and interest. Citizens by birth or choice of a common country, that country has a right to concentrate your affections. The name of American, which belongs to you in your national capacity, must always exalt the just pride of patriotism more than any appellation derived from local discriminations. With slight shades of difference, you have the same religion, manners, habits, and political principles. You have in a common cause fought and triumphed together. The independence and liberty you possess are the work of joint councils and joint efforts, of common dangers, sufferings, and successes. . . .

• • •

In contemplating the causes which may disturb our union it occurs as matter of serious concern that any ground should have been furnished for characterizing parties by *geographical* discriminations—*Northern* and *Southern, Atlantic* and *Western*—whence designing men may endeavor to excite a belief that there is a real difference of local interests and views. One of the expedients of party to acquire influence within particular districts is to misrepresent the opinions and aims of other districts. You can not shield yourselves too much against the jealousies and heartburnings which spring from these misrepresentations; they tend to render alien to each other those who ought to be bound together by fraternal affection . . .

• • •

To the efficacy and permanency of your union a government for the whole is indispensable. No alliances, however strict, between the parts can be an adequate substitute. They must inevitably experience the infractions and interruptions which all alliances in all times have experienced. Sensible of this momentous truth, you have improved upon your first essay by the adoption of a Constitution of government better calculated than your former for an intimate union and for the efficacious management of your common concerns. This government, the offspring of our own choice, uninfluenced and unawed, adopted upon full investigation and mature deliberation, completely free in its principles, in the distribution of its powers, uniting security with energy, and containing within itself a provision for its own amendment, has a just claim to your confidence and your support. Respect for its authority, compliance with its laws, acquiescence in its measures, are duties enjoined by the fundamental maxims of true liberty. The basis of our political systems is the right of the people to make and to alter their constitutions of government. But the constitution which at any time exists till changed by an explicit and authentic act of the whole people is sacredly obligatory upon all. The very idea of the power and the right of the people to establish government presupposes the duty of every individual to obey the established government . . .

Toward the preservation of your government and the permanency of your present happy state, it is requisite not only that you steadily discountenance irregular oppositions to its acknowledged authority, but also that you resist with care the spirit of innovation upon its principles, however specious the pretexts. One method of assault may be to effect in the forms of the Constitution alterations which will impair the energy of the system, and thus to undermine what can not be directly overthrown. In all the changes to which you may be invited remember that time and habit are at least as necessary to fix the true character of governments as of other human institutions; that experience is the surest standard by which to test the real tendency of the existing constitution of a country; that facility in changes upon the credit of mere hypothesis and opinion exposes to perpetual change, from the endless variety of hypothesis and opinion; and remember especially that for the efficient management of your common interests in a country so extensive as ours a government of as much vigor as is consistent with the perfect security of liberty is indispensable . . .

• • •

I have already intimated to you the danger of parties in the state, with particular reference to the founding of them on geographical discriminations. Let me now take a more comprehensive view, and warn you in the most solemn manner against the baneful effects of the spirit of party generally.

This spirit, unfortunately, is inseparable from our nature, having its root in the strongest passions of the human mind. It exists under different shapes in all governments, more or less stifled, controlled, or repressed; but in those of the popular form it is seen in its greatest rankness and is truly their worst enemy . . .

It serves always to distract the public councils and enfeeble the public administration. It agitates the community with illfounded jealousies and false alarms; kindles the animosity of one part against another; foments occasionally riot and insurrection. It opens the door to foreign influence and corruption, which find a facilitated access to the government itself through the channels of party passion. Thus the policy and the will of one country are subjected to the policy and will of another . . .

• • •

Against the insidious wiles of foreign influence (I conjure you to believe me, fellow-citizens) the jealousy of a free people ought to be *constantly* awake, since history and experience prove that foreign influence is one of the most baneful foes of republican government. But that jealousy, to be useful, must be impartial, else it becomes the instrument of the very influence to be avoided, instead of a defense against it. Excessive partiality for one foreign nation and excessive dislike of another cause those whom that actuate to see danger only on one side, and serve to veil and even second the arts of influence on the other. Real patriots who may resist the intrigues of the favorite are liable to become suspected and odious, while its tools and dupes usurp the applause and confidence of the people to surrender their interests.

The great rule of conduct for us in regard to foreign nations is, in extending our commercial relations to have with them as little *political* connection as possible. So far as we have already formed engagements let them be fulfilled with perfect good faith. Here let us stop.

Europe has a set of primary interests which to us have none or a very remote relation. Hence she must be engaged in frequent controversies, the causes of which are essentially foreign to our concerns. Hence, therefore, it must be unwise in us to implicate ourselves to artificial ties in the ordinary vicissitudes of her politics or the ordinary combinations and collisions of her friendships or enmities.

Our detached and distant situation invites and enables us to pursue a different course. If we remain one people, under an efficient government, the period is not far off when we may defy material injury from external annoyance; when we may take such an attitude as will cause the neutrality we may at any time resolve upon to be scrupulously respected; when belligerent nations, under the impossibility of making acquisitions upon us, will not lightly hazard the giving us provocation; when we may choose peace or war, as our interest, guided by justice, shall counsel.

Why forego the advantages of so peculiar a situation? Why quit our own to stand upon foreign ground? Why, by interweaving our destiny with that of any part of Europe, entangle our peace and prosperity in the toils of European ambition, rivalship, interest, humor, or caprice?

• • •

Questions

1. Why does Washington warn Americans against "the spirit of parties"?

2. What European "interests" does Washington have in mind when he warns against forming permanent alliances with any foreign country?

49. George Tucker on Gabriel's Rebellion (1801)

Source: Letter to a Member of the General Assembly of Virginia on the Subject of the Late Conspiracy of the Slaves; With a Proposal for their Colonization *(Baltimore, 1801), pp. 5–18.*

In 1800, a plot by slaves in Virginia to gain their freedom was organized by a Richmond blacksmith, Gabriel. The plot was soon discovered and the leaders arrested. Twenty-six slaves, including Gabriel, were hanged and dozens more transported out of the state. The conspiracy, commented George Tucker, a member of one of the state's most prominent families, demonstrated that slaves possessed "the love of freedom" as fully as other men. Gabriel's language, he added, reflected "the advance of knowledge" among Virginia's slaves, which would inevitably continue.

Like Thomas Jefferson, James Madison, and many others of his generation, Tucker opposed slavery but could not envision the United States as a biracial society of free citizens. He proposed that the Virginia legislature adopt a plan to emancipate the slaves and settle them outside of the state, somewhere "on the western side" of the Mississippi River (an area then under the control of Spain). The legislature, however, moved in the opposite direction. It tightened controls over the black population and severely restricted the possibility of masters voluntarily freeing their slaves.

THERE IS OFTEN a progress in human affairs which may indeed be retarded, but which nothing can arrest. Moving on with slow and silent steps, it is marked only by comparing distant periods. The causes which produce it are either so minute as to be invisible, or, if preceived, are too numerous and complicated to be subject to human controul. Of such sort is the advancement of knowledge among the negroes of this country. It is so striking, as to be obvious to a man of the most ordinary observation. Every year adds to the number of those who can read and write; and he who has made any proficiency in letters, becomes a little centre of instruction to others. This increase of knowledge is the principal agent in evolving the spirit we have to fear. The love of freedom, sir, is an inborn sentiment, which the God of nature has planted deep in the heart: long may it be kept under by the arbitrary institutions of society; but, at the first favourable moment, it springs forth, and flourishes with a vigour that defies all check. This celestial spark, which fires the breast of the savage, which glows in that of the philosopher, is not extinguished in the bosom of the slave. It may be buried in the embers; but it still lives; and the breath of knowledge kindles it into flame. Thus we find, sir, there never have been slaves in any country, who have not seized the first favorable opportunity to revolt.

• • •

In our infant country, where population and wealth increase with unexampled rapidity, the progress of liberal knowledge is proportionally great. In this vast march of the mind, the blacks, who are far behind us, may be supposed to advance at a pace equal to our own; but, sir, the fact is, they are likely to advance much faster. The growth and multiplication of our towns tend a thousand ways to enlighten and inform them. The very nature of our government, which leads us to recur perpetually to the discussion of natural rights, favors speculation and enquiry.

• • •

There is one argument to which I have not even hinted; but which some may think of more weight than any other;—I mean the ease with which they may become the tools of a foreign enemy. Granting that the danger from themselves is slight or remote, this, it must be confessed, depends upon an event that is altogether uncertain. War is sometimes inevitable; no human prudence can guard against an event that may be brought about by the insolence, the injustice, or the caprice of *any* nation. Whenever we are involved in this calamity, if our enemies hold out the lure of freedom, they will have, in every negro, a decided friend. The passage is easy from friends to auxiliaries: little address would be necessary to excite insurrection; to put arms into their hands, and to convert a willing multitude into a compact and disciplined army.

• • •

The following hints I submit to your serious and candid consideration.

That application be made to the United States, to procure from the Spanish government, or to furnish from its own territory, such a tract of country as shall be deemed sufficient for the colony proposed. The consideration of future peace would recommend the western side of the Mississipi. Present convenience and economy would advise a purchase of some part of the Indian country, comprehended within the limits of the state of Georgia.

That this colony be under the protection and immediate government of this state, or the United States, until it contained a number of inhabitants sufficient to manage their own concerns: and that it be exclusively appropriated to the colonization and residence of people of colour.

Questions

1. Why does Tucker think that "progress in human affairs" will inevitably lead slaves to become more discontented?

2. In what ways does Tucker believe that living in Virginia has affected the ideas of the slaves?

50. Tecumseh on Indians and Land (1810)

Source: Samuel G. Drake, The Book of the Indians; or, Biography and History of the Indians of North America *(8th ed.: Boston, 1841), Book 5, pp. 121–22.*

By 1800, nearly 400,000 American settlers lived west of the Appalachian Mountains. They far outnumbered remaining Indians. Some Indians determined to root out European influences and resist further white encroachment on Indian lands. The most militant were two Shawnee brothers, Tecumseh, a chief who had refused to sign the Treaty of Greenville in 1795, and Tenskwatawa, a religious prophet who called for complete separation from whites, the revival of traditional Indian culture, and resistance to federal policies.

In 1810, Tecumseh met with William Henry Harrison, territorial governor of Indiana. He predicted war if white incursions on Indian land continued and condemned chiefs who had sold land to the federal government. Indians, he proclaimed, should "unite in claiming a common and equal right in the land, as it was at first." During the War of 1812, Tecumseh was commissioned an officer in the British army. He died at the Battle of the Thames, near Detroit.

• • •

IT IS TRUE I am a Shawanee. My forefathers were warriors. Their son is a warrior. From them I only take my existence; from my tribe I take nothing. I am the maker of my own fortune; and oh! that I could make that of my red people, and of my country, as great as the conceptions of my mind, when I think of the Spirit that rules the universe. I would not then come to Governor *Harrison*, to ask him to tear the treaty, and to obliterate the landmark; but I would say to him, Sir, you have liberty to return to your own country. The being within, communing with past ages, tells me, that once, nor until lately, there was no white man on this continent. That it then all belonged to red men, children of the same parents, placed on it by the Great Spirit that made them, to keep it, to traverse it, to enjoy its productions, and to fill it with the same race. Once a happy race. Since made miserable by the white people, who are never contented, but always encroaching. The way, and the only way to check and to stop this evil, is, for all the red men to unite in claiming a common and equal right in the land, as it was at first, and should be yet; for it never was divided, but belongs to all, for the use of each. That no part has a right to sell, even to each other, much less to strangers; those who want all, and will not do with less. The white people have no right to take the land from the Indians, because they had it first; it is theirs. They may sell, but all must join. Any sale not made by all is not valid. The late sale is bad. It was made by a part only. Part do not know how to sell. It requires all to make a bargain for all. All red men have equal rights to the unoccupied land. The right of occupancy is as good in one place as in another. There cannot be two occupations in the same place. The first excludes all others. It is not so in hunting or travelling; for there the same ground will serve many, as they may follow each other all day; but the camp is stationary, and that is occupancy. It belongs to the first who sits down on his blanket or skins, which he has thrown upon the ground, and till he leaves it no other has a right.

• • •

Questions

1. How does Tecumseh's speech illustrate differences between Indian and American views of land as private property?

2. What evidence does he offer that whites cannot be trusted by the Indians?

---

51. Felix Grundy, Battle Cry of the War Hawks (1811)

Source: Annals of Congress, *12th Congress, 1st Session, pp. 425–27 (December 10, 1811).*

In the months leading up to the War of 1812, a group of younger congress-men, mostly from the West, called for war with Britain. Known as the War Hawks, this new generation of political leaders had come of age after the winning of independence and were ardent nationalists. Their leaders in-cluded Henry Clay of Kentucky, elected Speaker of the House of Representa-tives in 1810, and John C. Calhoun of South Carolina. The War Hawks spoke passionately of defending the national honor against British insults, but also had more practical goals in mind, notably the annexation of Canada. Their views were expressed in a speech in the House of Representa-tives by Felix Grundy of Tennessee. To British interference with American shipping, the main concern of the Madison administration, Grundy added the aim of adding Canada (British territory) and Florida (owned by Spain) to the United States, thereby expanding the Union and undermining the re-maining power of Indian tribes.

WHAT, MR. SPEAKER, are we now called on to decide? It is, whether we will resist by force the attempt, made by [the British] Government, to subject our maritime rights to the arbitrary and capricious rule of her will; for my part I am not prepared to say that this country shall submit to have her commerce interdicted or regu-lated, by any foreign nation. Sir, I prefer war to submission.

Over and above these unjust pretensions of the British Government, for many years past they have been in the practice of impressing our seamen, from merchant vessels; this unjust and lawless invasion of personal liberty, calls loudly for the interposition of this Government. To those better acquainted with the facts in relation to it, I leave it to fill up the picture. My mind is irresistibly drawn to the West. . . .

It cannot be believed by any man who will reflect, that the savage tribes, uninfluenced by other Powers, would think of making war on the United States. They understand too well their own weakness, and our strength. They have already felt the weight of our arms; they know they hold the very soil on which they live as tenants at suffer-ance. How, then, sir, are we to account for their late conduct? In one way only; some powerful nation must have intrigued with them, and turned their peaceful disposition towards us into hostilities. Great Britain alone has intercourse with those Northern tribes; I therefore infer, that if British gold has not been employed, their baubles and trinkets, and the promise of support and a place of refuge if necessary, have had their effect. . . .

This war, if carried on successfully, will have its advantages. We shall drive the British from our Continent—they will no longer have an opportunity of intriguing with our Indian neighbors, and setting on the ruthless savage to tomahawk our women and children. That nation will lose her Canadian trade, and, by having no resting place in this country, her means of annoying us will be diminished. . . . I am willing to receive the Canadians as adopted brethren; it will have beneficial political effects; it will preserve the equilibrium of the Government. When Louisiana shall be fully peopled, the Northern States will lose their power; they will be at the discretion of others; they can be depressed at pleasure, and then this Union might be endangered—I therefore feel anxious not only to add the Floridas to the South, but the Canadas to the North of this empire. . . .

Questions

1. Why does Grundy think that acquiring Canada will strengthen the American Union?

2. Who does Grundy hold responsible for Tecumseh's uprising (the "late conduct" of the Indian tribes he mentions)?

CHAPTER 9

The Market Revolution, 1800-1840

52. Josephine L. Baker, "A Second Peep at Factory Life" (1840)

Source: Josephine L, Baker, "A Second Peep at Factory Life," the Lowell Offering, Vol. 5 (1845), pp. 97–100.

The early industrial revolution centered on factories producing cotton textiles with water-powered spinning and weaving machinery. In the 1820s, a group of merchants created an entirely new factory town near Boston, incorporated as the city of Lowell in 1836. Here, they built a group of modern textile factories that brought together all phases of production from the spinning of thread to the weaving and finishing of cloth. By 1850, Lowell's fifty-two mills employed more than 10,000 workers.

At Lowell, young unmarried women from Yankee farm families dominated the workforce that tended spinning machines. To persuade parents to allow their daughters to leave their homes for work in the mills, Lowell owners set up boarding houses with strict rules regulating personal behavior, as well as lecture halls, schools, and even a periodical edited by factory workers, the *Lowell Offering*. The magazine printed articles by workers, like the one excerpted here by Josephine L. Baker, about the difficulties of factory life—long hours, monotonous work, and downward pressure on wages. But Baker also noted that the young women valued the educational opportunities available in Lowell and the ability to earn money independently.

THERE IS AN old saying, that "When we are with the Romans, we must do as the Romans do." And now, kind friend, as we are about to renew our walk, I beg that you will give heed to it, and do as factory girls do. After this preliminary, we will proceed to the factory.

• • •

There is a group of girls yonder, going our way; let us overtake them, and hear what they are talking about. Something unpleasant I dare say, from their earnest gestures and clouded brows.

"Well, I do think it is too bad," exclaims one.

"So do I," says another. "This cutting down wages *is not* what they cry it up to be. I wonder how they'd like to work as hard as we do, digging and drudging day after day, from morning till night, and then, every two or three years, have their wages reduced. I rather guess it wouldn't set very well."

"And, besides this, who ever heard, of such a thing as their being raised again," says the first speaker. "I confess that I never did, so long as I've worked in the mill, and that's been these ten years."

"Well, it is real provoking any how," returned the other, "for my part I should think they had made a clean sweep this time. I wonder what they'll do next."

• • •

You ask, if there are so many things objectionable, why we work in the mill. Well, simply for this reason,—every situation in life, has its trials which must be borne, and factory life has no more than any other. There are many things we do not like; many occurrences that send the warm blood mantling to the cheek when they must be borne in silence, and many harsh words and acts that are not called for. There are objections also to the number of hours we work, to the length of time allotted to our meals, and to the low wages allowed for labor; objections that must and will be answered; for the time has come when something, besides the clothing and feeding of the body is to be thought of; when the mind is to be clothed and fed; and this cannot be as it should be, with the present system of labor. Who, let me ask, can find that pleasure in life which they should, when it is spent in this way. Without time for the laborer's own work, and the improvement of the mind, save the few evening hours; and even then if the mind is enriched and stored with useful knowledge, it must be at the expense of health. And the feeling too, that comes over us (there is no use in denying it) when we hear the bell calling us away from repose that tired nature loudly claims—the feeling, that we are *obliged to go*. And these few hours, of which we have spoken, are far too short, three at the most at the close of day. Surely, methinks, every heart that lays claim to humanity will feel 'tis not enough. But this, we hope will, ere long, be done away with, and labor made what it should be; pleasant and inviting to every son and daughter of the human family.

There is a brighter side to this picture, over which we would not willingly pass without notice, and an answer to the question, why we work here? The time we *do* have is our own. The money we earn comes promptly; more so than in any other situation; and our work, though laborious is the same from day to day; we know what it is, and when finished we feel perfectly free, till it is time to commence it again.

Besides this, there are many pleasant associations connected with factory life, that are not to be found elsewhere.

There are lectures, evening schools and libraries, to which all may have access. The one thing needful here, is the time to improve them as we ought.

There is a class, of whom I would speak, that work in the mills, and will while they continue in operation. Namely, the many who have no home, and who come here to seek, in this busy, bustling "City of Spindles," a competency [economic independence] that shall enable them in after life, to live without being a burden to society,—the many who toil on, without a murmur, for the support of an aged mother or orphaned brother and sister. For the sake of them, we earnestly hope labor may be reformed; that the miserable, selfish spirit of competition, now in our midst, may be thrust from us and consigned to eternal oblivion.

There is one other thing that must be mentioned ere we part, that is the practice of sending agents through the country to decoy girls away from their homes with the promise of high wages, when the market is already stocked to overflowing. This is certainly wrong, for it lessens the value of labor, which should be ever held in high estimation, as the path marked out by the right hand of GOD, in which man should walk with dignity.

• • •

Questions

1. Is Baker's overall impression of life in Lowell positive or negative?

2. How does she define freedom for women?

[handwritten annotation]

53. Immigrants Arriving in New York City (1853)

Source: "Walks among the New York Poor," New York Times (June 23, 1853).

America's economic expansion fueled a demand for labor, which was met, in part, by increased immigration from abroad. Between 1840 and 1860, over 4 million people (more than the entire population of 1790) entered the United States, the majority from Ireland and Germany. About 90 percent headed for the northern states, where job opportunities were most abundant and the new arrivals would not have to compete with slave labor. In 1860, the 814,000 residents of New York City, the major port of entry, included over 384,000 immigrants.

A reporter for the *New York Times* captured the colorful spectacle of the arrival of immigrant ships in 1853, listing some of their European countries of origin. Many factors, economic, political, and religious, inspired this massive flow of population across the Atlantic. But the *Times* reporter identified something less specific—the hope inspired by coming to "the New Free World."

———

IF YOU WOULD see, for a moment, one of the streams in the great current which is always pouring through New-York, go down a Summer afternoon to the North River wharves. A German emigrant ship has just made fast. The long wharf is crowded full of trucks and carts, and drays, waiting for the passengers. As you approach the end you come upon a noisy crowd of strange faces and stranger costumes. Moustached peasants in Tyrolese hats are arguing in unintelligible English with truck-drivers; runners from the German hotels are pulling the confused women hither and thither; peasant girls with bare heads, and the rich-flushed, nut brown faces you never see here, are carrying huge bundles to the heaps of baggage; children in doublets and hose, and queer little caps, are mounted on the trunks, or swung off amid the laughter of the crowd with ropes from the ship's sides. Some are just welcoming an old face, so dear in the strange land, some are letting down the huge trunks, some swearing in very genuine low Dutch, at the endless noise and distractions. They bear the plain marks of the Old World. Healthy, stout frames, and low, degraded faces with many stamps of inferiority; dependence, servitude on them; little graces of costume too—a colored headdress or a fringed coat—which never could have originated here; and now and then a sweet face, with the rich bloom and the dancing blue eye, that seem to reflect the very glow and beauty of the vine hills of the Rhine.

It is a new world to them—oppression, bitter poverty behind— here, hope, freedom, and a chance to work, and food to the laboring man. They may have the vaguest ideas of it all—still, to the dullest some thoughts come of the New Free World.

Every one in the great City, who can make a living from the freshly arrived immigrant, is here. Runners, sharpers, peddlers, agents of boarding-houses, of forwarding-offices, and worst of all, of the houses where many a simple emigrant girl, far from friends and home, comes to a sad end. Very many of these, who are now arriving, will start tomorrow at once for the far West. Some will hang about the German boarding-houses in Greenwich-street, each day losing their money, their children getting out of control, until they at last seek a refuge in Ward's island, or settle down on the Eleventh Ward, to add to the great mass of the poverty and misery there gathered. From there we shall see their children sallying out these early mornings, as soon as light, to do the petty work of the City, rag-picking, bone-gathering, selling and peddling by the thousands, radishes, strawberries and fruit through every street.

Questions

1. What tone does the reporter adopt regarding the immigrants—hostile or generous?

2. What aspirations does the reporter think are uppermost in the immigrants' minds?

---

54. Ralph Waldo Emerson, "The American Scholar" (1837)

Source: *"The American Scholar [1837]," in Ralph Waldo Emerson,* Nature, Addresses, and Lectures *(Boston, 1892), pp. 79–80, 99–103.*

Ralph Waldo Emerson was perhaps the most prominent member of a group of New England intellectuals known as the Transcendentalists, who insisted on the primacy of individual judgment over existing social traditions and institutions. Emerson was a proponent of "individualism," a word that entered the language in the 1820s. The keynote of the times, he declared, was "the new importance given to the single person." In a widely reprinted

1837 address, "The American Scholar," delivered at Harvard College, he called on Americans engaged in writing and thinking to trust their own judgment and "never defer to the popular cry." In Emerson's own definition, rather than a preexisting set of rights or privileges, freedom was an openended process of self-realization by which individuals could remake themselves and their own lives. He particularly urged young scholars to free themselves from European literary and artistic ideas and create their own intellectual traditions based on American life.

Mr. President, and Gentlemen,

I greet you on the re-commencement of our literary year. Our anniversary is one of hope, and, perhaps, not enough of labor. We do not meet for games of strength or skill, for the recitation of histories, tragedies and odes, like the ancient Greeks; for parliaments of love and poesy, like the Troubadours; nor for the advancement of science, like our contemporaries in the British and European capitals. Thus far, our holiday has been simply a friendly sign of the survival of the love of letters amongst a people too busy to give to letters any more. As such, it is precious as the sign of an indestructible instinct. Perhaps the time is already come, when it ought to be, and will be something else; when the sluggard intellect of this continent will look from under its iron lids and fill the postponed expectation of the world with something better than the exertions of mechanical skill. Our day of dependence, our long apprenticeship to the learning of other lands, draws to a close. The millions that around us are rushing into life, cannot always be fed on the sere remains of foreign harvests. Events, actions arise, that must be sung, that will sing themselves. Who can doubt that poetry will revive and lead in a new age, as the star in the constellation Harp which now flames in our zenith, astronomers announce, shall one day be the pole-star for a thousand years.

• • •

In self-trust, all the virtues are comprehended. Free should the scholar be,—free and brave. Free even to the definition of freedom, "without any hindrance that does not arise out of his own constitution." Brave; for fear is a thing which a scholar by his very function puts behind him. Fear always springs from ignorance. It is a shame to him if his tranquility, amid dangerous times, arise from the presumption that like children and women, his is a protected class; or if he seek a temporary peace by the diversion of his thoughts from politics or vexed questions, hiding his head like an ostrich in the flowering bushes, peeping into microscopes, and turning rhymes, as a boy whistles to keep his courage up. So is the danger a danger still: so is the fear worse. Manlike let him turn and face it. Let him look into its eye and search its nature, inspect its origin—see the whelping of this lion,—which lies no great way back; he will then find in himself a perfect comprehension of its nature and extent; he will have made his hands meet on the other side, and can henceforth defy it, and pass on superior. The world is his who can see through its pretension. What deafness, what stoneblind custom, what overgrown error you behold, is there only by sufferance,—by your sufferance. See it to be a lie, and you have already dealt it its mortal blow.

Yes, we are the cowed,—we the trustless. It is a mischievous notion that we are come late into nature; that the world was finished a long time ago. As the world was plastic and fluid in the hands of God, so it is ever to so much of his attributes as we bring to it. To ignorance and sin, it is flint. They adapt themselves to it as they may; but in proportion as a man has anything in him divine, the firmament flows before him, and takes his signet [seal] and form. Not he is great who can alter matter, but he who can alter my state of mind. They are the kings of the world who give the color of their present thought to all nature and all art, and persuade men by the cheerful serenity of their carrying the matter, that this thing which they do, is the apple which the ages have desired to pluck, now at last ripe, and inviting nations to the harvest. The great man makes the great thing. . . . The day is always his, who works in it with serenity and great aims. The unstable estimates of men crowd to him whose mind is filled with a truth, as the heaped waves of the Atlantic follow the moon.

• • •

Another sign of our times, also marked by an analogous political movement is, the new importance given to the single person. Every thing that tends to insulate the individual,—to surround him with barriers of natural respect, so that each man shall feel the world is his, and man shall treat with man as a sovereign state with a sovereign state:—tends to true union as well as greatness. "I learned," said the melancholy Pestalozzi, [a Swiss educator] "that no man in God's wide earth is either willing or able to help any other man." Help must come from the bosom alone. The scholar is that man who must take up into himself all the ability of the time, all the contributions of the past, all the hopes of the future. He must be an university of knowledges. If there be one lesson more than another which should pierce his ear, it is, The world is nothing, the man is all; in yourself is the law of all nature, and you know not yet how a globule of sap ascends; in yourself slumbers the whole of Reason; it is for you to know all, it is for you to dare all. Mr. President and Gentlemen, this confidence in the unsearched might of man, belongs by all motives, by all prophecy, by all preparation, to the American Scholar, We have listened too long to the courtly muses of Europe. The spirit of the American freeman is already suspected to be timid, imitative, tame. Public and private avarice make the air we breathe thick and fat. The scholar is decent, indolent, complaisant. See already the tragic consequence. The mind of this country taught to aim at low objects, eats upon itself. There is no work for any but the decorous and the complaisant. Young men of the fairest promise, who begin life upon our shores, inflated by the mountain winds, shined upon by all the stars of God, find the earth below not in unison with these,—but are hindered from action by the disgust which the principles on which business is managed inspire, and turn drudges, or die of disgust,—some of them suicides. What is the remedy? They did not yet see, and thousands of young men as hopeful now crowding to the barriers for the career, do not yet see, that if the single man plant himself indomitably on his instincts, and there abide, the huge world will come round to him. Patience—patience;—with the shades of all the good and great for company; and for solace, the perspective of your own infinite life; and for work, the study and the communication of principles, the making those instincts prevalent, the conversion of the world. It is not the chief disgrace in the world, not to be an unit;—not to be reckoned one character;—not to yield that peculiar fruit which each man was created to bear, but to be reckoned in the gross, in the hundred, or the thousand, of the party, the section, to which we belong; and our opinion predicted geographically, as the north, or the south. Not so, brothers and friends,—please God, ours shall not be so. We will walk on our own feet; we will work with our own hands; we will speak our own minds. Then shall man be no longer a name for pity, for doubt, and for sensual indulgence. The dread of man and the love of man shall be a wall of defence and a wreath of love around all. A nation of men will for the first time exist, because each believes himself inspired by the Divine Soul which also inspires all men.

Questions

1. Why does Emerson feel that American writers and artists are "cowed" and need to develop more boldness and originality?

2. Why does Emerson describe self-reliance as a "manlike" quality?

───────

55. Henry David Thoreau, *Walden* (1854)

Source: Henry David Thoreau, Walden *(Boston, 1854), pp. 10–17.*

Henry David Thoreau, Emerson's neighbor in Concord, Massachusetts, became persuaded that modern society stifled individual judgment by making men "tools of their tools," trapped in stultifying jobs by their obsession with acquiring wealth. Americans, he believed, were so preoccupied with material things that they had no time to contemplate the beauties of nature.

To escape this fate, Thoreau retreated from 1845 to 1847 to a cabin on Walden Pond in Concord, where he could enjoy the freedom of isolation from the misplaced values he believed ruled American society. He subsequently wrote *Walden* (1854), an account of his experiences. Unlike writers who celebrated the market revolution, Thoreau insisted that it was degrading both Americans' values and the natural environment. Americans, he believed, should adopt a pace of life more attuned to the rhythms of nature. Genuine freedom, he insisted, lay not in the accumulation of material goods, but within. One of the most influential works of American literature ever written, *Walden* would be rediscovered by later generations who criticized social conformity, materialism, and the degradation of the natural environment.

• • •

THE MASS OF men lead lives of quiet desperation. What is called resignation is confirmed desperation. From the desperate city you go into the desperate country, and have to console yourself with the bravery of minks and muskrats. A stereotyped but unconscious despair is concealed even under what are called the games and amusements of mankind. There is no play in them, for this comes after work. But it is a characteristic of wisdom not to do desperate things.

The greater part of what my neighbours call good I believe in my soul to be bad, and if I repent of anything, it is very likely to be my good behaviour. What demon possessed me that I behaved so well? You may say the wisest thing you can, old man—you who have lived seventy years, not without honour of a kind—I hear an irresistible voice which invites me away from all that. One generation abandons the enterprises of another like stranded vessels.

I think that we may safely trust a good deal more than we do. We may waive just so much care of ourselves as we honestly bestow elsewhere. Nature is as well adapted to our weakness as to our strength ... Let us consider for a moment what most of the trouble and anxiety which I have referred to is about, and how much it is necessary that we be troubled, or at least, careful. It would be some advantage to live a primitive and frontier life, though in the midst of an outwards civilisation, if only to learn what are the gross necessaries of life and what methods have been taken to obtain them; or even to look over the old day-books of the merchants, to see what it was that the men most commonly bought at the stores, what they stored, that is, what are the grossest groceries. For the improvements of ages have had but little influence on the essential laws of man's existence: as our skeletons, probably, are not to be distinguished from those of our ancestors.

By the words, *necessary of life,* I mean whatever, of all that man obtains by his own exertions, has been from the first, or from long use has become, so important to human life that few, if any, whether from savageness, or poverty, or philosophy, ever attempt to do without it.... Most of the luxuries, and many of the so-called comforts of life, are not only not indispensable, but positive hindrances to the elevation of mankind. With respect to luxuries and comforts, the wisest have ever lived a more simple and meagre life than the poor. The ancient philosophers, Chinese, Hindoo, Persian, and Greek, were a class than which none has been poorer in outward riches, none so rich in inward...

• • •

I went to the woods because I wished to live deliberately, to [confront] only the essential facts of life, and see if I could not learn what it had to teach, and not, when I came to die, discover that I had not lived. I did not wish to live what was not life, living is so dear, nor did I wish to practice resignation, unless it was quite necessary. I wanted to live deep and suck out all the marrow of life, to live so sturdily and Spartan-like as to put rout all that was not life, to cut a broad swath and shave close, to drive life into a corner, and reduce it to its lowest terms, and, if it proved to be mean, why then to get the whole and genuine meanness of it, and publish its meanness to the world; or if it were sublime, to know it by experience, and be able to give a true account of it in my next excursion. For most men, it appears to me, are in a strange uncertainty about it, whether it is of the devil or of God, and have somewhat hastily concluded that it is the chief end of man here to "glorify God and enjoy him forever."

Still we live meanly, like ants; though the fable tells us that we were long ago changed into men; like pygmies we fight with cranes; it is error upon error, and clout upon clout, and our best virtue has for its occasion a superfluous and inevitable wretchedness. Our life is frittered away by detail. An honest man has hardly need to count more than his ten fingers, or in extreme cases he may add his ten toes, and lump the rest. Simplicity, simplicity, simplicity! I say, let your affairs be as two or three, and not a hundred or a thousand; instead of a million, count half a dozen, and keep your accounts on your thumb nail. . . . Simplify, simplify. Instead of three meals a day, if it be necessary eat but one; instead of a hundred dishes, five; and reduce other things in proportion. . . .

The nation itself, with all its so called internal improvements, which, by the way, are all external and superficial, is just such an unwieldy and overgrown establishment, cluttered with furniture and tripped up by its own traps, ruined by luxury and heedless expense, by want of calculation and a worthy aim, as the million households in the land; and the only cure for them is in a rigid economy, a stern and more than Spartan simplicity of life and elevation of purpose. It lives too fast. Men think that it is essential that the Nation have commerce, and export ice, and talk through a telegraph, and ride thirty miles an hour, without a doubt, whether they do or not; but whether we should live like baboons or like men, is a little uncertain.

If we do not get our sleepers, and forge rails, and devote days and nights to the work, but go tinkering upon our lives to improve them, who will build railroads? And if railroads are not built, how shall we get to heaven in season? But if we stay at home and mind our business, who will want railroads? We do not ride on the railroad; it rides upon us. Did you ever think what those sleepers are that underlie the railroad? Each one is a man, an Irishman, or a Yankee man. The rails are laid on them, and they are covered with sand, and the cars run smoothly over them. They are sound sleepers, I assure you. And every few years a new lot is laid down and run over; so that if some have the pleasure of riding on a rail, others have the misfortune to be ridden upon.

Why should we live with such a hurry and waste of life? We are determined to be starved before we are hungry. Men say that a stitch in time saves nine, and so they take a thousand stitches today to save nine tomorrow.

· · ·

Questions

1. Thoreau's statement, "The mass of men lead lives of quiet desperation," is one of the most famous lines in American literature. What does he mean, and what does he think is the cause?

2. What does Thoreau mean when he writes, "We do not ride on the railroad; it rides upon us"?

═══════════

56. Charles G. Finney, "Sinners Bound to Change Their Own Hearts" (1836)

Source: "Sinners Bound to Change Their Own Hearts," in Charles G. Finney, **Sermons on Important Subjects** *(3rd ed.: New York, 1836), pp. 3–42.*

Beginning in the early nineteenth century, a series of religious revivals, known as the Second Great Awakening, swept over the United States. They reached a crescendo in the 1820s and early 1830s, when the Rev. Charles Grandison Finney held months-long revival meetings in upstate New York and New York City. His sermons warned of hell in vivid language while offering the promise of salvation to converts who abandoned their sinful ways. He rejected the idea that man is a sinful creature with a preordained fate, promoting instead the doctrine of free will and the possibility of salvation. Every person, Finney insisted, was a moral free agent, that is, a person free to choose between a Christian life and a life of sin.

The Second Great Awakening democratized American Christianity, making it a truly mass enterprise. At the time of independence, fewer than 2,000 Christian ministers preached in the United States. In 1845, they numbered 40,000. Americans, wrote Alexis de Tocqueville when he visited the United States in the 1830s, "combine the notions of Christianity and of liberty so intimately in their minds that it is impossible to make them conceive the one without the other."

———

Ezek. xviii, 31: Make you a new heart and a new spirit, for why will ye die?
• • •

... A change of heart ... consists in changing the controlling preference of the mind in regard to the *end* of pursuit. The selfish heart is a preference of self-interest to the glory of God and the interests of his kingdom. A new heart consists in a preference of the glory of God and the interests of his kingdom to one's own happiness. In other words, it is a change from selfishness to benevolence, from having a supreme regard to one's own interest to an absorbing and controlling choice of the happiness and glory of God and his kingdom.

It is a change in the choice of a *Supreme Ruler*. The conduct of impenitent sinners demonstrates that they prefer Satan as the ruler of the world, they obey his laws, electioneer for him, and are zealous for his interests, even to martyrdom. They carry their attachment to him and his government so far as to sacrifice both body and soul to promote his interest and establish his dominion. A new heart is the choice of JEHOVAH as the supreme ruler; a deep-seated and abiding preference of his laws, and government, and character, and person, as the supreme Legislator and Governor of the universe.

Thus the world is divided into two great political parties; the difference between them is, that one party choose Satan as the god of this world, yield obedience to his laws, and are devoted to his interest. Selfishness is the law of Satan's empire, and all impenitent sinners yield it a willing obedience. The other party choose Jehovah for their governor, and consecrate themselves, with all their interests, to his service and glory. Nor does this change imply a constitutional alteration of the powers of body or mind, any more than a change of mind in regard to the form or administration of a human government....

God has established a government, and proposed by the exhibition of his own character, to produce the greatest practicable amount of happiness in the universe. He has enacted laws wisely calculated to promote this object, to which he conforms all his own conduct, and to which he requires all his subjects perfectly and undeviatingly to conform theirs. After a season of obedience, Adam changed his heart, and set up for himself. So with every sinner, although he *does not first obey, as Adam did;* yet his wicked heart consists in setting up his own interest in opposition to the interest and government of God. In aiming to promote his own private happiness, in a way that is opposed to the general good. Self-gratification becomes the law to which he conforms his conduct. It is that minding of the flesh, which is enmity against God. A change of heart, therefore, is to prefer a different *end.* To prefer supremely the glory of God and the public good, to the promotion of his own interest; and whenever this preference is changed, we see of course a corresponding change of conduct. If a man change sides in politics, you will see him meeting with those that entertain the same views and feelings with himself; devising plans and using his influence to elect the candidate which he has now chosen. He has new political friends on the one side, and new political enemies on the other. So with a sinner; if his heart is changed, you will see that Christians become his friends—Christ his candidate. He aims at honoring him and promoting his interest in all his ways. Before, the language of his conduct was, "Let Satan govern the world." Now, the language of his heart and of his life is, "Let Christ rule King of nations, as he is King of saints."

Before, his conduct said, "O Satan, let thy kingdom come, and let thy will be done." Now, his heart, his life, his lips cry out, "O Jesus, let thy kingdom come, let thy will be done on earth as it is in heaven." . . .

• • •

As God requires men to make to themselves a new heart, on pain of eternal death, it is the strongest possible evidence that they are able to do it. To say that he has commanded them to do it, without telling them they are able, is consummate trifling. Their ability is implied as strongly as it can be, in the command itself. . . .

The strivings of the Spirit of God with men, is not a physical scuffling, but a debate; a strife not of body with body, but of mind with mind; and that in the action and reaction of vehement argumentation. From these remarks, it is easy to answer the question sometimes put by individuals who seem to be entirely in the dark upon this subject, whether in converting the soul the Spirit acts directly on the mind, or on the truth. This is the same nonsense as if you should ask, whether an earthly advocate who had gained his cause, did it by acting directly and physically on the jury, or on his argument. . . .

You see from this subject that a sinner, under the influence of the Spirit of God, is just as free as a jury under the arguments of an advocate. . . .

• • •

So if a minister goes into a desk to preach to sinners, believing that they have no power to obey the truth, and under the impression that a direct physical influence must be exerted upon them before they *can* believe, and if his audience be of the same opinion, in vain does he preach, and in vain do they hear, "for they are yet in their sins;" they sit and quietly wait for some invisible hand to be stretched down from heaven, and perform some surgical operation, infuse some new principle, or implant some constitutional taste; *after* which they suppose they shall be *able* to obey God. Ministers should labor with sinners, as a lawyer does with a jury, and upon the same principles of mental philosophy; and the sinner should weigh his arguments, and make up his mind as upon oath and for his life, and give a verdict upon the spot, according to law and evidence. . . .

Sinner! instead of waiting and praying for God to change your heart, you should at once summon up your powers, put forth the effort, and change the governing preference of your mind. . . .

Sinner! your obligation to love God is equal to the excellence of his character, and your guilt in not obeying him is of course equal to your obligation. You cannot therefore for an hour or a moment defer obedience to the commandment in the text, without deserving eternal damnation. . . .

And now, sinner; while the subject is before you, will you yield? To keep yourself away from under the motives of the gospel, by neglecting church, and neglecting your Bible, will prove fatal to your soul. And to be careless when you do attend, or to hear with attention and refuse to make up your mind and yield, will be equally fatal. And now, "I beseech you, by the mercies of God, that you at *this time* render your body and soul, a living sacrifice to God, which is your reasonable service." Let the truth take hold upon your conscience—throw down your rebellious weapons—give up your refuges of lies—fix your mind steadfastly upon the world of considerations that should instantly decide you to close in with the offer of reconciliation while it now lies before you. Another moment's delay, and it may be too late forever. The Spirit of God may depart from you—the offer of life may be made no more, and this one more slighted offer of mercy may close up your account, and seal you over to all the horrors of eternal death. Hear, then, O sinner, I beseech you, and obey the word of the Lord—"Make you a new heart and a new spirit, for why will ye die?"

Questions

1. What precisely does Finney mean by a "change of heart?"

2. How does the fact that he is preaching in an era of mass political democracy affect Finney's language?

57. Orestes Brownson, "The Laboring Classes" (1840)

Source: Orestes Brownson, "The Laboring Classes," Boston Quarterly Review, Vol. 3 (July 1840), pp. 358–95.

Although many Americans welcomed the market revolution, others experienced it as a loss of freedom. Especially in the growing cities of the Northeast, economic growth was accompanied by a significant widening of the gap between wealthy merchants and industrialists, on the one hand, and impoverished factory workers, unskilled dock workers, and seamstresses laboring at home, on the other.

American society, wrote Orestes Brownson in his influential essay "The Laboring Classes," faced a "crisis," a war between "wealth and labor." Brownson embraced the traditional identification of freedom with economic independence and identified not simply poverty but the system of wage labor itself as the fundamental problem. Brownson directly challenged the idea that individual improvement—Emerson's self-reliance and self-realization—could produce "equality between man and man." Workers' problems, he insisted, had their root in "social arrangements," not the limitations of individuals—"you must abolish the system or accept its consequences."

No one can observe the signs of the times with much care, without perceiving that a crisis as to the relation of wealth and labor is approaching. It is useless to shut our eyes to the fact, and like the ostrich fancy ourselves secure because we have so concealed our heads that we see not the danger.

We or our children will have to meet this crisis. The old war between the King and the Barons is well nigh ended, and so is that between the Barons and the Merchants and Manufacturers,—landed capital and commercial capital. The business man has become the peer of my Lord. And now commences the new struggle between the operative and his employer, between wealth and labor. Every day does this struggle extend further and wax stronger and fiercer; what or when the end will be God only knows . . .

• • •

All over the world this fact stares us in the face, the workingman is poor and depressed, while a large portion of the non-workingmen, in the sense we now use the term, are wealthy. It may be laid down as a general rule, with but few exceptions, that men are rewarded in an inverse ratio to the amount of actual service they perform. Under every government on earth the largest salaries are annexed to those offices, which demand of their incumbents the least amount of actual labor either mental or manual. And this is in perfect harmony with the whole system of repartition of the fruits of industry, which obtain in every department of society. Now here is the system which prevails, and here is its result. The whole class of simple laborers are poor, and in general unable to procure anything beyond the bare necessaries of life . . .

• • •

Now, what is the prospect of those who fall under the operations of this system? We ask, is there a reasonable chance that any considerable portion of the present generation of laborers, shall ever become owners of a sufficient portion of the funds of production, to be able to sustain themselves by laboring on their own capital, that is, as independent laborers? We need not ask this question, for everybody knows there is not. Well, is the condition of a laborer at wages the best that the great mass of the working people ought to be able to aspire to? Is it a condition,—nay can it be made a condition,—with which a man should be satisfied; in which he should be contented to live and die? . . . .

• • •

Now the great work for this age and the coming, is to raise up the laborer, and to realize in our own social arrangements and in the actual condition of all men, that equality between man and man, which God has established between the rights of one and those of another. In other words, our business is to emancipate the proletaries, as the past has emancipated the slaves. This is our work. There must be no class of our fellow men doomed to toil through life as mere workmen at wages. If wages are tolerated it must be, in the case of the individual operative, only under such conditions that by the time he is of a proper age to settle in life, he shall have accumulated enough to be an independent laborer on his own capital,—on his own farm or in his own shop. Here is our work. How is it to be done?....

The truth is, the evil we have pointed out is not merely individual in its character. It is not, in the case of any single individual, of any one man's procuring, nor can the efforts of any one man, directed solely to his own moral and religious perfection, do aught to remove it. What is purely individual in its nature, efforts of individuals to perfect themselves, may remove. But the evil we speak of is inherent in all our social arrangements, and cannot be cured without a radical change of those arrangements. Could we convert all men to Christianity in both theory and practice, as held by the most enlightened sect of Christians among us, the evils of the social state would remain untouched. Continue our present system of trade, and all its present evil consequences will follow, whether it be carried on by your best men or your worst. Put your best men, your wisest, most moral, and most religious men, at the head of your paper money banks, and the evils of the present banking system will remain scarcely diminished. The only way to get rid of its evils is to change the system, not its managers. The evils of slavery do not result from the personal characters of slave masters. They are inseparable from the system, let who will be masters. Make all your rich men good Christians, and you have lessened not the evils of existing inequality in wealth. The mischievous effects of this inequality do not result from the personal character of either rich or poor, but from itself, and they will continue, just so long as there are rich men and poor men in the same community. You must abolish the system or accept its consequences. No man can serve both God and Mammon. If you will serve the devil, you must look to the devil for your wages; we know no other way.

Questions

1. How does Brownson explain the fact that "the workingman is poor and depressed," while many "non-workingmen" are wealthy?

2. How does Brownson define economic freedom for workers?

CHAPTER 10

Democracy in America, 1815–1840

58. "The Memorial of the Non-Freeholders of the City of Richmond" (1829)

Source: Proceedings and Debates of the Virginia State Convention of 1829–1830 *(Richmond, 1830), pp. 25–31.*

The challenge to property qualifications for voting, which began during the American Revolution, reached its culmination in the first part of the nineteenth century. No state that entered the Union after the original thirteen required ownership of property to vote. In the older states, constitutional conventions during the 1820s and 1830s debated once again who should be able to participate in American democracy.

By the 1820s, only North Carolina, Rhode Island, and Virginia still retained property qualifications for voting. One of the first actions of Virginia's constitutional convention of 1829–1830 was to consider a memorial from "non-freeholders" of Richmond—men who did not possess enough land to enable them to vote. The large slaveholders who dominated Virginia politics successfully resisted demands for changes in voting qualifications in 1829, but a subsequent constitutional convention, in 1850, eliminated the property requirement.

Your memorialists, as their designation imports, belong to that class of citizens, who, not having the good fortune to possess a certain

193

portion of land, are, for that cause only, debarred from the enjoyment of the right of suffrage. Experience has but too clearly evinced, what, indeed, reason had always foretold, by how frail a tenure they hold every other right, who are denied this, the highest prerogative of freemen. The want of it has afforded both the pretext and the means of excluding the entire class, to which your memorialists belong, from all participation in the recent election of the body, they now respectfully address. Comprising a very large part, probably a majority of male citizens of mature age, they have been passed by, like aliens or slaves, as if destitute of interest, or unworthy of a voice, in measures involving their future political destiny: whilst the freeholders, sole possessors, under the existing Constitution, of the elective franchise, have, upon the strength of that possession alone, asserted and maintained in themselves, the exclusive power of new-modelling the fundamental laws of the State: in other words, have seized upon the sovereign authority.

It cannot be necessary, in addressing the Convention now assembled, to expatiate on the momentous importance of the right of suffrage, or to enumerate the evils consequent upon its unjust limitation. Were there no other than that your memorialists have brought to your attention, and which has made them feel with full force their degraded condition, well might it justify their best efforts to obtain the great privilege they now seek, as the only effectual method of preventing its recurrence. To that privilege they respectfully contend, they are entitled equally with its present possessors. Many are bold enough to deny their title. None can show a better. It rests upon no subtle or abstruse reasoning; but upon grounds simple in their character, intelligible to the plainest capacity, and such as appeal to the heart, as well as the understanding, of all who comprehend and duly appreciate the principles of free Government. . . .

• • •

How do the principles thus proclaimed, accord with the existing regulation of suffrage? A regulation, which, instead of the equality nature ordains, creates an odious distinction between members of the same community; robs of all share, in the enactment of the laws, a large portion of the citizens, bound by them, and whose blood and treasure are pledged to maintain them, and vests in a favoured class, not in consideration of their public services, but of their private possessions, the highest of all privileges . . .

• • •

Surely it were much to be desired that every citizen should be qualified for the proper exercise of all his rights, and the due performance of all his duties. But the same qualifications that entitle him to assume the management of his private affairs, and to claim all other privileges of citizenship, equally entitle him, in the judgment of your memorialists, to be entrusted with this, the dearest of all his privileges, the most important of all his concerns. But if otherwise, still they cannot discern in the possession of land any evidence of peculiar merit, or superior title. To ascribe to a landed possession, moral or intellectual endowments, would truly be regarded as ludicrous, were it not for the gravity with which the proposition is maintained, and still more for the grave consequences flowing from it. Such possession no more proves him who has it, wiser or better, than it proves him taller or stronger, than him who has it not. That cannot be a fit criterion for the exercise of any right, the possession of which does not indicate the existence, nor the want of it the absence, of any essential qualification. . . .

Your memorialists do not design to institute a comparison; they fear none that can be fairly made between the privileged and the proscribed classes. They may be permitted, however, without disrespect, to remark, that of the latter, not a few possess land: many, though not proprietors, are yet cultivators of the soil: others are engaged in avocations of a different nature, often as useful, presupposing no less integrity, requiring as much intelligence, and as fixed a residence, as agricultural pursuits. Virtue, intelligence, are not among the products of the soil. Attachment to property, often a sordid sentiment, is not to be confounded with the sacred flame of patriotism. The love of country, like that of parents and offspring, is engrafted in our nature.

It exists in all climates, among all classes, under every possible form of Government. Riches oftener impair it than poverty. Who has it not is a monster. . . .

• • •

Let us concede that the right of suffrage is a social right; that it must of necessity be regulated by society. Still the question recurs, is the existing limitation proper? For obvious reasons, by almost universal consent, women and children, aliens and slaves, are excluded. It were useless to discuss the propriety of a rule that scarcely admits of diversity of opinion. What is concurred in by those who constitute the society, the body politic, must be taken to be right. But the exclusion of these classes for reasons peculiarly applicable to them, is no argument for excluding others to whom no one of those reasons applies.

It is said to be *expedient*, however, to exclude non-freeholders also. Who shall judge of this expediency? The society: and does that embrace the proprietors of certain portions of land only? Expedient, for whom? for the freeholders. A harsh appellation would he deserve, who, on the plea of expediency, should take from another his property: what, then, should be said of him who, on that plea, takes from another his rights, upon which the security, not of his property only, but of his life and liberty depends? . . .

• • •

They alone deserve to be called free, or have a guarantee for their rights, who participate in the formation of their political institutions, and in the control of those who make and administer the laws.

Questions

1. What "obvious reasons" exclude women, children, non-citizens, and slaves" from the right to vote?

2. How do the writers define political freedom?

59. John Quincy Adams on the Role of the National Government (1825)

Source: James D. Richardson, ed., A Compilation of the Messages and Papers of the Presidents *(Washington, D. C., 1896–1899), Vol. 2., pp. 878–82.*

Many Americans in the first half of the nineteenth century saw a powerful federal government as a threat to individual liberty. Others, however, believed that by promoting economic development and encouraging the development of the arts and sciences, the government would enhance Americans' freedom. Among the proponents of an activist federal government was John Quincy Adams, who served as president from 1825 to 1829.

In his first annual message to Congress, in December 1825, he set forth a comprehensive program for government action. He called for legislation promoting agriculture, commerce, and manufacturing, and "the mechanical and elegant arts." His plans included government-financed improvements in transportation, scientific expeditions, and the establishment of a national astronomical observatory. Adams astonished many listeners with his bold statement, "liberty is power." The United States, the freest nation on earth, he predicted, would also become the mightiest.

Adams's proposals alarmed all believers in strict construction of the constitution. Few of his ambitious ideas received support in Congress. Not until the twentieth century would the kind of national economic planning and educational and scientific involvement envisioned by Adams be realized.

—————

IN ASSUMING HER station among the civilized nations of the earth it would seem that our country had contracted the engagement to contribute her share of mind, of labor, and of expense to the improvement of those parts of knowledge which lie beyond the reach of individual acquisition, and particularly to geographical and astronomical science. Looking back to the history only of the half century since the declaration of our independence, and observing the generous emulation with which the Governments of France, Great Britain, and Russia have devoted the genius, the intelligence, the treasures of their respective nations to the common improvement of the species in these branches of science, is it not incumbent upon us to inquire whether we are not bound by obligations of a high and honorable character to contribute our portion of energy and exertion to the common stock? The voyages of discovery prosecuted in the course of that time at the expense of those nations have not only redounded to their glory, but to the improvement of human knowledge. We have been partakers of that improvement and owe for it a sacred debt, not only of gratitude, but of equal or proportional exertion in the same common cause. Of the cost of these undertakings, if the mere expenditures of outfit, equipment, and completion of the expeditions were to be considered the only charges, it would be unworthy of a great and generous nation to take a second thought. One hundred expeditions of circumnavigation . . . would not burden the exchequer of the nation fitting them out so much as the ways and means of defraying a single campaign in war. But if we take into the account the lives of those benefactors of mankind of which their services in the cause of their species were the purchase, how shall the cost of those heroic enterprises be estimated, and what compensation can be made to them or to their countries for them? Is it not by bearing them in affectionate remembrance? Is it not still more by imitating their example by enabling countrymen of our own to pursue the same career and to hazard their lives in the same cause?

• • •

In inviting the attention of Congress to the subject of internal improvements upon a view thus enlarged it is not my design to recommend the equipment of an expedition for circumnavigating the globe for purposes of scientific research and inquiry. We have objects of useful investigation nearer home, and to which our cares may be more beneficially applied. The interior of our own territories has yet been very imperfectly explored. Our coasts along many degrees of latitude upon the shores of the Pacific Ocean, though much frequented by our spirited commercial navigators, have been barely visited by our public ships. The River of the West, first fully discovered and navigated by a countryman of our own, still bears the name of the ship in which he ascended its waters, and claims the protection of our armed national flag at its mouth. With the establishment of a military post there or at some other point of that coast, recommended by my predecessor and already matured in the deliberations of the last Congress, I would suggest the expediency of connecting the equipment of a public ship for the exploration of the whole northwest coast of this continent ...

• • •

Connected with the establishment of an university, or separate from it, might be undertaken the erection of an astronomical observatory, with provision for the support of an astronomer, to be in constant attendance of observation upon the phenomena of the heavens, and for the periodical publication of his observations. It is with no feeling of pride as an American that the remark may be made that on the comparatively small territorial surface of Europe there are existing upward of 130 of these light-houses of the skies, while throughout the whole American hemisphere there is not one. If we reflect a moment upon the discoveries which in the last four centuries have been made in the physical constitution of the universe by the means of these buildings and of observers stationed in them, shall we doubt of their usefulness to every nation? And while scarcely a year passes over our heads without bringing some new astronomical discovery to light, which we must fain receive at second hand from Europe, are we not cutting ourselves off from the means of returning light for light while we have neither observatory nor observer upon our half of the globe and the earth revolves in perpetual darkness to our unsearching eyes?

The Constitution under which you are assembled is a charter of limited powers. After full and solemn deliberation upon all or any of the objects which, urged by an irresistible sense of my own duty, I have recommended to your attention should you come to the conclusion that, however desirable in themselves, the enactment of laws for effecting them would transcend the powers committed to you by that venerable instrument which we are all bound to support, let no consideration induce you to assume the exercise of powers not granted to you by the people. But if the power to exercise exclusive legislation in all cases whatsoever over the District of Columbia; if the power to lay and collect taxes, duties, imposts, and excises, to pay the debts and provide for the common defense and general welfare of the United States; if the power to regulate commerce with foreign nations and among the several States and with the Indian tribes, to fix the standard of weights and measures, to establish post-offices and post-roads, to declare war, to raise and support armies, to provide and maintain a navy, to dispose of and make all needful rules and regulations respecting the territory or other property belonging to the United States, and to make all laws which shall be necessary and proper for carrying these powers into execution—if these powers and others enumerated in the Constitution may be effectually brought into action by laws promoting the improvement of agriculture, commerce, and manufactures, the cultivation and encouragement of the mechanic and of the elegant arts, the advancement of literature, and the progress of the sciences, ornamental and profound, to refrain from exercising them for the benefit of the people themselves would be to hide in the earth the talent committed to our charge—would be treachery to the most sacred of trusts.

The spirit of improvement is abroad upon the earth. It stimulates the hearts and sharpens the faculties not of our fellow-citizens alone, but of the nations of Europe and of their rulers. While dwelling with pleasing satisfaction upon the superior excellence of our political institutions, let us not be unmindful that liberty is power; that the nation blessed with the largest portion of liberty must in proportion to its numbers be the most powerful nation upon earth, and that the tenure of power by man is, in the moral purposes of his Creator, upon condition that it shall be exercised to ends of beneficence, to improve the condition of himself and his fellowmen. While foreign nations less blessed with that freedom which is power than ourselves are advancing with gigantic strides in the career of public improvement, were we to slumber in indolence or fold up our arms and proclaim to the world that we are palsied by the will of our constituents, would it not be to cast away the bounties of Providence and doom ourselves to perpetual inferiority? In the course of the year now drawing to its close we have beheld, under the auspices and at the expense of one State of this Union, a new university unfolding its portals to the sons of science and holding up the torch of human improvement to eyes that seek the light. We have seen under the persevering and enlightened enterprise of another State the waters of our Western lakes mingle with those of the ocean. If undertakings like these have been accomplished in the compass of a few years by the authority of single members of our Confederation, can we, the representative authorities of the whole Union, fall behind our fellow-servants in the exercise of the trust committed to us for the benefit of our common sovereign by the accomplishment of works important to the whole and to which neither the authority nor the resources of any one State can be adequate?

Questions

1. Why does President Adams believe that the federal government should promote the sciences and arts?

2. What does he mean by the remark, "liberty is power"?

---

60. John C. Calhoun, the Concurrent Majority (ca. 1845)

Source: "A Disquisition on Government," in Richard K. Crallé, ed., The Works of John C. Calhoun *(New York, 1854–57), Vol. 1, pp. 28–29.*

The Nullification Crisis of the early 1830s pitted South Carolina, which claimed the right to nullify a national tariff law of which it disapproved, against President Andrew Jackson. John C. Calhoun, once a strong nationalist, emerged as the leading theorist of nullification. The national government, he insisted, had been created by an agreement between sovereign states, each of which retained the right to prevent the enforcement within its borders of acts of Congress that exceeded the powers spelled out in the Constitution.

In the aftermath of the crisis, Calhoun began thinking about other constitutional mechanisms that could preserve both the Union and the South's rights within a nation in which it was becoming a distinct minority. He developed the theory of the "concurrent majority." Rather than relying on a simple numerical majority to ascertain the popular will, Calhoun argued, the only way to ensure the stability of a large, diverse nation was for each major interest (including slaveowners) to have the right to veto all measures that affected it. Calhoun began writing his *Disquisition on Government*, from which the excerpt below is taken, during the 1840s, but it was not published until after his death in 1850.

THERE ARE TWO different modes in which the sense of the community may be taken; one, simply by the right of suffrage, unaided; the other, by the right through a proper organism. Each collects the sense of the majority. But one regards numbers only, and considers the whole community as a unit, having but one common interest throughout; and collects the sense of the greater number of the whole, as that of the community. The other, on the contrary, regards interests as well as numbers;—considering the community as made up of different and conflicting interests, as far as the action of the government is concerned; and takes the sense of each, through its majority or appropriate organ, and the united sense of all, as the sense of the entire community. The former of these I shall call the numerical, or absolute majority; and the latter, the concurrent, or constitutional majority. I call it the constitutional majority, because it is an essential element in every constitutional government,—be its form what it may. So great is the difference, politically speaking, between the two majorities, that they cannot be confounded, without leading to great and fatal errors; and yet the distinction between them has been so entirely overlooked, that when the term *majority* is used in political discussions, it is applied exclusively to designate the numerical,—as if there were no other. Until this distinction is recognized, the better understood, there will continue to be great liability to error in properly constructing constitutional governments, especially of the popular form, and of preserving them when properly constructed. Until then, the latter will have a strong tendency to slide, first, into the government of the numerical majority, and finally, into absolute government of some other form. To show that such must be the case, and at the same time to mark more strongly the difference between the two, in order to guard against the danger of overlooking it, I propose to consider the subject more at length.

The first and leading error which naturally arises from overlooking the distinction referred to, is, to confound the numerical majority with the people; and this so completely as to regard them as identical. This is a consequence that necessarily results from considering the numerical as the only majority. All admit, that a popular government, or democracy, is the government of the people; for the terms imply this. A perfect government of the kind would be one which would embrace the consent of every citizen or member of the community; but as this is impracticable, in the opinion of those who regard the numerical as the only majority, and who can perceive no other way by which the sense of the people can be taken,—they are compelled to adopt this as the only true basis of popular government, in contradistinction to governments of the aristocratical or monarchical form. Being thus constrained, they are, in the next place, forced to regard the numerical majority, as, in effect, the entire people. . . .

• • •

The necessary consequence of taking the sense of the community by the concurrent majority is, as has been explained, to give to each interest or portion of the community a negative on the others. It is this mutual negative among its various conflicting interests, which invests each with the power of protecting itself;—and places the rights and safety of each, where only they can be securely placed, under its own guardianship. Without this there can be no systematic, peaceful, or effective resistance to the natural tendency of each to come into conflict with the others: and without this there can be no constitution. It is this negative power,—the power of preventing or arresting the action of the government,—be it called by what term it may,—veto, interposition, nullification, check, or balance of power,—which, in fact, forms the constitution. They are all but different names for the negative power.

Questions

1. How does Calhoun distinguish between the "numerical" and "concurrent" majorities?

2. Which Americans would be most likely to object to Calhoun's proposed constitutional system?

---

61. Chief Sharitarish on Changes in Indian Life (1822)

Source: James Buchanan, Sketches of the History, Manners, and Customs of the North American Indians (New York, 1824), pp. 38–42.

In 1821, a large delegation of Indians arrived in Washington to meet with President James Monroe. Among them was Sharitarish, principal chief of the Great Pawnees, a hunting tribe of the Great Plains. In his speech, excerpted here, Sharitarish describes the lives of his people and how they had changed as they came into contact with white traders and hunters. Although relatively few whites lived west of the Mississippi River in 1821,

Sharitarish seemed to understand that the days of his people's traditional way of life were numbered.

———

My Great Father:—I have travelled a great distance to see you—I have seen you and my heart rejoices. I have heard your words—they have entered one ear and shall not escape the other, and I will carry them to my people as pure as they came from your mouth.

My Great Father— . . . If I am here now and have seen your people, your houses, your vessels on the big lake, and a great many wonderful things far beyond my comprehension, which appear to have been made by the Great Spirit and placed in your hands, I am indebted to my Father [Major Benjamin O'Fallon] here, who invited me from home, under whose wings I have been protected . . . but there is still another Great Father to whom I am much indebted—it is the Father of us all. . . . The Great Spirit made us all—he made my skin red, and yours white; he placed us on this earth, and intended that we should live differently from each other.

He made the whites to cultivate the earth, and feed on domestic animals; but he made us, red skins, to rove through the uncultivated woods and plains; to feed on wild animals; and to dress with their skins. He also intended that we should go to war—to take scalps— steal horses from and triumph over our enemies—cultivate peace at home, and promote the happiness of each other.

My Great Father:—Some of your good chiefs, as they are called [missionaries], have proposed to send some of their good people among us to change our habits, to make us work and live like the white people. . . . You love your country—you love your people— you love the manner in which they live, and you think your people brave. I am like you, my Great Father, I love my country—I love my people—I love the manner in which we live, and think myself and warriors brave. Spare me then, my Father; let me enjoy my country, and I will trade skins with your people. I have grown up, and lived thus long without work—I am in hopes you will suffer me to die without it. We have plenty of buffalo, beaver, deer, and other wild animals—we have an abundance of horses—we have everything we want—we have plenty of land, if you will keep your people off of it. . . .

There was a time when we did not know the whites—our wants were then fewer than they are now. They were always within our control—we had then seen nothing which we could not get. Before our intercourse with the whites, who have caused such a destruction in our game, we could lie down to sleep, and when we awoke we would find the buffalo feeding around our camp—but now we are killing them for their skins, and feeding the wolves with their flesh, to make our children cry over their bones.

Here, my Great Father, is a pipe which I present you, as I am accustomed to present pipes to all the red skins in peace with us. It is filled with such tobacco as we were accustomed to smoke before we knew the white people. It is pleasant, and the spontaneous growth of the most remote parts of our country. I know that the robes, leggings, moccasins, bear claws, etc., are of little value to you, but we wish you to have them deposited and preserved in some conspicuous part of your lodge, so that when we are gone and the sod turned over our bones, if our children should visit this place, as we do now, they may see and recognize with pleasure the deposits of their fathers; and reflect on the times that are past.

Questions

1. How, according to Sharitarish, has "our intercourse with the whites" affected the Indians' way of life?

2. What is Sharitarish's aspiration for his people?

62. Appeal of the Cherokee Nation (1830)

Source: E. C. Tracy, Memoir of the Life of Jeremiah Evarts *(Boston, 1845), pp. 149–58.*

One of the early laws of Jackson's administration, the Indian Removal Act of 1830, provided for uprooting the Cherokee and four other tribes, with a total population of around 60,000 living in the Southeast. The Cherokee had made great efforts to become citizens, establishing schools, adopting a constitution modeled on that of the United States, and becoming successful farmers, many of whom owned slaves. But in his messages to Congress, Jackson referred to them as "savages" and supported Georgia's effort to seize Cherokee land and nullify the tribe's laws.

Cherokee leaders petitioned Congress, proclaiming their desire to "remain on the land of our fathers," as guaranteed in treaties with the federal government. They also went to court to protect their rights. Chief Justice John Marshall held that Georgia's action in extending its jurisdiction over the Cherokee violated the tribe's treaties with Washington. But presidents Jackson and Van Buren refused to recognize the ruling's validity. Eventually, nearly all the Cherokee, along with the other "civilized tribes," were forced to leave their homes. Over 4,000 Indians perished during the winter of 1838–39 on the Trail of Tears, as the removal route to present-day Oklahoma came to be called.

WE ARE AWARE that some persons suppose it will be for our advantage to remove beyond the Mississippi. We think otherwise. Our people universally think otherwise. Thinking that it would be fatal to their interests, they have almost to a man sent their memorial to Congress, deprecating the necessity of a removal. This question was distinctly before their minds when they signed their memorial. Not an adult person can be found, who has not an opinion on the subject; and if the people were to understand distinctly, that they could be protected against the laws of the neighboring States, there is probably not an adult person in the nation, who would think it best to remove;

though possibly a few might emigrate individually. There are doubtless many who would flee to an unknown country, however beset with dangers, privations and sufferings, rather than be sentenced to spend six years in a Georgia prison for advising one of their neighbors not to betray his country. And there are others who could not think of living as outlaws in their native land, exposed to numberless vexations, and excluded from being parties or witnesses in a court of justice. It is incredible that Georgia should ever have enacted the oppressive laws to which reference is here made, unless she had supposed that something extremely terrific in its character was necessary, in order to make the Cherokees willing to remove. We are not willing to remove; and if we could be brought to this extremity, it would be, not by argument; not because our judgment was satisfied; not because our condition will be improved—but only because we cannot endure to be deprived of our national and individual rights, and subjected to a process of intolerable oppression.

We wish to remain on the land of our fathers. We have a perfect and original right to claim this, without interruption or molestation. The treaties with us, and laws of the United States made in pursuance of treaties, guaranty our residence, and our privileges, and secure us against intruders. Our only request is, that these treaties may be fulfilled, and these laws executed.

But if we are compelled to leave our country, we see nothing but ruin before us. The country west of the Arkansas territory is unknown to us. From what we can learn of it, we have no prepossessions in its favor. All the inviting parts of it, as we believe, are preoccupied by various Indian nations, to which it has been assigned. They would regard us as intruders, and look upon us with an evil eye. The far greater part of that region is, beyond all controversy, badly supplied with wood and water; and no Indian tribe can live as agriculturists without these articles. All our neighbors, in case of our removal, though crowded into our near vicinity, would speak a language totally different from ours, and practice different customs. The original possessors of that region are now wandering savages, lurking for prey in the neighborhood. They have always been at war, and would be easily tempted to turn their arms against peaceful emigrants. Were the country to which we are urged much better than it is represented to be, and were it free from the objections which we have made to it, still it is not the land of our birth, nor of our affections. It contains neither the scenes of our childhood, nor the graves of our fathers.

Questions

1. What reasons do the Cherokee give for rejecting the idea of moving beyond the Mississippi River?

2. How do the Cherokee understand their "national and individual rights"?

63. Andrew Jackson, Veto of the Bank Bill (1832)

Source: James D. Richardson, ed., A Compilation of the Messages and Papers of the Presidents *(Washington, D.C., 1896–99), Vol. 3, pp. 1139–54.*

The central political struggle of the Age of Jackson was the president's war on the Bank of the United States. The Second Bank of the United States, a private corporation that conducted the federal government's financial business and regulated currency issued by state banks, had been given a twenty-year charter by Congress in 1816. The issue of the bank's future came to a head in 1832, when the institution's allies persuaded Congress to approve a bill extending it for another twenty years. Jackson vetoed the bill. His veto message is perhaps the central document of what would come to be called "Jacksonian democracy."

    The proper role of government, Jackson insisted, was to offer "equal protection" to all citizens. In a democracy, it was unacceptable for Congress to create a source of economic power and privilege unaccountable to the people. Jackson presented himself to "humble" Americans as their defender against entrenched economic interests. Jackson's effective appeal to popular sentiments helped him win reelection in 1832. His victory en-sured the death of the Bank of the United States.

THE BILL "TO modify and continue" the act [to recharter the Second Bank of the U.S.] . . . ought not to become a law. . . . The powers and privileges possessed by the existing bank are unauthorized by the Constitution, subversive to the rights of the States, and dangerous to the liberties of the people. . . . The present corporate body . . . enjoys an exclusive privilege of banking under the authority of the General Government, a monopoly of its favor and support. . . . The powers, privileges, and favors bestowed upon it in the original charter, by in-creasing the value of the stock far above its par value, operated as a gratuity of many millions to its stockholders. . . . Every monopoly and all exclusive privileges are granted at the expense of the public, which ought to receive a fair equivalent. The many millions which this act proposes to bestow on the stockholders of the existing bank must come directly or indirectly out of the earnings of the American people. . . . It is not conceivable how the present stockholders can have any claim to the special favor of Government. Should [the bank's] influence become concentered, as it may under the operation of such an act as this, in the hands of a self-elected directory . . . will there not be cause to tremble for the purity of our elections.

It is maintained by the advocates of the bank that its constitu-tionality in all its features ought to be considered as settled by pre-cedent and by the decision of the Supreme Court. To this conclusion I can not assent . . . The Congress, the Executive, and the Court must each for itself be guided by its own opinion of the Con-stitution. Each public officer who takes an oath to support the Con-stitution swears that he will support it as he understands it, and not as it is understood by others. . . . The opinion of the judges has no more authority over Congress than the opinion of Congress has over the judges, and on that point the president is independent of both....

• • •

It is to be regretted that the rich and powerful too often bend the acts of government to their selfish purposes. Distinctions in society will always exist under every just government. Equality of talents, of education, or of wealth cannot be produced by human institutions. In the full enjoyment of the gifts of Heaven and the fruits of superior industry, economy, and virtue, every man is equally entitled to protection by law; but when the laws undertake to add to these natural and just advantages artificial distinctions, to grant titles, gratuities, and exclusive privileges, to make the rich richer and the potent more powerful, the humble members of our society—the farmers, mechanics and laborers—who have neither the time nor the means of securing like favors to themselves, have a right to complain of the injustice of their Government. There are no necessary evils in government. Its evils exist only in its abuses. If [the government] would confine itself to equal protection ... it would be an unqualified blessing. In the [Bank Bill] ... there seems to be a wide and unnecessary departure from these just principles....

Nor is our Government to be maintained or our Union preserved by invasions of the rights and power of the several States. In thus attempting to make our General Government strong we make it weak. Its true strength consists in leaving individuals and States as much as possible to themselves—in making itself felt, not in its power, but in its beneficence; not in its control, but in its protection; not in binding the States more closely to the center, but leaving each to move unobstructed in its proper orbit.

Experience should teach us wisdom. Most of the difficulties our Government now encounters ... have sprung from an abandonment of the legitimate objects of Government.... Many of our rich men have not been content with equal protection and equal benefits, but have besought us to make them richer by act of Congress. By attempting to gratify their desires we have ... arrayed section against section, interest against interest, and man against man.... We [must] at least take a stand against all new grants of monopolies and exclusive privileges, against any prostitution of our Government to the advancement of the few at the expense of the many....

Questions

1. Why does Jackson distinguish between just and unjust "distinctions in society"?

2. What does Jackson see as the legitimate scope of government action?

CHAPTER 11

The Peculiar Institution

64. Frederick Douglass on the Desire for Freedom (1845)

Source: **Narrative of the Life of Frederick Douglass, an American Slave** *(Boston, 1845), pp. 39–43.*

No American of the nineteenth century spoke more eloquently or effectively against slavery and racial inequality than Frederick Douglass. Born into slavery in 1818, he became a major figure in the crusade for abolition, the drama of emancipation, and the effort during Reconstruction to give meaning to black freedom. He was also active in other reform movements, such as the campaign for women's rights.

Douglass experienced slavery in all its variety, from work as a house servant and as a skilled craftsman in a Baltimore shipyard to labor as a plantation field hand. In 1838, having borrowed the free papers of a black sailor, he escaped to the North. He went on to become perhaps the era's most prominent antislavery orator and editor, and wrote three versions of his autobiography. The first, which appeared in 1845, offered an eloquent brief account of his experiences in slavery and his escape.

———

I WAS NOW about twelve years old, and the thought of being *a slave for life* began to bear heavily upon my heart. Just about this time, I got hold of a book entitled "The Columbian Orator." Every opportunity I got, I used to read this book. Among much of other interesting matter,

I found in it a dialogue between a master and his slave. The slave was represented as having run away from his master three times. The dialogue represented the conversation which took place between them, when the slave was retaken the third time. In this dialogue, the whole argument in behalf of slavery was brought forward by the master, all of which was disposed of by the slave. The slave was made to say some very smart as well as impressive things in reply to his master—things which had the desired though unexpected effect; for the conversation resulted in the voluntary emancipation of the slave on the part of the master.

In the same book, I met with one of [British politician Richard B.] Sheridan's mighty speeches on and in behalf of Catholic emancipation. These were choice documents to me. I read them over and over again with unabated interest. They gave tongue to interesting thoughts of my own soul, which had frequently flashed through my mind, and died away for want of utterance. The moral which I gained from the dialogue was the power of truth over the conscience of even a slaveholder. What I got from Sheridan was a bold denunciation of slavery, and a powerful vindication of human rights. The reading of these documents enabled me to utter my thoughts, and to meet the arguments brought forward to sustain slavery; but while they relieved me of one difficulty, they brought on another even more painful than the one of which I was relieved. The more I read, the more I was led to abhor and detest my enslavers. I could regard them in no other light than a band of successful robbers, who had left their homes, and gone to Africa, and stolen us from our homes, and in a strange land reduced us to slavery. I loathed them as being the meanest as well as the most wicked of men. As I read and contemplated the subject, behold! that very discontentment which Master Hugh had predicted would follow my learning to read had already come, to torment and sting my soul to unutterable anguish. As I writhed under it, I would at times feel that learning to read had been a curse rather than a blessing. It had given me a view of my wretched condition, without the remedy. It opened my eyes to the horrible pit, but to no ladder upon which to get out. In moments of agony, I envied my fellow-slaves for their stupidity. I have often wished myself a beast. I preferred the condition of the meanest reptile to my own. Any thing, no matter what, to get rid of thinking! It was this everlasting thinking of my condition that tormented me. There was no getting rid of it. It was pressed upon me by every object within sight or hearing, animate or inanimate. The silver trump of freedom had roused my soul to eternal wakefulness. Freedom now appeared, to disappear no more forever. It was heard in every sound, and seen in every thing. It was ever present to torment me with a sense of my wretched condition. I saw nothing without seeing it, I heard nothing without hearing it, and felt nothing without feeling it. It looked from every star, it smiled in every calm, breathed in every wind, and moved in every storm.

I often found myself regretting my own existence, and wishing myself dead; and but for the hope of being free, I have no doubt but that I should have killed myself, or done something for which I should have been killed. While in this state of mind, I was eager to hear any one speak of slavery. I was a ready listener. . . .

• • •

I went one day down on the wharf of Mr. Waters; and seeing two Irishmen unloading a scow of stone, I went, unasked, and helped them. When we had finished, one of them came to me and asked me if I were a slave. I told him I was. He asked, "Are ye a slave for life?" I told him that I was. The good Irishman seemed to be deeply affected by the statement. He said to the other that it was a pity so fine a little fellow as myself should be a slave for life. He said it was a shame to hold me. They both advised me to run away to the north; that I should find friends there, and that I should be free. I pretended not to be interested in what they said, and treated them as if I did not understand them; for I feared they might be treacherous. White men have been known to encourage slaves to escape, and then, to get the reward, catch them and return them to their masters. I was afraid that these seemingly good men might use me so; but I nevertheless remembered their advice, and from that time I resolved to run away. I looked forward to a time at which it would be safe for me to escape. I was too young to think of doing so immediately; besides, I wished to learn how to write, as I might have occasion to write my own pass. I consoled myself with the hope that I should one day find a good chance. Meanwhile, I would learn to write.

Questions

1. To whom is Douglass addressing his book, and how does the intended audience affect his argument?

2. Why does Douglass so strongly link education with freedom?

---

65. Rise of the Cotton Kingdom (1836)

Source: Fredrick Norcom to James C. Johnston, January 24, 1836. From Ira Parkers to John Sharpe, 12 August 1928, Folder 26, in the John Sharpe Papers #3592, Southern Historical Collection, Wilson Library, University of North Carolina at Chapel Hill. Reprinted with permission.

In some ways, the most dynamic feature of the American economy in the first forty years of the nineteenth century was the rise of the Cotton Kingdom. The early industrial revolution, which began in England and soon spread to parts of the North, generated an immense demand for cotton, a crop the Deep South was particularly suited to growing because of climate and soil fertility. Slavery, which many Americans had expected to die out because its major crop, tobacco, exhausted the soil, now embarked on a remarkable period of expansion. Settlers from the older southern states flooded into Alabama, Mississippi, and Louisiana.

The letter that follows was written by Fredrick Norcom, who migrated from North Carolina to Vicksburg, Mississippi, to a planter in Edenton, North Carolina. Norcom describes the feverish speculation in cotton, land, and slaves.

I HAVE MET with I suppose from 50 to 100 men who (many of them are entirely destitute of a common education) five years since could not get credit for a pair of shoes, now worth 100,000 to a million of dollars—I have seen a great number who came here rich, and now immensely rich; I have not seen but one single soul, nor have I heard of three, who have failed—and these were all merchants, who without much Capital went to speculating in Cotton—. It is in truth the only country I ever read or heard of, where a poor man could in two or three years without any aid, become wealthy—A few days of labour and lying out in the woods enabled them to find out a good body of land, and not having the money to enter it for themselves, they would sell their information to those who were too idle, or too rich to undergo the fatigue of hunting for it; by this means they would obtain money enough to enter one section, then two, and so on; soon sell that for ten or twenty times as much as they gave for it, and sometimes would absolutely make what is considered in the old States a fortune in five or six months....

At Pontotoc in the Chickasaw Nation, there was 4 to 5 millions of dollars lying last summer to be employed in land; at the sales in December at Columbus, there was more than 5 millions, how much at the other land offices I have not heard.

All the lands obtained from the Choctaw Indians in 1832 have now been offered for sale; the greater part of the choice land of course was taken up the first year or two, and that now sells from $50–75 to 100 per acre, according to location—the second rate is selling from 20 to 40 per acre, and the third rate of which there is much yet remaining, is selling from 8 to 20 per acre—you can thus see how easy it was to get rich here—a little labour would raise $800—that will enter a section of land, to sell that for 10, to $20,000, and lay that out again and get in return 10 or 20 for one, is an easy and rapid mode of getting rich.... The demand for all species of property here is great, constant and increasing—I cannot ascertain what amount of property has been sold in any one county. More than 6,000 Negroes and 10,000 horses and mules have been sold in Yazoo County alone, and from 1st

Sept. up to this time (and I am told it so continues until April) there are Negroes by the hundred in every little Log-Village for sale. . . .

I know of no point in the world with four times its population which sells so many goods, Negroes and provisions &c and if things go on at this rate long, we must soon have 20,000 population; goods are lying here in store in quantities, waiting for stores to be built, and all species of houses are going up as if by Magic weekly: property bought in the edge of Town twelve months since for $200 per acre sold for $4,000 per acre last week—. All species of labour here cost three times as much as at Edenton, and as a general rule most every thing costs about four times as much as in the old States, except Negroes—prime man and woman together sell for $2,000—the ordinary mode of selling here is man and wife.

Questions

1. How does Norcom's letter suggest the interconnection between the fate of Native Americans and the opportunities open to white migrants to Mississippi?

2. What were likely to have been the effect on slaves of the speculative process described in the letter?

---

66. J. D. B. De Bow, "The Non-Slaveholders of the South" (1860)

Source: J. D. B. De Bow, "The Non-Slaveholders of the South: Their Interests in the Present Sectional Controversy Identical with That of the Slaveholders," De Bow's Review, 30 (January 1861), 67–77.

The most important business publication in the South before the Civil War was *De Bow's Review*, edited by James De Bow. De Bow avidly defended the institution of slavery, while at the same time advocating a diversification of the southern economy to rely less fully on plantation agriculture. As the sectional controversy intensified, De Bow was well aware that a majority of white families in the South did not own slaves. Many, he feared, did not share the same commitment to the institution as planters and cotton merchants.

In 1860, De Bow delivered a speech in Nashville, reprinted the following January in his magazine, in which he outlined the benefits he claimed non-slaveholders derived from the system of slavery and attempted to convince them that they shared a common interest in defending the institution.

I WILL PROCEED to present several general considerations, which must be found powerful enough to influence the non-slaveholders, if the claims of patriotism were inadequate to resist any attempt to overthrow the institutions and industry of the section to which they belong.

1. *The non-slaveholder of the South is assured that the remuneration afforded by his labor, over and above the expense of living, is larger than that which is afforded by the same labor in the free States.* To be convinced of this, he has only to compare the value of labor in the Southern cities with those of the North, and to take note annually of the large number of laborers who are represented to be out of employment there, and who migrate to our shores, as well as to other sections. No white laborer, in return, has been forced to leave our midst, or remain without employment. . . .

2. *The non-slaveholders, as a class, are not reduced by the necessity of our condition, as is the case in the free States, to find employment in crowded cities, and come into competition in close and sickly workshops and factories, with remorseless and untiring machinery.* They have but to compare their condition, in this particular, with the mining and manufacturing operatives of the North and Europe, to be thankful that God has reserved them for a better fate. Tender women, aged men, delicate children, toil and labor there from early dawn until after candle-light,

from one year to another, for a miserable pittance, scarcely above the starvation point; and without hope of amelioration. . . .

3. *The non-slaveholder is not subjected to that competition with foreign pauper labor which has degraded the free labor of the North, and demoralized it to an extent which perhaps can never be estimated. . . .*

4. *The non-slaveholder of the South preserves the status of the white man, and is not regarded as an inferior or a dependant.* He is not told that the Declaration of Independence, when it says that all men are born free and equal, refers to the negro equally with himself. It is not proposed to him that the free negro's vote shall weigh equally with his own at the ballot-box, and that the little children of both colors shall be mixed in the classes and benches of the schoolhouse, and embrace each other filially in its outside sports. . . . No white man at the South serves another as a body-servant, to clean his boots, wait on his table, and perform the menial services of his household! His blood revolts against this, and his necessities never drive him to it. He is a companion and an equal. . . . The poor white laborer at the North is at the bottom of the social ladder, while his brother here has ascended several steps, and can look down upon those who are beneath him at an infinite remove!

5. *The non-slaveholder knows that as soon as his savings will admit, he can become a slaveholder, and thus relieve his wife from the necessities of the kitchen and the laundry, and his children from the labors of the field.* This, with ordinary frugality, can in general be accomplished in a few years, and is a process continually going on. . . .

6. *The large slaveholders and proprietors of the South begin life in great part as non-slaveholders. . . .* Cheap lands, abundant harvests, high prices, give the poor man soon a negro. His ten bales of cotton bring him another, a second crop increases his purchases, and so he goes on, opening land and adding labor, until in a few years his draft for $20,000 upon his merchant becomes a very marketable commodity.

7. *But should such fortune not be in reserve for the non-slaveholder, he will understand that by honesty and industry it may be realized to his children. . . .*

8. *The sons of the non-slaveholder are and have always been among the leading and ruling spirits of the South, in industry as well as in politics....* Nowhere else have intelligence and virtue, disconnected from ancestral estates, the same opportunities for advancement, and nowhere else is their triumph more speedy and signal.

9. *Without the institution of slavery the great staple products of the South would cease to be grown, and the immense annual results which are distributed among every class of the community, and which give life to every branch of industry, would cease.* The world furnishes no instances of these products being grown upon a large scale by free labor....

10. *If emancipation be brought about, as will, undoubtedly be the case, unless the encroachments of the fanatical majorities of the North are resisted now, the slaveholders, in the main, will escape the degrading equality which must result, by emigration, for which they have the means, by disposing of their personal chattels, while the non-slaveholders, without these resources, would be compelled to remain and endure the degradation.* This is a startling consideration. In Northern communities, where the free negro is one in a hundred of the total population, he is recognized and acknowledged often as a pest, and in many cases even his presence is prohibited by law. What would be the case in many of our States, where every other inhabitant is a negro, or in many of our communities, ... where there are from twenty to one hundred negroes to each white inhabitant? Low as would this class of people sink by emancipation in idleness, superstition, and vice, the white man compelled to live among them would, by the power exerted over him, sink even lower....

... They [southern non-slaveholders] fully understand the momentous questions which now agitate the land in all their relations. They perceive the inevitable drift of Northern aggression, and know that if necessity impel to it, as I verily believe it does at this moment, the establishment of a Southern confederation will be a sure refuge from the storm. In such a confederation our rights and possessions would be secure, and the wealth being retained at home, to build up our towns and cities, to extend our railroads, and increase our shipping, which now goes in tariffs or other involuntary or voluntary tributes to other sections, opulence would be diffused throughout all classes, and we should become the freest, the happiest, and the most prosperous and powerful nation upon earth.

Questions

1. What economic benefits does De Bow claim non-slaveholders derive from slavery?

2. Why should non-slaveholders, according to De Bow, fear the consequences of the emancipation of the slaves?

67. George Fitzhugh and the Proslavery Argument (1854)

Source: George Fitzhugh, Sociology for the South, or the Failure of Free Society *(Richmond, Va., 1854), pp. 225–55.*

In the thirty years before the outbreak of the Civil War, proslavery thought came to dominate southern public life. Racism—the belief that blacks were innately inferior to whites and unsuited for life in any condition other than slavery—formed one pillar of the proslavery ideology. Most slaveholders also found legitimation for slavery in biblical passages such as the injunction that servants should obey their masters. Still other defenders of slavery insisted that the institution guaranteed equality for whites. Some proslavery writers began to question the ideals of liberty, equality, and democracy so widely shared elsewhere in the nation. The Virginia writer George Fitzhugh took the argument to its most radical conclusion, explicitly repudiating Jeffersonian ideals of liberty and equality as proper foundations for a good society. Indeed, wrote Fitzhugh, slaveowners and slaves shared a community of interest unknown in "free society." All workers, white and black, North and South, according to Fitzhugh, would fare better having individual owners, rather than living as "slaves" of the economic marketplace.

TEN YEARS AGO [I] became satisfied that slavery, *black or white*, was right and necessary.... Liberty and equality are new things under the sun. The free states of antiquity abounded with slaves. The feudal system that supplanted Roman institutions changed the form of slavery, but brought with it neither liberty nor equality. France and the Northern States of our Union have alone fully and fairly tried the experiment of a social organization founded upon universal liberty and equality of rights.... The experiment has already failed, if we are to form our opinions from the discontent of the masses.... Liberty and equality have not conduced to enhance the comfort or the happiness of the people.... The struggle to better one's condition, to pull others down or supplant them is the great organic law of free society. All men being equal, all aspire to the highest honors and the largest possessions.... None but the selfish virtues are encouraged, because none other aid a man in the race of free competition.... The bestowing upon men of equality of rights, is but giving license to the strong to oppress the weak....

There is no rivalry, no competition to get employment among slaves, as among free laborers. Nor is there a war between master and slave. The master's interest prevents his reducing the slave's allowance or wages in infancy or sickness, for he might lose the slave by so doing. His feeling for his slave never permits him to stint him in old age. The slaves are all well fed, well clad, have plenty of fuel, and are happy. They have no dread of the future—no fear of want. A state of dependence is the only condition in which reciprocal affection can exist among human beings—the only situation in which the war of competition ceases, and peace, amity and good will arise. A state of independence always begets more or less of jealous rivalry and hostility. A man loves his children because they are weak, helpless and dependent; he loves his wife for similar reasons. . . .

• • •

At the slaveholding South all is peace, quiet, plenty and contentment. We have no mobs, no trades unions, no strikes for higher wages, no armed resistance to the law, but little jealousy of the rich by the poor. We have but few in our jails, and fewer in our poor houses. We produce enough of the comforts and necessaries of life for a population three or four times as numerous as ours. We are wholly exempt from the torrent of pauperism, crime, agrarianism, and infidelity which Europe is pouring from her jails and alms houses on the already crowded North. Population increases slowly, wealth rapidly. In the tide water region of Eastern Virginia, as far as our experience extends, the crops have doubled in fifteen years, whilst the population has been almost stationary. In the same period the lands, owing to improvements of the soil and the many fine houses erected in the country, have nearly doubled in value. This ratio of improvement has been approximated or exceeded wherever in the South slaves are numerous. . . . Wealth is more equally distributed than at the North, where a few millionaires own most of the property of the country. (These millionaires are men of cold hearts and weak minds; they know how to make money, but not how to use it, either for the benefit of themselves or of others.) High intellectual and moral attainments, refinement of head and heart, give standing to a man in the South, however poor he may be. Money is, with few exceptions, the only thing that ennobles at the North. We have poor among us, but none who are over-worked and under-fed. We do not crowd cities because lands are abundant and their owners kind, merciful and hospitable. The poor are as hospitable as the rich, the negro as the white man. Nobody dreams of turning a friend, a relative, or a stranger from his door. The very negro who deems it no crime to steal, would scorn to sell his hospitality. We have no loafers, because the poor relative or friend who borrows our horse, or spends a week under our roof, is a welcome guest. The loose economy, the wasteful mode of living at the South, is a blessing when rightly considered; it keeps want, scarcity and famine at a distance, because it leaves room for retrenchment. The nice, accurate economy of France, England and New England, keeps society always on the verge of famine, because it leaves no room to retrench, that is to live on a part only of what they now consume. Our society exhibits no appearance of precocity, no symptoms of decay. A long course of continuing improvement is in prospect before us, with no limits which human foresight can descry. Actual liberty and equality with our white population has been approached much nearer than in the free States. Few of our whites ever work as day laborers, none as cooks, scullions, ostlers, body servants, or in other menial capacities. One free citizen does not lord it over another; hence that feeling of independence and equality that distinguishes us; hence that pride of character, that self-respect, that give us ascendancy when we come in contact with Northerners. It is a distinction to be a Southerner, as it was once to be a Roman citizen. . . .

Questions

1. What are Fitzhugh's main criticisms of "free society"?

2. Why does he present an analogy between the condition of slaves and that of women?

---

68. Solomon Northup, The New Orleans Slave Market (1853).

Source: Solomon Northup, **Twelve Years a Slave** *(Auburn, N.Y., 1853), pp. 78–82.*

The ending of the slave trade from Africa in 1808 stimulated the rapid expansion of the domestic slave trade within the United States. Over 2 million slaves were sold between 1820 and 1860, a majority to local buyers but hundreds of thousands from older states to "importing" states of the lower South. The main business districts of southern cities contained the offices of slave traders, complete with signs reading "Negro Sales" or "Negroes Bought Here." The public slave market of New Orleans was one great center of the slave trade, where slaves were sold to work the plantations of the expanding Cotton Kingdom.

A free black resident of New York state, Solomon Northup was kidnaped in 1841 while in Washington, D.C., and sold as a slave. After twelve years, during which he labored on plantations in Louisiana, he managed to contact friends in the North who arranged for his release. His memoir, published in 1853, became one of the most widely read accounts of slavery by someone who had experienced it. In this passage, Northup describes a sale at the New Orleans slave market.

———

THE VERY AMIABLE, pious-hearted Mr. Theophilus Freeman, a partner or consignee of James H. Burch, and keeper of the slave pen in New-Orleans, was out among his animals early in the morning. With an occasional kick of the older men and women, and many a sharp crack of the whip about the ears of the younger slaves, it was not long before they were all astir, and wide awake. Mr. Theophilus Freeman bustled about in a very industrious manner, getting his property ready for the sales-room, intending, no doubt, to do that day a rousing business.

In the first place we were required to wash thoroughly, and those with beards, to shave. We were then furnished with a new suit each, cheap, but clean. The men had hat, coat, shirt, pants and shoes; the women frocks of calico, and handkerchiefs to bind about their heads. We were now conducted into a large room in the front part of the building to which the yard was attached, in order to be properly trained, before the admission of customers. The men were arranged on one side of the room, the women on the other. The tallest was placed at the head of the row, then the next tallest, and so on in the order of their respective heights. Emily was at the foot of the line of women. Freeman charged us to remember our places; exhorted us to appear smart and lively,—sometimes threatening, and again, holding out various inducements. During the day he exercised us in the art of "looking smart," and of moving to our places with exact precision. . . .

Next day many customers called to examine Freeman's "new lot." The latter gentleman was very loquacious, dwelling at much length upon our several good points and qualities. He would make us hold up our heads, walk briskly back and forth, while customers would feel of our hands and arms and bodies, turn us about, ask us what we could do, make us open our mouths and show our teeth, precisely as a jockey examines a horse which he is about to barter for or purchase. Sometimes a man or woman was taken back to the small house in the yard, stripped, and inspected more minutely. Scars upon a slave's back were considered evidence of a rebellious or unruly spirit, and hurt his sale.

One old gentleman, who said he wanted a coachman, appeared to take a fancy to me. From his conversation with Freeman, I learned he was a resident in the city. I very much desired that he would buy me, because I conceived it would not be difficult to make my escape from New-Orleans on some northern vessel. Freeman asked him fifteen hundred dollars for me. The old gentleman insisted it was too much, as times were very hard. Freeman, however, declared that I was sound and healthy, of good constitution, and intelligent. He made it a point to enlarge upon my musical attainments. The old gentleman argued quite adroitly that there was nothing extraordinary about the nigger, and finally, to my regret, went out, saying he would call again. During the day, however, a number of sales were made. David and Caroline were purchased together by a Natchez planter. They left us, grinning broadly, and in the most happy state of mind, caused by the fact of their not being separated. Lethe was sold to a planter of Baton Rouge, her eyes flashing with anger as she was led away.

The same man also purchased Randall. The little fellow was made to jump, and run across the floor, and perform many other feats, exhibiting his activity and condition. All the time the trade was going on, Eliza was crying aloud, and wringing her hands. She besought the man not to buy him, unless he also bought herself and Emily. She promised, in that case, to be the most faithful slave that ever lived. The man answered that he could not afford it, and then Eliza burst into a paroxysm of grief, weeping plaintively. Freeman turned round to her, savagely, with his whip in his uplifted hand, ordering her to stop her noise, or he would flog her. He would not have such work—such snivelling; and unless she ceased that minute, he would take her to the yard and give her a hundred lashes. Yes, he would take the nonsense out of her pretty quick—if he didn't, might he be d———d. Eliza shrunk before him, and tried to wipe away her tears, but it was all in vain. She wanted to be with her children, she said, the little time she had to live. All the frowns and threats of Freeman could not wholly silence the afflicted mother. She kept on begging and beseeching them, most piteously, not to separate the three. Over and over again she told them how she loved her boy. A great many times she repeated her former promises—how very faithful and obedient she would be; how hard she would labor day and night, to the last moment of her life, if he would only buy them all together. But it was of no avail; the man could not afford it. The bargain was agreed upon, and Randall must go alone. Then Eliza ran to him; embraced him passionately; kissed him again and again; told him to remember her—all the while her tears falling in the boy's face like rain.

Freeman damned her, calling her a blubbering, bawling wench, and ordered her to go to her place, and behave herself, and be somebody. He swore he wouldn't stand such stuff but a little longer. He would soon give her something to cry about, if she was not mighty careful, and *that* she might depend upon.

The planter from Baton Rouge, with his new purchases, was ready to depart.

"Don't cry, mama. I will be a good boy. Don't cry," said Randall, looking back, as they passed out of the door.

What has become of the lad, God knows. It was a mournful scene indeed. I would have cried myself if I had dared.

Questions

1. What aspects of the buying and selling of slaves does Northup single out for condemnation?

2. What light does Northup's account shed on the arguments in defense of slavery advanced by George Fitzhugh?

---

69. Letter by a Fugitive Slave (1840)

Source: Letter from Joseph Taper to Joseph Long, November 11, 1840 in the Joseph Long Papers located in the Rare Book, Manuscript, and Special Collections Library, Duke University. Reprinted with the permission of Duke University Manuscript Library.

No one knows how many slaves succeeded in escaping from bondage before the Civil War—a rough estimate would be around 1,000 per year. Some settled in northern cities like Boston, Cincinnati, and New York. But because the Constitution required that fugitives be returned to slavery, many continued northward until they reached Canada.

Formidable obstacles confronted fugitive slaves, including the presence of slave patrols in every southern county. Not surprisingly, most successful runaways originated in states that bordered on freedom, such as Maryland, Virginia, and Kentucky, rather than in the Deep South. One was Joseph Taper, a slave in Frederick County, Virginia, who in 1837 ran away to Pennsylvania with his wife and children. Two years later, learning that a "slave catcher" was in the neighborhood, he and his family fled to Canada. In 1840, Taper wrote the following letter to a white acquaintance in Virginia. He recounted some of his experiences, and rejoiced in finally living in a country where slavery did not exist and the law treated all persons equally regardless of race.

Dear Sir,

I now take this opportunity to inform you that I am in a land of liberty, in good health. After I left Winchester I staid in Pennsylvania two years, and there met some of your neighbors who lived in the house opposite you, & they were very glad to see me; from there I moved to this place where I arrived in the month of August 1839.

I worked in Erie Penn where I met many of our neighbors from New Town. I there recieved 26 dollars a month.

Since I have been in the Queens dominions I have been well contented, Yes well contented for Sure, man is as God intended he should be. That is, all are born free and equal. This is a wholesome law, not like the Southern laws which puts man made in the image of God, on level with brutes. O, what will become of the people, and where will they stand in the day of Judgment. Would that the 5th verse of the 3d chapter of Malachi were written as with the bar of iron, and the point of a diamond upon every oppressors heart that they might repent of this evil, and let the oppressed go free. I wish you might tell Addison, John, and Elias to begin to serve the Lord in their youth, and be prepared for death, which they cannot escape, and if they are prepared all will be well, if not they must according to scripture be lost forever, and if we do not meet in this world I hope we shall meet in a better world when parting shall be no more. . . .

We have good schools, and all the colored population supplied with schools. My boy Edward who will be six years next January, is now reading, and I intend keeping him at school until he becomes a good scholar.

I have enjoyed more pleasure with one month here than in all my life in the land of bondage. . . .

My wife and self are sitting by a good comfortable fire happy, knowing that there are none to molest [us] or make [us] afraid. God save Queen Victoria, The Lord bless her in this life, and crown her with glory in the world to come is my prayer,

Yours With much respect
most obt, Joseph Taper

Questions

1. How does Taper's letter reverse the common rhetoric of white America, which exalted American freedom and condemned the British empire as lacking in liberty?

2. What elements of freedom in Canada seem most valued by Taper?

---

70. *Confessions of Nat Turner* (1831)

Source: The Confessions of Nat Turner, the Leader of the Late Insurrection in Southampton, Va., as Fully and Voluntarily Made to Thomas R. Gray *(Baltimore, 1831), pp. 9–12.*

The most dramatic example of slaves' desire for freedom were slave rebellions. The best known was led by Nat Turner, a slave preacher in Southampton County, Virginia. Turner came to believe that God had chosen him to lead a black uprising. Perhaps from a sense of irony, he initially chose July 4, 1831, for his rebellion, only to fall ill. On August 22, he and a handful of followers marched from farm to farm killing the white inhabitants. By the time the militia put down the uprising, about eighty slaves had joined Turner's band, and some sixty whites had been killed.

While in prison awaiting execution, Turner was interviewed by a white lawyer, Thomas C. Gray, who subsequently published *The Confessions of Nat Turner*. Historians disagree over how much of this brief pamphlet should be attributed to Gray and how much to Turner. But the account of Turner's religious visions, of how he saw black and white angels fighting in the sky and the heavens running red with blood, rings true.

BY THIS TIME, having arrived to man's estate, and hearing the scriptures commented on at meetings, I was struck with that particular passage which says: "Seek ye the kingdom of Heaven and all things shall be added unto you." I reflected much on this passage, and prayed daily for light on this subject—As I was praying one day at my plough, the spirit spoke to me, saying "Seek ye the kingdom of Heaven and all things shall be added unto you." *Question*—what do you mean by the Spirit. *Ans.* The Spirit that spoke to the prophets in former days—and I was greatly astonished, and for two years prayed continually, whenever my duty would permit—and then again I had the same revelation, which fully confirmed me in the impression that I was ordained for some great purpose in the hands of the Almighty. Several years rolled round, in which many events occurred to strengthen me in this my belief. At this time I reverted in my mind to the remarks made of me in my childhood, and the things that had been shewn me—and as it had been said of me in my childhood by those by whom I had been taught to pray, both white and black, and in whom I had the greatest confidence, that I had too much sense to be raised, and if I was, I would never be of any use to any one as a slave.

Now finding I had arrived to man's estate, and was a slave, and these revelations being made known to me, I began to direct my attention to this great object, to fulfil the purpose for which, by this time, I felt assured I was intended. Knowing the influence I had obtained over the minds of my fellow servants, (not by the means of conjuring and such like tricks—for to them I always spoke of such things with contempt) but by the communion of the Spirit whose revelations I often communicated to them, and they believed and said my wisdom came from God. I now began to prepare them for my purpose, by telling them something was about to happen that would terminate in fulfilling the great promise that had been made to me.

About this time I was placed under an overseer, from whom I ran away—and after remaining in the woods thirty days, I returned, to the astonishment of the negroes on the plantation, who thought I had made my escape to some other part of the country, as my father had done before. But the reason of my return was, that the Spirit appeared to me and said I had my wishes directed to the things of this world, and not to the kingdom of Heaven, and that I should return to the service of my earthly master—"For he who knoweth his Master's will, and doeth it not, shall be beaten with many stripes, and thus have I chastened you." And the negroes found fault, and murmured against me, saying that if they had my sense they would not serve any master in the world. And about this time I had a vision—and I saw white spirits and black spirits engaged in battle, and the sun was darkened—the thunder rolled in the Heavens, and blood flowed in streams—and I heard a voice saying, "Such is your luck, such you are called to see, and let it come rough or smooth, you must surely bare it." I now withdrew myself as much as my situation would permit, from the intercourse of my fellow servants, for the avowed purpose of serving the Spirit more fully—and it appeared to me, and reminded me of the things it had already shown me, and that it would then reveal to me the knowledge of the elements, the revolution of the planets, the operation of tides, and changes of the seasons.

After this revelation in the year of 1825, and the knowledge of the elements being made known to me, I sought more than ever to obtain true holiness before the great day of judgment should appear, and then I began to receive the true knowledge of faith. And from the first steps of righteousness until the last, was I made perfect; and the Holy Ghost was with me, and said, "Behold me as I stand in the Heavens"—and I looked and saw the forms of men in different attitudes—and there were lights in the sky to which the children of darkness gave other names than what they really were—for they were the lights of the Savior's hands, stretched forth from east to west, even as they were extended on the cross on Calvary for the redemption of sinners. And I wondered greatly at these miracles, and prayed to be informed of a certainty of the meaning thereof—and shortly afterwards, while laboring in the field, I discovered drops of blood on the corn as though it were dew from heaven—and I communicated it to many, both white and black, in the neighborhood—and I then found on the leaves in the woods hieroglyphic characters, and numbers, with the forms of men in different attitudes, portrayed in blood, and representing the figures I had seen before in the heavens. And now the Holy Ghost had revealed itself to me, and made plain the miracles it had shown me—For as the blood of Christ had been shed on this earth, and had ascended to heaven for the salvation of sinners, and was now returning to earth again in the form of dew—and as the leaves on the trees bore the impression of the figures I had seen in the heavens, it was plain to me that the Savior was about to lay down the yoke he had borne for the sins of men, and the great day of judgment was at hand.

About this time I told these things to a white man, (Etheldred T. Brantley) on whom it had a wonderful effect—and he ceased from his wickedness, and was attacked immediately with a cutaneous eruption, and blood oozed from the pores of his skin, and after praying and fasting nine days, he was healed, and the Spirit appeared to me again, and said, as the Savior had been baptised so should we be also—and when the white people would not let us be baptised by the church, we went down into the water together, in the sight of many who reviled us, and were baptised by the Spirit—After this I rejoiced greatly, and gave thanks to God. And on the 12th of May, 1828, I heard a loud noise in the heavens, and the Spirit instantly appeared to me and said the Serpent was loosened, and Christ had laid down the yoke he had borne for the sins of men, and that I should take it on and fight against the Serpent, for the time was fast approaching when the first should be last and the last should be first. *Ques.* Do you not find yourself mistaken now? *Ans.* Was not Christ crucified?

And by signs in the heavens that it would make known to me when I should commence the great work—and until the first sign appeared, I should conceal it from the knowledge of men—And on the appearance of the sign, (the eclipse of the sun last February) I should arise and prepare myself, and slay my enemies with their own weapons. And immediately on the sign appearing in the heavens, the seal was removed from my lips, and I communicated the great work laid out for me to do, to four in whom I had the greatest confidence, (Henry, Hark, Nelson, and Sam)—It was intended by us to have begun the work of death on the 4th July last—Many were the plans formed and rejected by us, and it affected my mind to such a degree, that I fell sick, and the time passed without our coming to any determination how to commence—Still forming new schemes and rejecting them, when the sign appeared again, which determined me not to wait longer.

Since the commencement of 1830, I had been living with Mr. Joseph Travis, who was to me a kind master, and placed the greatest confidence in me; in fact, I had no cause to complain of his treatment to me. On Saturday evening, the 20th of August, it was agreed between Henry, Hark, and myself, to prepare a dinner the next day for the men we expected, and then to concert a plan, as we had not yet determined on any. Hark, on the following morning, brought a pig, and Henry brandy, and being joined by Sam, Nelson, Will and Jack, they prepared in the woods a dinner, where, about three o'clock, I joined them.

Q. Why were you so backward in joining them?

A. The same reason that had caused me not to mix with them for years before.

I saluted them on coming up, and asked Will how came he there, he answered, his life was worth no more than others, and his liberty as dear to him. I asked him if he thought to obtain it? He said he would, or lose his life. This was enough to put him in full confidence. Jack, I knew, was only a tool in the hands of Hark, it was quickly agreed we should commence at home (Mr. J. Travis') on that night, and until we had armed and equipped ourselves, and gathered sufficient force, neither age nor sex was to be spared, (which was invariably adhered to).

Questions

1. Why does Turner answer, in response to a question, "Was not Christ crucified?"

2. What reasons does Turner give for other slaves joining his rebellion?

CHAPTER 12

An Age of Reform, 1820–1840

71. Robert Owen, "The First Discourse on a New System of Society" (1825)

Source: Robert Owen, The First Discourse on a New System of Society, as Delivered in the Hall of Representatives, at Washington, on the 25th of February, 1825 (London, 1825), pp. 3–15.

The increasing economic inequality and intense economic competition promoted by the market revolution led some Americans to create their own miniature societies based on equality and harmony. Through their efforts, the words "socialism" and "communism," meaning societies in which productive property is owned by the community rather than private individuals, entered the language of politics.

The most important secular communitarian (meaning a person who plans or lives in a cooperative community) was Robert Owen, a British factory owner. In 1824, he purchased the Harmony community in Indiana originally founded by the Protestant religious leader George Rapp, and renamed it New Harmony. Early in 1825, Owen addressed a gathering of notable Americans in the hall of the House of Representatives—one of the few foreign citizens ever to speak there—and outlined his vision of "a new system of society."

THE RESULT OF ... [my] reading, reflection, experiments, and personal communication, has been to leave an irresistible impression on my mind, that society is in error; that the notions on which all its institutions are founded are not true; that they necessarily generate deception and vice; and that the practices which proceed from them are destructive of the happiness of human life.

The reflections which I am enabled to make upon the facts which the history of our race presented to me, led me to conclude that the great object intended to be attained, by the various institutions of every age and country, was, or ought to be, to secure happiness for the greatest number of human beings. That this object could be obtained only, first, by a proper training and education from birth, of the physical and mental powers of each individual; second, by arrangements to enable each individual to procure in the best manner at all times, a full supply of those things which are necessary and the most beneficial for human nature; and third, that all individuals should be so united and combined in a social system, as to give to each the greatest benefit from society. . . .

• • •

Man, through ignorance, has been, hitherto, the tormentor of man.

He is here, in a nation deeming itself possessed of more privileges than all other nations, and which pretensions, in many respects, must be admitted to be true. Yet, even here, where the laws are the most mild, and consequently the least unjust and irrational, individuals are punished even to death, for actions which are the natural and necessary effects arising from the injurious circumstances which the government and society, to which they belong, unwisely permit to exist; while other individuals are almost as much injured by being as unjustly rewarded for performing actions for which, as soon as they shall become rational beings, they must be conscious they cannot be entitled to a particle of merit. . . .

• • •

My desire now is to introduce into these States, and through them to the world at large, a new social system, formed in practice of an entire new combination of circumstances, all of them having a direct moral, intellectual, and beneficial tendency, fully adequate to effect the most important improvements throughout society. This system has been solely derived from the facts relative to our common nature, which I have previously explained.

In this new social arrangement, a much more perfect system of liberty and equality will be introduced than has yet any where existed, or been deemed attainable in practice. Within it there will be no privileged thoughts or belief; every one will be at full liberty to express the genuine impressions which the circumstances around them have made on their minds as well as all their own undisguised reflections thereon, and then no motive will exist for deception or insincerity of any kind....

The degrading and pernicious practices in which we are now trained, of buying cheap and selling dear, will be rendered wholly unnecessary; for so long as this principle shall govern the transactions of men, nothing really great or noble can be expected from mankind....

• • •

In the new system, union and co-operation will supersede individual interest, and the universal counteraction of each other's objects; and, by the change, the powers of one man will obtain for him the advantages of many, and all will become as rich as they will desire. The very imperfect experiments of the Moravians, Shakers, and Harmonites, give sure proof of the gigantic superiority of union over division, for the creation of wealth. But these associations have been hitherto subject to many disadvantages, and their progress and success have been materially counteracted by many obstacles which will not exist under a system, founded on a correct knowledge of the constitution of our nature....

Under this system, real wealth will be too easily obtained in perpetuity and full security to be much longer valued as it is now by society, for the distinctions which it makes between the poor and rich. For, when the new arrangements shall be regularly organized and completed, a few hours daily, of healthy and desirable employment, chiefly applied to direct modern mechanical and other scientific improvements, will be amply sufficient to create a full supply, at all times, of the best of every thing for every one, and then all things will be valued according to their intrinsic worth, will be used beneficially, and nothing will be wasted or abused. . . .

• • •

This is a revolution from a system in which individual reward and punishment has been the universal practice, to one, in which individual reward and punishment will be unpracticed and unknown, except as a grievous error of a past wretched system. On this account, my belief has long been, that wherever society should be fully prepared to admit of one experiment on the new system, it could not fail to be also prepared to admit the principle from which it has been derived, and to be ready for all the practice which must emanate from the principle; and, in consequence, that the change could not be one of slow progression, but it must take place at once, and make an immediate, and almost instantaneous resolution in the minds and manners of the society in which it shall be introduced—unless we can imagine that there are human beings who prefer sin and misery to virtue and happiness. . . .

It is to effect this change that I am here this night; that, if possible, a mortal blow shall be now given to the fundamental error which, till now, has governed this wretched world, and inflicted unnumbered cruelties and miseries upon its inhabitants. The time has passed, within the present hour, when this subject can be no longer mentioned or hidden from the public mind of this country. It must now be open to the most free discussion, and I well know what will be the result. . . .

Questions

1. What does Owen see as the greatest "errors" of society in the 1820s?

2. How does he plan to increase the enjoyment of "liberty and equality"?

72. Philip Schaff on Freedom as Self-Restraint (1855)

Source: *Philip Schaff,* America. A Sketch of the Political, Social, and Religious Character of the United States of North America *(New York, 1855), pp. 43–47.*

Numerous reform movements arose in the United States in the decades before the Civil War, promising to liberate Americans from social injustice and from evils like drink, poverty, or slavery. The reformers did not propose that individuals should simply follow their own desires without restraint. Their definition of the free individual was the person who internalized the practice of self-control.

Philip Schaff, a Swiss-German minister who emigrated to Pennsylvania in 1843 to teach in a small college and later worte a "sketch" of American society for a European audience, offered perceptive comments on reformers' understanding of freedom. "True national freedom, in the American view," Schaff observed, was "anything but an absence of restraint." Rather, it "rests upon a moral groundwork, upon the virtue of self-possession and self-control in individual citizens." As an example, Schaff offered the temperance movement, which sought to convince Americans to renounce intoxicating liquor. The conflict between freedom as following a moral code (imposed, if necessary, by the government) and freedom as choosing without outside interference how to conduct one's life would be repeated in many subsequent eras of American history.

═══

THE WHOLE ANGLO-AMERICAN conception of freedom is specifically different from the purely negative notion which prevails amongst the radicals and revolutionists on the continent of Europe. With the American, freedom is anything but a mere absence of restraint, an arbitrary, licentious indulgence, every one following his natural impulse, as the revolutionists would have it. It is a rational, moral self-determination, hand in hand with law, order, and authority. True national freedom, in the American view, rests upon a moral groundwork, upon the virtue of self-possession and self-control in individual citizens. He alone is worthy of this great blessing and capable of enjoying it, who holds his passions in check; is master of his sensual nature; obeys natural laws, not under pressure from without, but from inward impulse, cheerfully and joyfully. But the negative and hollow liberalism, or rather the radicalism, which undermines the authority of law and sets itself against Christianity and the church, necessarily dissolves all social ties, and ends in anarchy; which then passes very easily into the worst and most dangerous form of despotism.

These sound views of freedom, in connection with the moral earnestness and the Christian character of the nation, form the basis of the North American republic, and can alone secure its permanence. We also find there, indeed, beyond all question, utterly unsound and dangerous radical tendencies; in the political elections all wild passions, falsehood, calumny, bribery, and wickedness of all sorts, are let loose; and even the halls of the legislatures and of Congress are frequently disgraced by the misconduct of unprincipled demagogues, so that multitudes of the best citizens, disgusted with the wire-pulling and mean selfishness of self-styled friends of the people, shrink from any active participation in politics, or discharge their duty as citizens by nothing more, at most, than their vote at the ballot-box. But on the whole, there prevails undeniably among the people a sound conservative tone, which exerts a constant influence in favor of right and order; and it is an imposing spectacle, when immediately after the election of a president or governor, a universal calm at once succeeds the furious storm of party strife, and the conquered party patiently submits to the result, never dreaming of such a thing as asserting its real or supposed rights in any violent way. Any dissatisfaction—for such certainly has place there as well as elsewhere—reaches never to the republican form of government, but only to the manner of its exercise, not to the constitution of the land, but only to the measures of the dominant party; and it seeks redress of its wrong always in a lawful, constitutional way. So far as this goes, it may well be asserted, that the North American Union, with all the fluctuation and insecurity of its affairs in particular instances—which is to be expected in so new a country—stands in general more firmly on its feet, and is safer from violent revolutions, than any country on the continent of Europe.

A very characteristic proof of our assertion, that American freedom is different in principle from radicalism and licentiousness, and rests entirely on the basis of self-control and self-restraint, is presented in the really sublime temperance movement, particularly in the "Maine liquor law," as it is called. This law wholly forbids, not directly the drinking—for this would be an infringement of personal liberty,—but the manufacture and sale of all intoxicating drinks, including even wine and beer, except for medicinal, mechanical, and sacramental purposes. This law was first introduced a few years ago in the predominantly Puritanical, New England State of Maine, and has since been extended to several other states by a popular majority; and even in the great States of New York, Pennsylvania, and Ohio, the most zealous efforts are now making by public addresses, by tracts and periodicals, and other means of agitation, to secure the election of legislators favorable to the temperance cause, who will strike at the root of the terrible evil, and remove even the temptation to drunkenness. Even last fall, shortly before the election, I was personal witness of the zeal and earnestness, with which the agents of the temperance society, ministers and laymen, canvassed the countries of Pennsylvania, and spreading their tent under the open heaven, after a solemn introduction by singing and prayer, eloquently described the horrible consequences, temporal and eternal, of intemperance, and demonstrated to the people by the most convincing arguments, the duty of using their elective franchise in a way demanded by the public weal, in the consciousness of their high responsibility to God and the world.

It must be granted that this Maine temperance law, *in itself considered*, goes too far, and is to be ranked with radical legislation. . . .

• • •

Yet, think of the "Maine liquor law" as we may,—and we would here neither advocate nor condemn it,—we must admire the moral energy and self-denial of a free people, which would rather renounce an enjoyment in itself lawful, than see it drive thousands of weak persons to bodily and spiritual ruin.

To those, who see in America only the land of unbridled radicalism and of the wildest fanaticism for freedom, I take the liberty to put the modest question: In what European state would the government have the courage to enact such a prohibition of the traffic in all intoxicating drinks, and the people the self-denial to submit to it?

Questions

1. How does Schaff believe Christianity influences American understandings of freedom?

2. Why does Schaff have reservations about the "Maine law" prohibiting the manufacture and sale of liquor?

---

73. Opening Editorial of *The Liberator* (1831)

Source: The Liberator, *January 1, 1831.*

The appearance on January 1, 1831, of William Lloyd Garrison's weekly newspaper, *The Liberator*, marked a turning point in the crusade against slavery. Garrison became the most prominent spokesman for a new generation of reformers who rejected the traditional approach of gradual emancipation and demanded immediate abolition. Also unlike their predecessors, they directed explosive language against slavery and slaveholders and insisted that blacks, once free, should be incorporated as equal citizens of the republic rather than being deported.

Garrison was among the first to appreciate the key role of public opinion in a mass democracy. He focused his efforts not on infiltrating the existing political parties (he opposed voting, since the Constitution protected slavery) but on awakening the nation to the moral evil of slavery. Persuaded that northern sentiment about slavery was as much of an obstacle to abolition as southern, Garrison used deliberately provocative language, calculated to seize public attention. "I will be as harsh as truth," Garrison announced, "and as uncompromising as justice."

• • •

DURING MY RECENT tour for the purpose of exciting the minds of the people by a series of discourses on the subject of slavery, every place that I visited gave fresh evidence of the fact, that a greater revolution in public sentiment was to be effected in the free states—*and particularly in New-England*—than at the south. I found contempt more bitter, opposition more active, detraction more relentless, prejudice more stubborn, and apathy more frozen, than among slave owners themselves. Of course, there were individual exceptions to the contrary. This state of things afflicted, but did not dishearten me. I determined, at every hazard, to lift up the standard of emancipation in the eyes of the nation, *within sight of Bunker Hill and in the birth place of liberty*. That standard is now unfurled; and long may it float, unhurt by the spoliations of time or the missiles of a desperate foe—yea, till every chain be broken, and every bondman set free! Let southern oppressors tremble—let their secret abettors tremble—let their northern apologist tremble—let all the enemies of the persecuted blacks tremble.

I deem the publication of my original Prospectus unnecessary, as it has obtained a wide circulation. The principles therein inculcated will be steadily pursued in this paper, excepting that I shall not array myself as the political partisan of any man. In defending the great cause of human rights, I wish to derive the assistance of all religions and of all parties.

Assenting to the "self-evident truth" maintained in the American Declaration of Independence, "that all men are created equal, and endowed by their Creator with certain inalienable rights—among

which are life, liberty and the pursuit of happiness," I shall strenu-
ously contend for the immediate enfranchisement of our slave population. In Park-street Church, on the Fourth of July, 1829, in an
address on slavery, I unreflectingly assented to the popular but pernicious doctrine of *gradual* abolition. I seize this opportunity to
make a full and unequivocal recantation, and thus publicly to ask
pardon of my God, of my country, and of my brethren the poor
slaves, for having uttered a sentiment so full of timidity, injustice
and absurdity. A similar recantation, from my pen, was published in
the Genius of Universal Emancipation at Baltimore, in September,
1829. My conscience is now satisfied.

I am aware, that many object to the severity of my language; but is
there not cause for severity? I *will be* as harsh as truth, and as uncompromising as justice. On this subject, I do not wish to think, or speak,
or write, with moderation. No! no! Tell a man whose house is on fire,
to give a moderate alarm; tell him to moderately rescue his wife from
the hands of the ravisher; tell the mother to gradually extricate her
babe from the fire into which it has fallen;—but urge me not to use
moderation in a cause like the present. I am in earnest—I will not
equivocate—I will not excuse—I will not retreat a single inch—AND
I WILL BE HEARD. The apathy of the people is enough to make every
statue leap from its pedestal, and to hasten the resurrection of the
dead.

It is pretended, that I am retarding the cause of emancipation by
the coarseness of my invective, and the precipitancy of my measures. *The charge is not true.* On this question my influence,—
humble as it is,—is felt at this moment to a considerable extent, and
shall be felt in coming years—not perniciously, but beneficially—
not as a curse, but as a blessing; and posterity will bear testimony
that I was right. I desire to thank God, that he enables me to disre-
gard "the fear of man which bringeth a snare," and to speak his
truth in its simplicity and power. And here I close with this fresh
dedication:

Oppression! I have seen thee, face to face,
And met thy cruel eye and cloudy brow;
But thy soul-withering glance I fear not now—
For dread to prouder feelings doth give place
Of deep abhorrence! Scorning the disgrace
Of slavish knees that at thy footstool bow,
I also kneel—but with far other vow
Do hail thee and thy hord of hirelings base:—
I swear, while life-blood warms my throbbing veins,
Still to oppose and thwart, with heart and hand,
Thy brutalising sway—till Afric's chains
Are burst, and Freedom rules the rescued land,—
Trampling Oppression and his iron rod:
Such is the vow I take—SO HELP ME GOD!

Questions

1. Why does Garrison believe that the North is in greater need of a "revolution in public sentiment" regarding slavery than the South?

2. How does Garrison justify the "severity" of his language?

---

74. Frederick Douglass on the Fourth of July (1852)

Source: Frederick Douglass, **My Bondage and My Freedom** *(New York, 1855), pp. 441–45.*

The greatest oration on American slavery and American freedom was delivered in Rochester in 1852 by Frederick Douglass. Speaking just after the annual Independence Day celebration, Douglass posed the question, "What, to the Slave, is the Fourth of July?" He answered that July Fourth festivities revealed the hypocrisy of a nation that proclaimed its belief in liberty yet daily committed "practices more shocking and bloody" than any other country on earth. Like other abolitionists, however, Douglass also laid claim to the founders' legacy. The Revolution had proclaimed "the great principles of political freedom and of natural justice, embodied in [the] Declaration of Independence," from which subsequent generations had tragically strayed. Only by abolishing slavery and freeing the ideals of the Declaration from the bounds of race could the United States, he believed, recapture its original mission.

FELLOW-CITIZENS, PARDON me, allow me to ask, why am I called upon to speak here to-day? What have I, or those I represent, to do with your national independence? Are the great principles of political freedom and of natural justice, embodied in that Declaration of Independence, extended to us? and am I, therefore, called upon to bring our humble offering to the national altar, and to confess the benefits and express devout gratitude for the blessings resulting from your independence to us?

Would to God, both for your sakes and ours, that an affirmative answer could be truthfully returned to these questions! Then would my task be light, and my burden easy and delightful. For *who* is there so cold, that a nation's sympathy could not warm him? Who so obdurate and dead to the claims of gratitude, that would not thankfully acknowledge such priceless benefits? Who so stolid and selfish, that would not give his voice to swell the hallelujahs of a nation's jubilee, when the chains of servitude had been torn from his limbs? I am not that man. In a case like that, the dumb might eloquently speak, and the "lame man leap as an hart."

But, such is not the state of the case. I say it with a sad sense of the disparity between us. I am not included within the pale of this glorious anniversary! Your high independence only reveals the immeasurable distance between us. The blessings in which you, this day, rejoice, are not enjoyed in common. The rich inheritance of justice, liberty, prosperity and independence, bequeathed by your fathers, is shared by you, not by me. The sunlight that brought life and healing to you, has brought stripes and death to me. This Fourth [of] July is *yours*, not *mine.* You may rejoice, *I* must mourn. To drag a man in fetters into the grand illuminated temple of liberty, and call upon him to join you in joyous anthems, were inhuman mockery and sacrilegious irony. Do you mean, citizens, to mock me, by asking me to speak to-day? If so, there is a parallel to your conduct. And let me warn you that it is dangerous to copy the example of a nation whose crimes, towering up to heaven, were thrown down by the breath of the Almighty, burying that nation in irrecoverable ruin! I can to-day take up the plaintive lament of a peeled and woesmitten people!

• • •

Fellow-citizens; above your national, tumultuous joy, I hear the mournful wail of millions whose chains, heavy and grievous yesterday, are, today, rendered more intolerable by the jubilee shouts that reach them. If I do forget, if I do not faithfully remember those bleeding children of sorrow this day, "may my right hand forget her cunning, and may my tongue cleave to the roof of my mouth!" To forget them, to pass lightly over their wrongs, and to chime in with the popular theme, would be treason most scandalous and shocking, and would make me a reproach before God and the world. My subject, then fellow-citizens, is AMERICAN SLAVERY. I shall see, this day, and its popular characteristics, from the slave's point of view. Standing, there, identified with the American bondman, making his wrongs mine, I do not hesitate to declare, with all my soul, that the character and conduct of this nation never looked blacker to me than on this 4th of July! Whether we turn to the declarations of the past, or to the professions of the present, the conduct of the nation seems equally hideous and revolting. America is false to the past, false to the present, and solemnly binds herself to be false to the future. Standing with God and the crushed and bleeding slave on this occasion, I will, in the name of humanity which is outraged, in the name of liberty which is fettered, in the name of the constitution and the Bible, which are disregarded and trampled upon, dare to call in question and to denounce, with all the emphasis I can command, everything that serves to perpetuate slavery—the great sin and shame of America! "I will not equivocate; I will not excuse"; I will use the severest language I can command; and yet not one word shall escape me that any man, whose judgement is not blinded by prejudice, or who is not at heart a slaveholder, shall not confess to be right and just.

For the present, it is enough to affirm the equal manhood of the negro race. Is it not astonishing that, while we are ploughing, planting and reaping, using all kinds of mechanical tools, erecting houses, constructing bridges, building ships, working in metals of brass, iron, copper, silver and gold; that, while we are reading, writing and cyphering, acting as clerks, merchants and secretaries, having among us lawyers, doctors, ministers, poets, authors, editors, orators and teachers; that, while we are engaged in all manner of enterprises common to other men, digging gold in California, capturing the whale in the Pacific, feeding sheep and cattle on the hillside, living, moving, acting, thinking, planning, living in families as husbands, wives and children, and, above all, confessing and worshipping the Christian's God, and looking hopefully for life and immortality beyond the grave, we are called upon to prove that we are men!

Would you have me argue that man is entitled to liberty? that he is the rightful owner of his own body? You have already declared it. Must I argue the wrongfulness of slavery? Is that a question for Republicans? Is it to be settled by the rules of logic and argumentation, as a matter beset with great difficulty, involving a doubtful application of the principle of justice, hard to be understood? How should I look to-day, in the presence of Americans, dividing, and subdividing a discourse, to show that men have a natural right to freedom? speaking of it relatively, and positively, negatively, and affirmatively. To do so, would be to make myself ridiculous, and to offer an insult to your understanding. There is not a man beneath the canopy of heaven, that does not know that slavery is wrong *for him.*

What, am I to argue that it is wrong to make men brutes, to rob them of their liberty, to work them without wages, to keep them ignorant of their relations to their fellow men, to beat them with sticks, to flay their flesh with the lash, to load their limbs with irons, to hunt them with dogs, to sell them at auction, to sunder their families, to knock out their teeth, to burn their flesh, to starve them into obedience and submission to their masters? Must I argue that a system thus marked with blood, and stained with pollution, is *wrong?* No! I will not. I have better employments for my time and strength, than such arguments would imply.

What, then, remains to be argued? Is it that slavery is not divine; that God did not establish it; that our doctors of divinity are mistaken? There is blasphemy in the thought. That which is inhuman, cannot be divine! *Who* can reason on such a proposition? They that can, may; I cannot. The time for such argument is past.

At a time like this, scorching irony, not convincing argument, is needed. O! had I the ability, and could I reach the nation's ear, I would, to-day, pour out a fiery stream of biting ridicule, blasting reproach, withering sarcasm, and stern rebuke. For it is not light that is needed, but fire; it is not the gentle shower, but thunder. We need the storm, the whirlwind, and the earthquake. The feeling of the nation must be quickened; the conscience of the nation must be roused; the propriety of the nation must be startled; the hypocrisy of the nation must be exposed; and its crimes against God and man must be proclaimed and denounced.

What, to the American slave, is your 4th of July? I answer: a day that reveals to him, more than all other days in the year, the gross injustice and cruelty to which he is the constant victim. To him, your celebration is a sham; your boasted liberty, an unholy license; your national greatness, swelling vanity; your sounds of rejoicing are empty and heartless; your denunciations of tyrants, brass fronted impudence; your shouts of liberty and equality, hollow mockery; your prayers and hymns, your sermons and thanksgivings, with all your religious parade, and solemnity, are, to him, mere bombast, fraud, deception, impiety, and hypocrisy—a thin veil to cover up crimes which would disgrace a nation of savages. There is not a nation on the earth guilty of practices, more shocking and bloody, than are the people of these United States, at this very hour.

Go where you may, search where you will, roam through all the monarchies and despotisms of the old world, travel through South America, search out every abuse, and when you have found the last, lay your facts by the side of the everyday practices of this nation, and you will say with me, that, for revolting barbarity and shameless hypocrisy, America reigns without a rival.

Questions

1. What does Douglass hope to accomplish by accusing white Americans of injustice and hypocrisy?

2. What evidence does Douglass present to disprove the idea of black inferiority?

---

75. Catharine Beecher on the "Duty of American Females" (1837)

Source: *Catharine E. Beecher,* Essay on Slavery and Abolitionism, with Reference to the Duty of American Females *(Philadelphia, 1837), pp. 5–6, 27, 41, 101–08, 128.*

The abolitionist movement enabled women to carve out a place in the public sphere. Women attended antislavery meetings and circulated petitions to Congress. Most prominent during the 1830s were Angelina and Sarah Grimké, the daughters of a South Carolina slaveowner. The sisters had been converted to Quakerism and abolitionism while visiting Philadelphia. They began to deliver popular lectures that offered a scathing condemnation of slavery from the perspective of those who had witnessed its evils firsthand.

In 1836, Angelina Grimké wrote *Appeal to the Christian Women of the South,* urging them to take a stand against slavery.

The sight of women lecturing in public to mixed male-female audiences and taking part in public debate on political questions aroused considerable criticism. The prominent writer Catharine Beecher responded to Grimké's essay by reprimanding her for stepping outside "the domestic and social sphere," urging her to accept the fact that "heaven" had designated man "the superior" and woman "the subordinate."

⸺⸺⸺

MY DEAR FRIEND:

Your public address to Christian females at the South has reached me, and I have been urged to aid in circulating it at the North. I have also been informed, that you contemplate a tour, during the ensuing year, for the purpose of exerting your influence to form Abolition Societies among ladies of the non-slave-holding States.

Our acquaintance and friendship give me a claim to your private ear; but there are reasons why it seems more desirable to address you, who now stand before the public as an advocate of Abolition measures, in a more public manner.

The object I have in view, is to present some reasons why it seems unwise and inexpedient for ladies of the non-slave-holding States to unite themselves in Abolition Societies; and thus, at the same time, to exhibit the inexpediency of the course you propose to adopt. . . .

Now Abolitionists are before the community, and declare that all slavery is sin, which ought to be immediately forsaken; and that it is their object and intention to promote the *immediate emancipation* of all the slaves in this nation. . . . [R]eproaches, rebukes, and sneers, were employed to convince the whites that their prejudices were sinful. . . .

[T]he severing of the Union by the present mode of agitating the question . . . may be one of the results, and, if so, what are the probabilities for a Southern republic that has torn itself off for the purpose of excluding foreign interference, and for the purpose of perpetuating slavery? . . .

Heaven has appointed to one sex the superior, and to the other the subordinate station, and this without any reference to the character or conduct of either. It is therefore as much for the dignity as it is for the interest of females, in all respects to conform to the duties of this relation. . . . But while woman holds a subordinate relation in society to the other sex, it is not because it was designed that her duties or her influence should be any the less important, or all-pervading. But it was designed that the mode of gaining influence and of exercising power should be altogether different and peculiar. . . .

Woman is to win every thing by peace and love; by making herself so much respected, esteemed and loved, that to yield to her opinions and to gratify her wishes, will be the free-will offering of the heart. But this is to be all accomplished in the domestic and social circle. . . . But the moment woman begins to feel the promptings of ambition, or the thirst for power, her aegis of defence is gone. All the sacred protection of religion, all the generous promptings of chivalry, all the poetry of romantic gallantry, depend upon woman's retaining her place as dependent and defenceless, and making no claims, and maintaining no right but what are the gifts of honour, rectitude and love.

A woman may seek the aid of co-operation and combination among her own sex, to assist her in her appropriate offices of piety, charity, maternal and domestic duty; but whatever, in any measure, throws a woman into the attitude of a combatant either for herself or others—whatever binds her in a party conflict—whatever obliges her in any way to exert coercive influences, throws her out of her appropriate sphere. . . .

If it is asked, "May not woman appropriately come forward as a suppliant for a portion of her sex who are bound in cruel bondage?" It is replied, that, the rectitude and propriety of any such measure, depend entirely on its probable results. If petitions from females will operate to exasperate; if they will be deemed obtrusive, indecorous, and unwise, by those to whom they are addressed; . . . if they will be the opening wedge, that will eventually bring females as petitioners and partisans into every political measure that may tend to injure and oppress their sex . . . then it is neither appropriate nor wise, nor right, for a woman to petition for the relief of oppressed females. . . .

In this country, petitions to congress, in reference to the official duties of legislators, seem, IN ALL CASES, to fall entirely without the sphere of female duty. Men are the proper persons to make appeals to the rulers whom they appoint, and if their female friends, by arguments and persuasions, can induce them to petition, all the good that can be done by such measures will be secured. But if females cannot influence their nearest friends, to urge forward a public measure in this way, they surely are out of their place, in attempting to do it themselves. . . .

It is allowed by all reflecting minds, that the safety and happiness of this nation depends upon having the *children* educated, and not only intellectually, but morally and religiously. There are now nearly two millions of children and adults in this country who cannot read, and who have no schools of any kind. To give only a small supply of teachers to these destitute children, who are generally where the population is sparse, will demand *thirty thousand teachers* at the moment and an addition of *two thousand every year.* Where is this army of teachers to be found? Is it at all probable that the other sex will afford even a moderate portion of this supply? . . . Men will be educators in the college, in the high school, in some of the most honourable and lucrative common schools, but the *children,* the *little children* of this nation must, to a wide extent, be taught by females, or remain untaught. . . . And as the value of education rises in the public mind . . . women will more and more be furnished with those intellectual advantages which they need to fit them for such duties.

The result will be, that America will be distinguished above all other nations, for well-educated females and for the influence they will exert on the general interests of society. But if females, as they approach the other sex, in intellectual elevation, begin to claim, or to exercise in any manner, the peculiar prerogatives of that sex, education will prove a doubtful and dangerous blessing. But this will never be the result. For the more intelligent a woman becomes, the more she can appreciate the wisdom of that ordinance that appointed her subordinate station.

But it may be asked, is there nothing to be done to bring this national sin of slavery to an end? Must the internal slave-trade, a trade now ranked as piracy among all civilized nations, still prosper in our bounds? Must the very seat of our government stand as one of the chief slave-markets of the land; and must not Christian females open their lips, nor lift a finger, to bring such a shame and sin to an end? To this it may be replied, that Christian females may, and can say and do much to bring these evils to an end; and the present is a time and an occasion when it seems most desirable that they should know, and appreciate, and *exercise* the power which they do possess for so desirable an end. . . .

In the present aspect of affairs among us, when everything seems to be tending to disunion and distraction, it surely has become the duty of every female instantly to relinquish the attitude of a partisan, in every matter of clashing interests, and to assume the office of a mediator, and an advocate of peace. And to do this, it is not necessary that a woman should in any manner relinquish her opinion as to the evils or the benefits, the right or the wrong, of any principle of practice. But, while quietly holding her own opinions, and calmly avowing them, when conscience and integrity make the duty imperative, every female can employ her influence, not for the purpose of exciting or regulating public sentiment, but rather for the purpose of promoting a spirit of candour, forbearance, charity, and peace.

Questions

1. How does Beecher think women should exert power within American society?

2. Why does she believe that the abolitionist movement is dangerous?

76. Angelina Grimké on Women's Rights (1837)

Source: The Liberator, *August 2, 1837.*

In response to Catharine Beecher's criticism, Angelina Grimké wrote a series of twelve letters forthrightly defending the right of women to take part in political debate. The final one addressed the question of women's rights directly. "Since I engaged in the investigation of the rights of the slave," she wrote, "I have necessarily been led to a better understanding of my own." "I know nothing," she continued, "of men's rights and women's rights. My doctrine is that whatever is morally right for man to do, it is morally right for woman to do." The Grimké sisters soon retired from the fray, after Angelina married the abolitionist Theodore Weld. But their writings helped to spark the movement for women's rights that arose in the 1840s.

Since I engaged in the investigation of the rights of the slave, I have necessarily been led to a better understanding of my own; for I have found the Anti-Slavery cause to be the high school of morals in our land—the school in which human rights are more fully investigated, and better understood and taught, than in any other benevolent enterprise. Here one great fundamental principle is disinterred, which, as soon as it is uplifted to public view, leads the mind into a thousand different ramifications, into which the rays of this central light are streaming with brightness and glory. Here we are led to examine why human beings have any rights. It is because they are moral beings; the rights of all men, from the king to the slave, are built upon their moral nature: and as all men have this moral nature, so all men have essentially the same rights. These rights may be plundered from the slave, but they cannot be alienated: his right and title to himself is as perfect now, as is that of Lyman Beecher: they are written in his moral being, and must remain unimpaired as long as that being continues.

Now it naturally occurred to me, that if rights were founded in moral being, then the circumstance of sex could not give to man higher rights and responsibilities, than to woman. To suppose that it did, would be to deny the self-evident truth, "that the physical constitution is the mere instrument of the moral nature." To suppose that it did, would be to break up utterly the relations of the two natures, and to reverse their functions, exalting the animal nature into a monarch, and humbling the moral into a slave; "making the former a proprietor, and the latter its property." When I look at human beings as moral beings, all distinction in sex sinks to insignificance and nothingness; for I believe it regulates rights and responsibilities no more than the color of the skin or the eyes. My doctrine then is, that whatever it is morally right for man to do, it is morally right for woman to do. Our duties are governed, not by difference of sex, but by the diversity of our relative connections in life, and the variety of gifts and talents committed to our care, and the different eras in which we live.

This regulation of duty by the mere circumstance of sex, rather than by the fundamental principle of moral being, has led to all that multifarious train of evils flowing out of the anti-christian doctrine of masculine and feminine virtues. By this doctrine, man has been converted into the warrior, and clothed in sternness, and those other kindred qualities, which, in the eyes of many, belong to his character as a man; whilst woman has been taught to lean upon an arm of flesh, to sit as a soul arrayed "in gold and pearls, and costly array," to be admired for her personal charms, and caressed and humored like a spoiled child, or converted into a mere drudge to suit the convenience of her lord and master. This principle has spread desolation over the whole moral world, and brought into all the diversified relations of life, "confusion and every evil work." It has given to man a charter for the exercise of tyranny and selfishness, pride and arrogance, lust and brutal violence. It has robbed woman of essential rights, the right to think and speak and act on all great moral questions, just as men think and speak and act; the right to share their responsibilities, dangers, and toils; the right to fulfill the great end of her being, as a help meet for man, as a moral, intellectual and immortal creature, and of glorifying God in her body and her spirit which are His. Hitherto, instead of being a help meet to man, in the highest, noblest sense of the term, as a companion, a co-worker, an equal; she has been a mere appendage of his being, and instrument of his convenience and pleasure, the pretty toy, with which he wiled away his leisure moments, or the pet animal whom he humored into playfulness and submission. Woman, instead of being regarded as the equal of man, has uniformly been looked down upon as his inferior, a mere gift to fill up the measure of his happiness. In the poetry of "romantic gallantry," it is true, she has been called the "last best gift of God to man;" but I believe I speak forth the words of truth and soberness when I affirm, that woman never was given to man. She was created, like him, in the image of God, and crowned with glory and honor; created only a little lower than the angels,—not, as is too generally presumed, a little lower than man; on her brow, as well as on his, was placed the "diadem of beauty," and in her hand the scepter of universal dominion . . .

Measure her rights and duties by the sure, unerring standard of moral being, not by the false rights and measures of a mere circumstance of her human existence, and then will it become a self-evident truth, that whatever it is morally right for a man to do, it is morally right for a woman to do. I recognize no rights but human rights—I know nothing of men's rights and women's rights; for in Christ Jesus, there is neither male or female; and it is my solemn conviction, that, until this important principle of equality is recognized and carried out into practice, that vain will be the efforts of the church to do anything effectual for the permanent reformation of the world. Woman was the first transgressor, and the first victim of power. In all the heathen nations, she has been the slave of man, and no Christian nation has ever acknowledged her rights. Nay more, no Christian Society has ever done so either, on the broad and solid basis of humanity. I know that in some few denominations, she is permitted to preach the gospel; but this is not done from a conviction of her equality as a human being, but of her equality in spiritual gifts—for we find that woman, even in these Societies, is not allowed to make the Discipline by which she is to be governed. Now, I believe it is her right to be consulted in all the laws and regulations by which she is to be governed, whether in Church or State, and that the present arrangement of Society, on those points, are a violation of human rights, an usurpation of power over her, which is working mischief, great mischief, in the world. If Ecclesiastical and Civil governments are ordained of God, then I contend that woman has just as much right to sit in solemn counsel in Conventions, Conferences, Associations, and General Assemblies, as man—just as much right to sit upon the throne of England, or in the Presidential chair of the United States, as man. . . .

• • •

I believe the discussion of Human Rights at the North has already been of immense advantage to this country. It is producing the happiest influence upon the minds and hearts of those who are engaged in it; . . . Indeed, the very agitation of the question, which it involved, has been highly important. Never was the heart of man so expanded; never were its generous sympathies so generally and so perseveringly excited. These sympathies, thus called into existence, have been useful preservatives of national virtue. I therefore do wish very much to promote the Anti-Slavery excitement at the North, because I believe it will prove a useful preservative of national virtue. . . .

The discussion of the wrongs of slavery has opened the way for the discussion of other rights, and the ultimate result will most certainly be "the breaking of every yoke," the letting the oppressed of every grade and description go free—an emancipation far more glorious than any the world has ever yet seen, an introduction into that liberty wherewith Christ hath made his people free. . . .

Questions

1. Why does Angelina Grimké call the abolitionist movement the nation's foremost "school [of] human rights"?

2. What role does she think the difference between the sexes should play in determining a person's rights and obligations?

77. Declaration of Sentiments of the Seneca Falls Convention (1848)

Source: Elizabeth Cady Stanton, et al., eds., A History of Woman Suffrage (Rochester, N.Y., 1881–1922), Vol. 1, pp. 70–74.

The Seneca Falls convention of 1848 marked the beginning of the seventy-year struggle for women's suffrage. Elizabeth Cady Stanton, a veteran of the antislavery crusade, was the principal author of the Declaration of Sentiments adopted at Seneca Falls, the town in upstate New York where she lived. Modeled on the Declaration of Independence, the document added "women" to Jefferson's axiom, "all men are created equal." And in place of Jefferson's list of injustices committed by George III, Stanton condemned the "injuries and usurpations on the part of man toward woman." The first to be listed was denying her the right to vote. As Stanton told the convention, only the vote would make woman "free as man is free," since in a democratic society, freedom was impossible without the ballot. The vote, however, was hardly the only issue raised at the convention. Equal rights became the rallying cry of the early movement for women's rights, and equal rights meant claiming access to all the prevailing definitions of American freedom.

―――――――――

WHEN, IN THE course of human events, it becomes necessary for one portion of the family of man to assume among the people of the earth a position different from that which they have hitherto occupied, but one to which the laws of nature and of nature's God entitle them, a decent respect to the opinions of mankind requires that they should declare the causes that impel them to such a course.

We hold these truths to be self-evident: that all men and women are created equal; that they are endowed by their Creator with certain inalienable rights; that among these are life, liberty, and the pursuit of happiness; that to secure these rights governments are instituted, deriving their just powers from the consent of the governed. Whenever any form of government becomes destructive of these ends, it is the right of those who suffer from it to refuse allegiance to it, and to insist upon the institution of a new government, laying its foundation on such principles, and organizing its powers in such form, as to them shall seem most likely to effect their safety and happiness. Prudence, indeed, will dictate that governments long established should not be changed for light and transient causes; and accordingly all experience hath shown that mankind are more disposed to suffer, while evils are sufferable, than to right themselves by abolishing the forms to which they were accustomed. But when a long train of abuses and usurpations, pursuing invariably the same object evinces a design to reduce them under absolute despotism, it is their duty to throw off such government, and to provide new guards for their future security. Such has been the patient sufferance of the women under this government, and such is now the necessity which constrains them to demand the equal station to which they are entitled.

The history of mankind is a history of repeated injuries and usurpations on the part of man toward woman, having in direct object the establishment of an absolute tyranny over her. To prove this, let facts be submitted to a candid world.

He has never permitted her to exercise her inalienable right to the elective franchise.

He has compelled her to submit to laws, in the formation of which she had no voice.

He has withheld from her rights which are given to the most ignorant and degraded men—both natives and foreigners.

Having deprived her of this first right of a citizen, the elective franchise, thereby leaving her without representation in the halls of legislation, he has oppressed her on all sides.

He has made her, if married, in the eye of the law, civilly dead.

He has taken from her all right in property, even to the wages she earns.

He has made her, morally, an irresponsible being, as she can commit many crimes with impunity, provided they be done in the presence of her husband. In the covenant of marriage, she is compelled to promise obedience to her husband, he becoming, to all intents and purposes, her master—the law giving him power to deprive her of her liberty, and to administer chastisement.

He has so framed the laws of divorce, as to what shall be the proper causes, and in case of separation, to whom the guardianship of the children shall be given, as to be wholly regardless of the happiness of women—the law, in all cases, going upon a false supposition of the supremacy of man, and giving all power into his hands.

After depriving her of all rights as a married woman, if single, and the owner of property, he has taxed her to support a government which recognizes her only when her property can be made profitable to it.

He has monopolized nearly all the profitable employments, and from those she is permitted to follow, she receives but a scanty remuneration. He closes against her all the avenues to wealth and distinction which he considers most honorable to himself. As a teacher of theology, medicine, or law, she is not known.

He has denied her the facilities for obtaining a thorough education, all colleges being closed against her.

He allows her in Church, as well as State, but a subordinate position, claiming Apostolic authority for her exclusion from the ministry, and, with some exceptions, from any public participation in the affairs of the Church.

He has created a false public sentiment by giving to the world a different code of morals for men and women, by which moral delinquencies which exclude women from society, are not only tolerated, but deemed of little account in man.

He has usurped the prerogative of Jehovah himself, claiming it as his right to assign for her a sphere of action, when that belongs to her conscience and to her God.

He has endeavored, in every way that he could, to destroy her confidence in her own powers, to lessen her self-respect, and to make her willing to lead a dependent and abject life.

Now, in view of this entire disfranchisement of one-half the people of this country, their social and religious degradation—in view of the unjust laws above mentioned, and because women do feel themselves aggrieved, oppressed, and fraudulently deprived of their most sacred rights, we insist that they have immediate admission to all the rights and privileges which belong to them as citizens of the United States.

In entering upon the great work before us, we anticipate no small amount of misconception, misrepresentation, and ridicule; but we shall use every instrumentality within our power to effect our object. We shall employ agents, circulate tracts, petition the State and National legislatures, and endeavor to enlist the pulpit and the press in our behalf. We hope this Convention will be followed by a series of Conventions embracing every part of the country.

Questions

1. What are the key demands, other than the right to vote, put forward by the Seneca Falls convention?

2. How does the Declaration seem to define freedom for women?

CHAPTER 13

A House Divided, 1840–1861

78. John L. O'Sullivan, Manifest Destiny (1845)

Source, John L. O'Sullivan, "Annexation," United States Magazine, and Democratic Review, Vol. 17 (July/August 1845), pp. 5–10.

The expansionist spirit of the 1840s was captured in the phrase "manifest destiny," coined by John. L. O'Sullivan, a New York journalist. O'Sullivan, employed it to suggest that the United States had a divinely appointed mission to occupy all of North America. This right to the continent was provided by the nation's mission to extend the area of freedom. In the excerpt that follows, O'Sullivan defends the annexation of Texas, and suggests that California, then a province of Mexico, would be the next area to be absorbed into the United States, linked to the rest of the country by a new transcontinental road. O'Sullivan foresees the day when one government will control the entire North American continent. The spirit of manifest destiny would soon help to justify the Mexican War and, half a century later, the annexation of Puerto Rico and the Philippines as a result of the Spanish-American War.

━━━━━━━━

IT IS TIME now for all opposition to annexation of Texas to cease... Texas is now ours. Already before these records are written, her convention has undoubtedly ratified the acceptance, by her congress, of our proffered invitation into the Union; and made the requisite changes in her already republican form of constitution to adapt it to its future federal relations. Her star and stripe may already be said to have taken their place in the glorious blazon of our common nationality; and the sweep of our eagle's wing already includes within its circuit the wide extent of her fair and fertile land.

She is no longer to us a mere geographical space—a certain combination of coast, plain, mountain, valley, forest, and stream. She is no longer to us a mere country on the map ... It is time when all should cease to treat her as alien, and even adverse ... and cease ... thwarting our policy and hampering our power, limiting our greatness and checking the fulfillment of our manifest destiny to overspread the continent allotted by Providence for the free development of our yearly multiplying millions.

• • •

It is wholly untrue, and unjust to ourselves, the pretense that the annexation has been a measure of spoliation, unrightful and unrighteous of military conquest under forms of peace and law of territorial aggrandizement at the expense of justice. ...

The independence of Texas was complete and absolute. It was an independence, not only in fact, but of right. ... If Texas became peopled with an American population, it was by no contrivance of our government, but on the express invitation of that of Mexico herself; accompanied with such guaranties of state independence, and the maintenance of a federal system analogous to our own ... She was released, rightfully and absolutely released, from all Mexican allegiance, or duty of cohesion to the Mexican political body, by acts and fault of Mexico herself, and Mexico alone. There was never a clearer case. It was not revolution; it was resistance to revolution: and resistance under such circumstances as left independence the necessary resulting state, caused by the abandonment of those with whom her former federal association had existed.

Nor is there any just foundation for the charge that annexation is a great pro-slavery measure calculated to increase and perpetuate that institution. Slavery had nothing to do with it. Opinions were and are greatly divided, both at the North and South, as to the influence to be exerted by it on slavery and the slave states. ...

Every new slave state in Texas will make at least one free state from among those in which that institution now exists—to say nothing of those portions of Texas on which slavery cannot spring and grow—to say nothing of the far more rapid growth of new states in the free West and Northwest, as these fine regions are overspread by the emigration fast flowing over them from Europe, as well as from the Northern and Eastern states of the Union as it exists. . . .

California will, probably, next fall away from the loose adhesion which, in such a country as Mexico, holds a remote province in a slight equivocal kind of dependence on the metropolis. Imbecile and distracted, Mexico never can exert any real government authority over such a country. . . .

In the case of California this is now impossible. The Anglo-Saxon foot is already on its borders. Already the advance guard of the irresistible army of Anglo-Saxon emigration has begun to pour down upon it, armed with the plough and the rifle, and marking its trail with schools and colleges, courts and representative halls, mills and meetinghouses. A population will soon be in actual occupation of California, over which it will be idle for Mexico to dream of dominion. They will necessarily become independent. All this without agency of our government, without responsibility of our people . . .

And they will have a right to independence—to self-government—to the possession of the homes conquered from the wildness of their own labors and dangers, sufferings and sacrifices—a better and a truer right than the artificial title of sovereignty in Mexico, a thousand miles distant, inheriting from Spain a title good only against those who have none better. Their right to independence will be the natural right of self-government belonging to any community strong enough to maintain it. . . . This will be their title to independence; and by this title, there can be no doubt that the population now fast streaming down upon California will both assert and maintain that independence.

Whether they will attach themselves to our Union or not is not to be predicted with any certainty. Unless the projected railroad across the continent to the Pacific be carried into effect, perhaps they may not; though even in that case, the day when the empires of the Atlantic and Pacific would again flow together into one, as soon as their inland border should approach each other. But that great work, colossal as appears the plan on its first suggestion, cannot remain long unbuilt.

Its [the transcontinental railroad] necessity for this very purpose of binding and holding together in its iron clasp our fast settling Pacific region with that of the Mississippi Valley, the natural facility of the route, the ease with which any amount of labor for the construction can be drawn in from the overcrowded populations of Europe, to be paid in the lands made valuable by the progress of the work itself and its immense utility, to the whole commerce of the world with the whole eastern coast of Asia, alone almost sufficient for the support of such a road—these considerations give assurance that the day cannot be distant which shall witness the conveyance of representatives from Oregon and California to Washington [D.C.] within less time than a few years ago was devoted to a similar journey by those from Ohio; while the magnetic telegraph will enable the editors of the San Francisco Union, the Astoria Evening Post, or the Nootka Morning News, to set up in type the first half of the President's inaugural before the echoes of the latter half shall have died away beneath the lofty porch of the Capitol, as spoken from his lips.

Away, then, with all idle French talk of balances of power on the American continent. There is no growth in Spanish America! Whatever progress of population may be in British Canada, is only for their own early severance of their present colonial relation to the little island 3,000 miles across the Atlantic; soon to be followed by annexation, and destined to swell the still accumulating momentum of our progress.

And whosoever may hold the balance, though they should cast into the opposite scale all the bayonets and cannon, not only of France and England, but of Europe entire, how would it kick the beam against the simple, solid weight of the 250, or 300 million, and American millions destined to gather beneath the flutter of the stars and stripes, in the fast hastening year of the Lords 1845!

Questions

1. What connection does O'Sullivan see between manifest destiny and the idea of American freedom?

2. What does O'Sullivan mean when he describes America's destiny to rule the entire continent as "manifest"?

━━━━━━━━━

79. Henry David Thoreau, "Resistance to Civil Government" (1849)

Source: Henry David Thoreau, "Resistance to Civil Government," in **Aesthetic Papers** *(Boston, 1849), pp. 189–200.*

The Mexican-American War of 1846–1848 was the first American conflict to be fought primarily on foreign soil and the first in which American troops occupied a foreign capital. It resulted in the absorption by the United States of about one third of the territory of Mexico—the present-day states of Arizona, California, New Mexico, Nevada, and Utah. The war pushed to the center of political debate the question of whether slavery should be allowed to expand into this vast new territory.

Inspired by the expansionist fervor of manifest destiny, a majority of Americans supported the war. But a significant minority in the North feared that, far from expanding the "empire of liberty," the real aim of the administration of James K. Polk was to acquire new land for the expansion of slavery. In Massachusetts, Henry David Thoreau was jailed in 1846 for refusing to pay taxes as a protest against the war. Defending his action, Thoreau wrote the essay, "On Civil Disobedience." The essay would inspire such later advocates of nonviolent resistance to unjust laws as Martin Luther King Jr.

━━━━━━━━━

I HEARTILY ACCEPT the motto,—"That government is best which governs least," and I should like to see it acted up to more rapidly and systematically. Carried out, it finally amounts to this, which also I believe,—"That government is best which governs not at all," and when men are prepared for it, that will be the kind of government which they will have. Government is at best but an expedient; but most governments are usually, and all governments are sometimes, inexpedient. The objections which have been brought against a standing army, and they are many and weighty, and deserve to prevail, may also at last be brought against a standing government. The standing army is only an arm of the standing government. The government itself, which is only the mode which the people have chosen to execute their will, is equally liable to be abused and perverted before the people can act through it. Witness the present Mexican war, the work of comparatively a few individuals using the standing government as their tool; for, in the outset, the people would not have consented to this measure.

This American government,—what is it but a tradition, though a recent one, endeavoring to transmit itself unimpaired to posterity, but each instant losing some of its integrity? It has not the vitality and force of a single living man; for a single man can bend it to his will. It is a sort of wooden gun to the people themselves; and, if ever they should use it in earnest as a real one against each other, it will surely split. But it is not the less necessary for this; for the people must have some complicated machinery or other, and hear its din, to satisfy that idea of government which they have. Governments show thus how successfully men can be imposed on, even impose on themselves, for their own advantage. It is excellent, we must all allow; yet this government never of itself furthered any enterprise, but by the alacrity with which it got out of its way. *It* does not keep the country free. *It* does not settle the West. *It* does not educate. The character inherent in the American people has done all that has been accomplished; and it would have done somewhat more, if the government had not sometimes got in its way. For government is an expedient by which men would fain succeed in letting one another alone; and, as has been said, when it is most expedient, the governed are most let alone by it. Trade and commerce, if they were not made of India rubber, would never manage to bounce over the obstacles which legislators are continually putting in their way; and, if one were to judge these men wholly by the effects of their actions, and not partly by their intentions, they would deserve to be classed and punished with those mischievous persons who put obstructions on the railroads.

But, to speak practically and as a citizen, unlike those who call themselves no-government men, I ask for, not at once no government, but *at once* a better government. Let every man make known what kind of government would command his respect, and that will be one step toward obtaining it.

After all, the practical reason why, when the power is once in the hands of the people, a majority are permitted, and for a long period continue, to rule, is not because they are most likely to be in the right, nor because this seems fairest to the minority, but because they are physically the strongest. But a government in which the majority rule in all cases cannot be based on justice, even as far as men understand it. Can there not be a government in which majorities do not virtually decide right and wrong, but conscience?—in which majorities decide only those questions to which the rule of expediency is applicable? Must the citizen ever for a moment, or in the least degree, resign his conscience to the legislator? Why has every man a conscience, then? I think that we should be men first, and subjects afterward. It is not desirable to cultivate a respect for the law, so much as for the right. The only obligation which I have a right to assume, is to do at any time what I think right. It is truly enough said, that a corporation has no conscience; but a corporation of conscientious men is a corporation *with* a conscience. Law never made men a whit more just; and, by means of their respect for it, even the well-disposed are daily made the agents of injustice. A common and natural result of an undue respect for law is, that you may see a file of soldiers, colonel, captain, corporal, privates, powder-monkeys and all, marching in admirable order over hill and dale to the wars, against their wills, aye, against their common sense and consciences, which makes it very steep marching indeed, and producing palpitation of the heart . . .

• • •

Unjust laws exist: shall we be content to obey them, or shall we endeavor to amend them, and obey them until we have succeeded, or shall we transgress them at once? Men generally, under such a government as this, think that they ought to wait until they have persuaded the majority to alter them. They think that, if they should resist, the remedy would be worse than the evil. But it is the fault of the government itself that the remedy *is* worse than the evil. *It* makes it worse. Why is it not more apt to anticipate and provide for reform? Why does it not cherish its wise minority? Why does it cry and resist before it is hurt? Why does it not encourage its citizens to be on the alert to point out its faults, and *do* better than it would have them? Why does it always crucify Christ, and excommunicate Copernicus and Luther, and pronounce Washington and Franklin rebels?

One would think, that a deliberate and practical denial of its authority was the only offence never contemplated by government; else, why has it not assigned its definite, its suitable and proportionate penalty? If a man who has no property refuses but once to earn nine shillings for the State, he is put in prison for a period unlimited by any law that I know, and determined only by the discretion of those who placed him there; but if I should steal ninety times nine shillings from the State, he is soon permitted to go at large again.

If the injustice is part of the necessary friction of the machine of government, let it go, let it go: perchance it will wear smooth,— certainly the machine will wear out. If the injustice has a spring, or a pulley, or a rope, or a crank, exclusively for itself, then perhaps you may consider whether the remedy will not be worse than the evil; but if it is of such a nature that it requires you to be the agent of injustice to another, then, I say, break the law. Let your life be a counter friction to stop the machine. What I have to do is to see, at any rate, that I do not lend myself to the wrong which I condemn . . .

• • •

Under a government which imprisons any unjustly, the true place for a just man is also a prison. The proper place to-day, the only place which Massachusetts has provided for her freer and less desponding spirits, is in her prisons, to be put out and locked out of the State by her own act, as they have already put themselves out by their principles. It is there that the fugitive slave, and the Mexican prisoner on parole, and the Indian come to plead the wrongs of his race, should find them; on that separate, but more free and honorable ground, where the State places those who are not *with* her but *against* her,— the only house in a slave-state in which a free man can abide with honor. If any think that their influence would be lost there, and their voices no longer afflict the ear of the State, that they would not be as an enemy within its walls, they do not know by how much truth is stronger than error.

Questions

1. What does Thoreau see as the relationship between government and freedom?

2. How does he justify an individual deciding to break the law?

---

80. George Henry Evans, "Freedom of the Soil" (1844)

Source: **Working Man's Advocate** *(New York, June 1, 1844).*

The economic depression that lasted from 1837 into the early 1840s inspired a rash of plans to improve the conditions of American workers. One idea, popularized by George Henry Evans, was land reform. An immigrant from England who in 1829 became the editor of *The Working Man's*

Advocate, a pro-labor newspaper published in New York City, Evans argued that the monopolization of land by large owners was destroying ordinary citizens' prospects for economic independence. Appealing to the traditional equation of landownership with economic freedom, Evans pointed to access to western land as a way of combating unemployment and low wages in the East and the only alternative to permanent economic dependence for American workers. Evans's plan for the government to provide free land in the West to settlers would be enacted into law in the Homestead Act of 1862.

AFTER THE REVOLUTION, which placed a vast increase of power in the hands of the people in this country, the masses thought, and thought truly, that they had the means of establishing the best government that the world ever saw. They made their first essay, they completed their machine, and its workings were so far superior to the operations of the old monarchial machinery, that they thought their machine had attained perfection, and they began to grow vain of the applause of the great and good throughout the world. Land was cheap and easily accessible, and every thing went on prosperously for a time.... Yet... although *national* improvements progressed rapidly, and *national* wealth increased, yet the condition of the working man was not improved! *The rich were growing richer and the poor poorer!* The non-producer was getting *more* and the producer *less* of the fruits of industry! How was this?... A simple remedy is now discovered, and one that will go far toward *perfecting* this machine of self government. The great defect, which has hitherto enabled a few to live sumptuously without labor on the labor of the many... is now discovered to be the Monopoly of the Soil....

It is urged by the aristocracy in England, as an argument against universal suffrage, that we have *made no use of it* to ameliorate our condition, and that we still tolerate slavery.... Monarchy, to use a comprehensive phrase of a black writer, "stole the black man from his land, and his land from the red man," and then he apportioned the stolen bodies and the stolen land among a few of his own color to whom he made the remainder of the whites as dependent for the means of existence as were the blacks themselves. And now, because in seventy years Democracy has not freed itself from the gigantic, complicated trifold scheme of plunder entailed upon her, she is to be taunted as though the original sin was hers! We hurl back the charge in old Monarchy's teeth, and tell him that infant Democracy is now perfecting a plan that will not only restore their rights to the blacks, the Indians, and the landless whites of this continent, but will contribute essentially, we trust, to the liberation of universal man; for all this good will result from a restoration of the Equal right to the Land. . . .

Evidently, it seems to us, it is the *first* duty of Democracy to decree the freedom of the soil.

Questions

1. How does Evans try to explain the existence of economic inequality in a country of political democracy?

2. Does Evans appear to be a critic of slavery as well as land monopoly?

———

81. William Henry Seward, "The Irrepressible Conflict" (1858)

Source: The Irrepressible Conflict: A Speech by William H. Seward, Delivered at Rochester, Monday, Oct. 25, 1858 *(New York, 1858), pp. 1–6.*

As the controversy over the expansion of slavery intensified during the 1850s, a new political party, the Republican, rose to dominance in the North. The party's appeal rested on the idea of "free labor." Republicans glorified the North as the home of progress, opportunity, and freedom.

One of the most powerful statements of the Republican outlook was delivered in 1858 by William H. Seward, a senator from New York. Seward described the nation's division into free and slave societies as an "irrepressible conflict" between two fundamentally different social systems. Although Seward condemned slavery as immoral, his essential argument had to do with economic development and national unity. The market revolution, he argued, was drawing the entire nation closer together in a web of transportation and commerce, thus heightening the tension between freedom and slavery. The United States, he predicted, "must and will, sooner or later, become either entirely a slaveholding nation, or entirely a free-labor nation."

OUR COUNTRY IS a theater, which exhibits, in full operation, two radically different political systems; the one resting on the basis of servile or slave labor, the other on the basis of voluntary labor of freemen.

The laborers who are enslaved are all Negroes, or persons more or less purely of African derivation. But this is only accidental. The principle of the system is, that labor in every society, by whomsoever performed, is necessarily unintellectual, groveling and base; and that the laborer, equally for his own good and for the welfare of the State, ought to be enslaved. The white laboring man, whether native or foreigner, is not enslaved, only because he cannot, as yet, be reduced to bondage. . . .

• • •

One of the chief elements of the value of human life is freedom in the pursuit of happiness. The slave system is not only intolerant, unjust, and inhuman, toward the laborer, whom, only because he is a laborer, it loads down with chains and converts into merchandise, but is scarcely less severe upon the freeman, to whom, only because he is a laborer from necessity, it denies facilities for employment, and whom it expels from the community because it cannot enslave and convert him into merchandise also. It is necessarily improvident and ruinous, because, as a general truth, communities prosper and flourish or droop and decline in just the degree that they practice or neglect to practice the primary duties of justice and humanity. The free-labor system conforms to the divine law of equality, which is written in the hearts and consciences of men, and therefore is always and everywhere beneficent.

The slave system is one of constant danger, distrust, suspicion, and watchfulness. It debases those whose toil alone can produce wealth and resources for defense, to the lowest degree of which human nature is capable, to guard against mutiny and insurrection, and thus wastes energies which otherwise might be employed in national development and aggrandizement.

The free-labor system educates all alike, and by opening all the fields of industrial employment, and all the departments of authority, to the unchecked and equal rivalry of all classes of men, at once secures universal contentment, and brings into the highest possible activity all the physical, moral, and social energies of the whole State. In States where the slave system prevails, the masters, directly or indirectly, secure all political power, and constitute a ruling aristocracy. In States where the free-labor system prevails, universal suffrage necessarily obtains, and the State inevitably becomes, sooner or later, a republic or democracy. . . .

• • •

The two systems are at once perceived to be incongruous. But they are more than incongruous—they are incompatible. They never have permanently existed together in one country, and they never can. It would be easy to demonstrate this impossibility, from the irreconcilable contrast between their great principles and characteristics. But the experience of mankind has conclusively established it. . . .

Hitherto, the two systems have existed in different States, but side by side within the American Union. This has happened because the Union is a confederation of States. But in another aspect the United States constitute only one nation. Increase of population, which is filling the States out to their very borders, together with a new and extended network of railroads and other avenues, and an internal commerce which daily becomes more intimate, is rapidly bringing the States into a higher and more perfect social unity or consolidation. Thus, these antagonistic systems are continually coming into closer contact, and collision results.

Shall I tell you what this collision means? . . . It is an irrepressible conflict between opposing and enduring forces, and it means that the United States must and will, sooner or later, become either entirely a slaveholding nation, or entirely a free-labor nation. Either the cotton and rice fields of South Carolina and the sugar plantations of Louisiana will ultimately be filled by free labor, and Charleston and New Orleans become marts for legitimate merchandise alone, or else the rye-fields and wheat-fields of Massachusetts and New York must again be surrendered by their farmers to slave culture and to the production of slaves, and Boston and New York become once more markets for trade in the bodies and souls of men. . . .

Thus far, the course of that contest has not been according to the humane anticipations and wishes [of the founding fathers]. In the field of federal policies, Slavery, deriving unlooked-for advantages from commercial changes, and energies unforeseen from the facilities of combination between members of the slaveholding class and between that class and other property classes, early rallied, and has at length made a stand, not merely to retain its original defensive position, but to extend its sway throughout the whole Union. . . . This is a Constitution of Freedom. It is being converted into a Constitution of Slavery.

Questions

1. How does Seward expand the antislavery argument beyond the moral appeal of the abolitionists?

2. To whom does Seward seem to be addressing his remarks?

82. Hinton R. Helper, "The Impending Crisis" (1857)

Source: Hinton R. Helper, The Impending Crisis of the South *(New York, 1857), pp. 21–41.*

Northerners were not the only ones to criticize slavery during the 1850s. In 1857, the North Carolinian Hinton R. Helper wrote *The Impending Crisis of the South*, which argued that slavery was responsible for the South lagging further and further behind the northern states in economic and social development. Non-slaveholding whites, Helper insisted, were as much victims of the system as slaves—both were oppressed by the planter aristocracy. Helper called on poorer whites to use their right to vote to take power in the South, abolish slavery, colonize blacks outside the country, and transform the region into an area of small farms and thriving manufacturing centers modeled on the North. Although Helper won little support in his own region, his book was widely circulated by northern Republicans to demonstrate the superiority of free society.

───────

IT IS A fact well known to every intelligent Southerner that we are compelled to go to the North for almost every article of utility and adornment, from matches, shoepegs and paintings up to cotton-mills, steamships and statuary; that we have no foreign trade, no princely merchants, nor respectable artists; that, in comparison with the free states, we contribute nothing to the literature, polite arts and inventions of the age; that, for want of profitable employment at home, large numbers of our native population find themselves necessitated to emigrate to the West, whilst the free states retain not only the larger proportion of those born within their own limits, but induce, annually, hundreds of thousands of foreigners to settle and remain amongst them; . . . that, owing to the absence of a proper system of business amongst us, the North becomes, in one way or another, the proprietor and dispenser of all our floating wealth, and that we are dependent on Northern capitalists for the means necessary to build our railroads, canals and other public improvements; . . . and that nearly all the profits arising from the exchange of commodities, from insurance and shipping offices, and from the thousand and one industrial pursuits of the country, accrue to the North, and are there invested in the erection of those magnificent cities and stupendous works of art which dazzle the eyes of the South, and attest the superiority of free institutions! . . .

All the world sees . . . that, in comparison with the Free States, our agricultural resources have been greatly exaggerated, misunderstood and mismanaged; and that, instead of cultivating among ourselves a wise policy of mutual assistance and co-operation with respect to individuals, and of self-reliance with respect to the South at large, instead of giving countenance and encouragement to the industrial enterprises projected in our midst, and instead of building up, aggrandizing and beautifying our own States, cities and towns, we have been spending our substance at the North, and are daily augmenting and strengthening the very power which now has us so completely under its thumb. . . .

The causes which have impeded the progress and prosperity of the South, which have dwindled our commerce, and other similar pursuits, into the most contemptible insignificance; sunk a large majority of our people in galling poverty and ignorance, rendered a small minority conceited and tyrannical, and driven the rest away from their homes; entailed upon us a humiliating dependence on the Free States; disgraced us in the recesses of our own souls, and brought us under reproach in the eyes of all civilized and enlightened nations— may all be traced to one common source . . . *Slavery!*

Reared amidst the institution of slavery, believing it to be wrong both in principle and in practice, and having seen and felt its evil influences upon individuals, communities and states, we deem it a duty, no less than a privilege, to enter our protest against it, and to use our most strenuous efforts to overturn and abolish it! . . . We are not only in favor of keeping slavery out of the territories, but, carrying our opposition to the institution a step further, we here unhesitatingly declare ourself in favor of its immediate and unconditional abolition, in every state in this confederacy, where it now exists! Patriotism makes us a freesoiler; state pride makes us an emancipationist; a profound sense of duty to the South makes us an abolitionist; a reasonable degree of fellow feeling for the negro, makes us a colonizationist. . . .

Nothing short of the complete abolition of slavery can save the South from falling into the vortex of utter ruin. Too long have we yielded a submissive obedience to the tyrannical domination of an inflated oligarchy; too long have we tolerated their arrogance and self-conceit; too long have we submitted to their unjust and savage exactions. Let us now wrest from them the sceptre of power, establish liberty and equal rights throughout the land, and henceforth and forever guard our legislative halls from the pollutions and usurpations of pro-slavery demagogues. . . .

It is not so much in its moral and religious aspects that we propose to discuss the question of slavery, as in its social and political character and influences. To say nothing of the sin and the shame of slavery, we believe it is a most expensive and unprofitable institution; and if our brethren of the South will but throw aside their unfounded prejudices and preconceived opinions, and give us a fair and patient hearing, we feel confident that we can bring them to the same conclusion. Indeed, we believe we shall be enabled—not alone by our own contributions, but with the aid of incontestable facts and arguments which we shall introduce from other sources—to convince all true-hearted, candid and intelligent Southerners . . . that slavery, and nothing but slavery, has retarded the progress and prosperity of our portion of the Union; depopulated and impoverished our cities by forcing the more industrious and enterprising natives of the soil to emigrate to the free states; brought our domain under a sparse and inert population by preventing foreign immigration; made us tributary to the North, and reduced us to the humiliating condition of mere provincial subjects in fact, though not in name. . . .

Agriculture, it is well known, is the sole boast of the South; and, strange to say, many pro-slavery Southerners, who, in our latitude,

pass for intelligent men, are so puffed up with the idea of our importance in this respect, that they speak of the North as a sterile region,
unfit for cultivation, and quite dependent on the South for the necessaries of life! Such rampant ignorance ought to be knocked in the
head! We can prove that the North produces greater qualities of
bread-stuffs than the South! Figures shall show the facts. Properly,
the South has nothing left to boast of; the North has surpassed her in
everything, and is going farther and farther ahead of her every day....

We have two objects in view; the first is to open the eyes of the non-
slaveholders of the South, to the system of deception, that has so long
been practiced upon them, and the second is to show slaveholders
themselves—we have reference only to those who are not too per-
verse, or ignorant, to perceive naked truths—that free labor is far more
respectable, profitable, and productive, than slave labor. In the South,
unfortunately, no kind of labor is either free or respectable. Every
white man who is under the necessity of earning his bread, by the
sweat of his brow, or by manual labor, in any capacity, no matter how
unassuming in deportment, or exemplary in morals, is treated as if he
was a loathsome beast, and shunned with the utmost disdain. His soul
may be the very seat of honor and integrity, yet without slaves—
himself a slave—he is accounted as nobody, and would be deemed in-
tolerably presumptuous, if he dared to open his mouth, even so wide
as to give faint utterance to a three-lettered monosyllable, like yea or
nay, in the presence of an august knight of the whip and the lash.

Questions

1. How does Helper describe the economic and social conditions of non-
slaveholding white southerners?

2. How does Helper explain what he considers the South's economic
backwardness?

83. The Lincoln-Douglas Debates (1858)

Source: Political Debates Between Honorable Abraham Lincoln and
Honorable Stephen Douglas, in the Celebrated Campaign of 1858
(Columbus, Ohio, 1860), pp. 71, 75, 178–82, 204, 209, 234, 238.

The depth of Americans' divisions over slavery were brought into sharp focus in 1858 in the election campaign that pitted Illinois senator Stephen A.
Douglas, the North's most prominent Democratic leader, against the then
little-known Abraham Lincoln.

The Lincoln-Douglas debates, held in seven Illinois towns and attended
by tens of thousands of listeners, remain classics of American political
oratory. Clashing definitions of freedom lay at their heart. To Lincoln,
freedom meant opposition to slavery. Douglas insisted that the essence of
freedom lay in local self-government. A large, diverse nation could survive
only by respecting the right of each locality to determine its own
institutions. He attempted to portray Lincoln as a dangerous radical whose
positions threatened to degrade white Americans by reducing them to
equality with blacks.

Douglas was reelected. But the campaign created Lincoln's national
reputation.

• • •

DOUGLAS: Do you desire to strike out of our state constitution that
clause which keeps slaves and free negroes out of the state, and allow
the free negroes to flow in, and cover your prairies with black settlements? Do you desire to turn this beautiful state into a free negro
colony, in order that when Missouri abolishes slavery she can send
one hundred thousand emancipated slaves into Illinois, to become
citizens and voters, on an equality with yourselves? If you desire negro citizenship, if you desire to allow them to come into the state and
settle with the white man, if you desire them to vote on an equality
with yourselves, and to make them eligible to office, to serve on juries, and to adjudge your rights, then support Mr. Lincoln and the

Black Republican party, who are in favor of the citizenship of the negro. For one, I am opposed to negro citizenship in any and every form. I believe this government was made on the white basis. I believe it was made by white men, for the benefit of white men and their posterity for ever, and I am in favor of confining citizenship to white men, men of European birth and descent, instead of conferring it upon negroes, Indians and other inferior races.

Mr. Lincoln, following the example and lead of all the little Abolition orators, who go around and lecture in the basements of schools and churches, reads from the Declaration of Independence, that all men were created equal, and then asks how can you deprive a negro of that equality which God and the Declaration of Independence awards to him. He and they maintain that negro equality is guaranteed by the laws of God, and that it is asserted in the Declaration of Independence. If they think so, of course they have a right to say so, and so vote. I do not question Mr. Lincoln's conscientious belief that the negro was made his equal, and hence is his brother, (laughter,) but for my own part, I do not regard the negro as my equal, and positively deny that he is my brother or any kin to me whatever.

• • •

LINCOLN: Now gentlemen, I don't want to read at any greater length, but this is the true complexion of all I have ever said in regard to the institution of slavery and the black race. This is the whole of it, and anything that argues me into his idea of perfect social and political equality with the negro, is but a specious and fantastic arrangement of words, by which a man can prove a horse chestnut to be a chestnut horse. I will say here, while upon this subject, that I have no purpose directly or indirectly to interfere with the institution of slavery in the states where it exists. I believe I have no lawful right to do so, and I have no inclination to do so. I have no purpose to introduce political and social equality between the white and the black races. There is a physical difference between the two, which in my judgment will probably forever forbid their living together upon the footing of perfect equality, and inasmuch as it becomes a necessity that there must be a difference, I, as well as Judge Douglas, am in favor of the race to which I belong, having the superior position. I have never said anything to the contrary, but I hold that notwithstanding all this, there is no reason in the world why the negro is not entitled to all the natural rights enumerated in the Declaration of Independence, the right to life, liberty and the pursuit of happiness. I hold that he is as much entitled to these as the white man. I agree with Judge Douglas he is not my equal in many respects—certainly not in color, perhaps not in moral or intellectual endowment. But in the right to eat the bread, without leave of anybody else, which his own hand earns, *he is my equal and the equal of Judge Douglas, and the equal of every living man.*

• • •

DOUGLAS: He tells you that I will not argue the question whether slavery is right or wrong. I tell you why I will not do it. I hold that under the Constitution of the United States, each state of this Union has a right to do as it pleases on the subject of slavery. In Illinois we have exercised that sovereign right by prohibiting slavery within our own limits. I approve of that line of policy. We have performed our whole duty in Illinois. We have gone as far as we have a right to go under the Constitution of our common country. It is none of our business whether slavery exists in Missouri or not. Missouri is a sovereign state of this Union, and has the same right to decide the slavery question for herself that Illinois has to decide it for herself. ("Good.") Hence I do not choose to occupy the time allotted to me discussing a question that we have no right to act upon.

• • •

LINCOLN: The real issue in this controversy—the one pressing upon every mind—is the sentiment on the part of one class that looks upon the institution of slavery *as a wrong,* and of another class that *does not* look upon it as a wrong. The sentiment that contemplates the institution of slavery in this country as a wrong is the sentiment of the Republican party. It is the sentiment around which all their actions—all their arguments circle—from which all their propositions radiate.

They look upon it as being a moral, social and political wrong; and while they contemplate it as such, they nevertheless have due regard for its actual existence among us, and the difficulties of getting rid of it in any satisfactory way and to all the constitutional obligations thrown about it. Yet having a due regard for these, they desire a policy in regard to it that looks to its not creating any more danger. They insist that it should as far as may be, *be treated* as a wrong, and one of the methods of treating it as a wrong is to *make provision that it shall grow no larger.* They also desire a policy that looks to a peaceful end of slavery at sometime, as being wrong. . . .

That is the real issue. That is the issue that will continue in this country when these poor tongues of Judge Douglas and myself shall be silent. It is the eternal struggle between these two principles—right and wrong—throughout the world. They are the two principles that have stood face to face from the beginning of time; and will ever continue to struggle. The one is the common right of humanity and the other the divine right of kings. It is the same principle in whatever shape it develops itself. It is the same spirit that says, "You work and toil and earn bread, and I'll eat it." [Loud applause.] No matter in what shape it comes, whether from the mouth of a king who seeks to bestride the people of his own nation and live by the fruit of their labor, or from one race of men as an apology for enslaving another race, it is the same tyrannical principal. I was glad to express my gratitude at Quincy, and I re-express it here to Judge Douglas—*that he looks to no end of the institution of slavery.* That will help the people to see where the struggle really is. It will hereafter place with us all men who really do wish the wrong may have an end. And whenever we can get rid of the fog which obscures the real question—when we can get Judge Douglas and his friends to avow a policy looking to its perpetuation—we can get out from among them that class of men and bring them to the side of those who treat it as a wrong. Then there will soon be an end of it, and that end will be its "ultimate extinction." Whenever the issue can be distinctly made, and all extraneous matter thrown out so that men can fairly see the real difference between the parties, this controversy will soon be settled, and it will be done peaceably too.

• • •

Questions

1. How do Douglas and Lincoln differ in their views on what rights black Americans ought to enjoy?

2. What is Douglas's response to antislavery criticism of slavery in the southern states?

---

84. South Carolina Ordinance of Secession (1860)

Source: Frank H. Moore, ed., The Rebellion Record *(New York, 1861–1868), Vol. 1, pp. 3–5.*

In the three months that followed Abraham Lincoln's election as president in November 1860, seven states seceded from the Union. First to act was South Carolina, the state with the highest percentage of slaves in its population and a long history of political radicalism. On December 20, 1860, the legislature unanimously voted to leave the Union. In justifying the right to secede, the legislature issued an *Ordinance of Secession.* It restated the compact theory of the Constitution that had become more and more central to southern political thought during the three decades since the nullification controversy and placed the issue of slavery squarely at the center of the crisis. Rather than accept permanent minority status in a nation governed by their opponents, South Carolina's leaders boldly struck for their region's independence. At stake, they believed, was not a single election but an entire way of life based on slavery.

THE STATE OF South Carolina having resumed her separate and equal place among nations, deems it due to herself, to the remaining United States of America, and to the nations of the world, that she should declare the immediate causes which have led to this act.

In 1787, Deputies were appointed by the States to revise the Articles of Confederation; and on 17th September, 1787, these Deputies recommended, for the adoption of the States, the Articles of Union, known as the Constitution of the United States. . . .

Thus was established by compact between the States, a Government with defined objects and powers, limited to the express words of the grant. . . . We hold that the Government thus established is subject to the two great principles asserted in the Declaration of Independence; and we hold further, that the mode of its formation subjects it to a third fundamental principle, namely, the law of compact. We maintain that in every compact between two or more parties, the obligation is mutual; that the failure of one of the contracting parties to perform a material part of the arrangement, entirely releases the obligation of the other, and that, where no arbiter is provided, each party is remitted to his own judgment to determine the fact of failure, with all its consequences.

• • •

We affirm that the ends for which this Government was instituted have been defeated, and the Government itself has been made destructive of them by the action of the non-slaveholding States. Those States have assumed the right of deciding upon the propriety of our domestic institutions, and have denied the rights of property established in fifteen of the States and recognized by the Constitution; they have denounced as sinful the institution of Slavery; they have permitted the open establishment among them of societies, whose avowed object is to disturb the peace of and eloin [take away] the property of the citizens of other States. They have encouraged and assisted thousands of our slaves to leave their homes; and those who remain, have been incited by emissaries, books, and pictures, to servile insurrection.

For twenty-five years this agitation has been steadily increasing, until it has now secured to its aid the power of the common Government. Observing the *forms* of the Constitution, a sectional party has found within that article establishing the Executive Department, the means of subverting the Constitution itself. A geographical line has been drawn across the Union, and all the States north of that line have united in the election of a man to the high office of President of the United States whose opinions and purposes are hostile to Slavery. He is to be intrusted with the administration of the common Government, because he has declared that "Government cannot endure permanently half slave, half free," and that the public mind must rest in the belief that Slavery is in the course of ultimate extinction.

This sectional combination for the subversion of the Constitution has been aided, in some of the States, by elevating to citizenship persons who, by the supreme law of the land are incapable of becoming citizens; and their votes have been used to inaugurate a new policy, hostile to the South, and destructive of its peace and safety.

On the 4th of March next this party will take possession of the Government. It has announced that the South shall be excluded from the common territory, that the Judicial tribunal shall be made sectional, and that a war must be waged against Slavery until it shall cease throughout the United States.

The guarantees of the Constitution will then no longer exist; the equal rights of the States will be lost. The Slaveholding States will no longer have the power of self-government, or self-protection, and the Federal Government will have become their enemy.

Sectional interest and animosity will deepen the irritation; and all hope of remedy is rendered vain, by the fact that the public opinion at the North has invested a great political error with the sanctions of a more erroneous religious belief.

We, therefore, the people of South Carolina, by our delegates in Convention assembled, appealing to the Supreme Judge of the world for the rectitude of our intentions, have solemnly declared that the

Union heretofore existing between this State and the other States of North America is dissolved, and that the State of South Carolina has resumed her position among the nations of the world as a separate and independent state, with full power to levy war, conclude peace, contract alliances, establish commerce, and to do all other acts and things which independent States may of right do.

Questions

1. Why do secessionists place so much emphasis on the growth of antislavery public opinion in the North?

2. What appears to be the main motivation for South Carolina's secession?

CHAPTER 14

A New Birth of Freedom: The Civil War, 1861–1865

85. Alexander H. Stephens, The Cornerstone of the Confederacy (1861)

Source: Frank H. Moore, ed., **The Rebellion Record** *(New York, 1861–1868), Vol. 1, pp. 45–46.*

Alexander H. Stephens, one of Georgia's most prominent political leaders, opposed secession in the winter of 1860–1861, but once his state had acted, agreed to serve as the vice president of the Confederacy. In March, 1861, he delivered a speech in Savannah that laid out his explanation for the dissolution of the Union and argued that the Confederate Constitution represented a significant improvement over that of the United States. After the war, Stephens would write a long book arguing that the Civil War was caused not by slavery but by a constitutional question—the South's insistence on preserving state sovereignty against an overly powerful national government. In his 1861 speech, however, he forthrightly identified the defense of slavery and white supremacy as the fundamental motivation of the Confederacy, the "cornerstone" of the new southern nation. Apparently, Stephens's speech embarrassed Confederate President Jefferson Davis, who hoped to gain recognition from European powers by downplaying the role of slavery in the secession movement.

WE ARE IN the midst of one of the greatest epochs in our history. The last ninety days will mark one of the most memorable eras in the history of modern civilization. . . .

We are passing through one of the greatest revolutions in the annals of the world—seven States have, within the last three months, thrown off an old Government and formed a new. This revolution has been signally marked, up to this time, by the fact of its having been accomplished without the loss of a single drop of blood. [Applause.] This new Constitution, or form of government, constitutes the subject to which your attention will be partly invited.

In reference to it, I make this first general remark: It amply secures all our ancient rights, franchises, and privileges. All the great principles of Magna Charta are retained in it. No citizen is deprived of life, liberty, or property, but by the judgment of his peers, under the laws of the land. The great principle of religious liberty, which was the honor and pride of the old Constitution, is still maintained and secured. All the essentials of the old Constitution, which have endeared it to the hearts of the American people, have been preserved and perpetuated. . . . So, taking the whole new Constitution, I have no hesitancy in giving it as my judgment, that it is decidedly better than the old. [Applause.] Allow me briefly to allude to some of these improvements. The question of building up class interests, or fostering one branch of industry to the prejudice of another, under the exercise of the revenue power, which gave us so much trouble under the old Constitution, is put at rest forever under the new. We allow the imposition of no duty with a view of giving advantage to one class of persons, in any trade or business, over those of another. All, under our system, stand upon the same broad principles of perfect equality. Honest labor and enterprise are left free and unrestricted in whatever pursuit they may be engaged in . . .

But not to be tedious in enumerating the numerous changes for the better, allow me to allude to one other—though last, not least: the new Constitution has put at rest *forever* all the agitating questions relating to our peculiar institutions—African slavery as it ex-

ists among us—the proper *status* of the negro in our form of civilization. *This was the immediate cause of the late rupture and present revolution.* Jefferson, in his forecast, had anticipated this, as the "rock upon
which the old Union would split." He was right. What was conjec-
ture with him, is now a realized fact. But whether he fully comprehended the great truth upon which that rock *stood* and *stands*, may be
doubted. *The prevailing ideas entertained by him and most of the leading
statesmen at the time of the formation of the old Constitution were, that the
enslavement of the African was in violation of the laws of nature; that it was
wrong in principle, socially, morally and politically.* It was an evil they
knew not well how to deal with; but the general opinion of the men
of that day was, that, somehow or other, in the order of Providence,
the institution would be evanescent and pass away. This idea,
though not incorporated in the Constitution, was the prevailing idea
at the time. The Constitution, it is true, secured every essential guarantee to the institution while it should last, and hence no argument
can be justly used against the constitutional guarantees thus secured, because of the common sentiment of the day. *Those ideas, however, were fundamentally wrong. They rested upon the assumption of the
equality of races. This was an error.* It was a sandy foundation, and the idea
of a Government built upon it—when the "storm came and the wind
blew, it *fell.*"

   *Our new Government is founded upon exactly the opposite ideas; its foun-
dations are laid, its cornerstone rests, upon the great truth that the negro is
not equal to the white man; that slavery, subordination to the superior race,
is his natural and moral condition.* [Applause.] *This, our new Government,
is the first, in the history of the world, based upon this great physical, philo-
sophical, and moral truth.* This truth has been slow in the process of its
development, like all other truths in the various departments of science. It is so even amongst us. Many who hear me, perhaps, can recollect well that this truth was not generally admitted, even within
their day. The errors of the past generation still clung to many as late
as twenty years ago. Those at the North who still cling to these errors
with a zeal above knowledge, we justly denominate fanatics. All

fanaticism springs from an aberration of the mind; from a defect in reasoning. It is a species of insanity. One of the most striking characteristics of insanity, in many instances, is, forming correct conclusions from fancied or erroneous premises; so with the *anti-slavery* fanatics: their conclusions are right if their premises are. They assume that the negro is equal, and hence conclude that he is entitled to equal privileges and rights, with the white man.... I recollect once of having heard a gentleman from one of the Northern States, of great power and ability, announce in the House of Representatives, with imposing effect, that we of the South would be compelled, ultimately, to yield upon this subject of slavery; that it was as impossible to war successfully against a principle in politics, as it was in physics or mechanics. That the principle would ultimately prevail. That we, in maintaining slavery as it exists with us, were warring against a principle—a principle founded in nature, the principle of the equality of man. The reply I made to him was, that upon his own grounds we should succeed, and that he and his associates in their crusade against our institutions would ultimately fail. The truth announced, that it was as impossible to war successfully against a principle in politics as well as in physics and mechanics, I admitted, but told him it was he and those acting with him who were warring against a principle. They were attempting to make things equal which the Creator had made unequal.

In the conflict thus far, success has been on our side, complete throughout the length and breadth of the Confederate States. It is upon this, as I have stated, our social fabric is firmly planted; and I cannot permit myself to doubt the ultimate success of a full recognition of this principle throughout the civilized and enlightened world.

As I have stated, the truth of this principle may be slow in development, as all truths are, and ever have been, in the various branches of science. It was so with the principles announced by Galileo—it was so with Adam Smith and his principles of political economy. It was so with Harvey, and his theory of the circulation of the blood. It is stated that not a single one of the medical profession, living at the time of the announcement of the truths made by him, admitted them. Now, they are universally acknowledged. May we not therefore look with confidence to the ultimate universal acknowledgment of the truths upon which our system rests? It is the first Government ever instituted upon principles in strict conformity to nature, and the ordination of Providence, in furnishing the materials of human society. Many Governments have been founded upon the principles of certain classes; but the classes thus enslaved, were of the same race, and in violation of the laws of nature. Our system commits no such violation of nature's laws. The negro by nature, or by the curse against Canaan, [*A reference to* Genesis, 9:20–27, *which was used as a justification for slavery*] is fitted for that condition which he occupies in our system. The architect, in the construction of buildings, lays the foundation with the proper material—the granite—then comes the brick or the marble. The substratum of our society is made of the material fitted by nature for it, and by experience we know that it is the best, not only for the superior but for the inferior race, that it should be so. It is, indeed, in conformity with the Creator. *It is not for us to inquire into the wisdom of His ordinances or to question them.* For His own purposes He has made one race to differ from another, as He has made "one star to differ from another in glory."

The great objects of humanity are best attained, when conformed to his laws and degrees [sic], in the formation of Governments as well as in all things else. Our Confederacy is founded upon principles in strict conformity with these laws. This stone which was rejected by the first builders "is *become the chief stone of the corner*" in our new edifice.

Questions

1. What argument does Stephens offer for the idea that blacks are innately suited for the condition of slaves?

2. Why does Stephens believe the U.S. Constitution is fundamentally flawed?

86. Marcus M. Spiegel, Letter of a Civil War Soldier (1864)

Source: Reprinted from A Jewish Colonel in the Civil War: Marcus M. Spiegel of the Ohio Volunteers, *edited by Jean Powers Soman and Frank L. Byrne. By permission of the University of Nebraska Press. Copyright © 1985 by The Kent State University Press. Copyright © 1994 by Jean P. Soman. Reprinted with permission.*

Born into a Jewish family in Germany in 1829, Marcus Spiegel took part in the failed German revolution of 1848. In the following year, he emigrated to Ohio, where he married the daughter of a local farmer. He enlisted in the Union army in 1861. He went to war, he wrote to his brother-in-law, to defend "the flag that was ever ready to protect you and me and every one who sought its protection from oppression." Spiegel rose to the rank of colonel in the 120th Ohio Infantry and saw action in Virginia, Mississippi, and Louisiana. He was an ardent Democrat, who shared the era's racist attitudes and thought Lincoln's Emancipation Proclamation a serious mistake. Yet, as the Union army penetrated the heart of the Deep South, Spiegel became increasingly antislavery. Spiegel died in a minor engagement in Louisiana in May 1864, one of the 620,000 Americans to perish in the Civil War.

━━━━━

PLAQUEMINE LA JAN 22/64

My dear Wife, my sweet Cary!

• • •

... You must not expect any news inasmuch as this [is] as monotonous a place as ever Millersburg can be. We are living here right on the Mississippi River and with exception of three or four Steamboats landing here every day which are called Coast Packets and travel from Baton Rouge to New Orleans and back, we have no news. When I first came here we had four Regiments of Infantry, three Batteries of Artillery and one Company of Cavelery. Since then two Regiments of Infantry, the 22nd and 7th Kentucky and two Batteries have been moved to Baton Rouge where they got up a big scare the other day.

This leaves us the 42nd Ohio and the 120th Ohio, one Battery and one Company of Cavelery, sufficient to hold this place against all marauding forces they can bring; we are building a very large and formidable Fort here. The weather here is beautiful, just like our June; it is very warm and the air is mild, wholesome and refreshing. I wish to God you could be here. Colonel L. A. Sheldon of the 42nd Ohio is in command here; you know if you remember what I think of him; he commanded our Brigade last year at Chickasaw and Arkansas Post. Yet he is a very clever man and extremely kind to me. He has his wife here; she is from Lorain County; a regular build Western Reserve Yankee Girl. I do not see her often, though very much pressed to call. I saw her twice in four weeks.

Dr. Stanton, Adjutand, Uncle Josey, Sinsheimer and myself spend most of our time together. There was a report yesterday that there were a lot of Rebels twelve miles from here, so I started out with a Company of Cavelery. Uncle Josey and Doctor Stanton and my friend Lieutenant Miller (whom you saw at home) acted as volunteer Aids, but we found "nary Reb" after a hard ride. I managed to get four dozend Eggs and we came home. We are living in a House all together (i.e. field and Staff); our boy does the cooking for our Mess. Uncle Josey's business does not go very well just now; there are so very few troops here and they have no money and the lines are closed.

I have at present twelve Sergeants in Ohio on the recruiting Service; I do not know how well or whether at all, they succeed. It takes so long somehow to hear from Ohio and the North generally that we do not know what is going on. In New Orleans they have news once a week at least but here it is very irregular.

Captain Moffit sent in his resignation Papers about three months ago and a few days ago they came back accepted. I am very sorry for them indeed. Since I am here I have learned and seen more of what the horrors of Slavery was than I ever knew before and I am glad indeed that the signs of the times show, towards closing out the accursed institution. You know it takes me long to say anything that sounds antidemocratic and it goes hard, but whether I stay in the Army or come home, I am [in] favor of doing away with the institution of Slavery. I am willing for the Planters to hire them and in favor of making the negro work at all events; inasmuch as he is naturally lazy and indolent, but never hereafter will I either speak or vote in favor of Slavery; this is no hasty conclusion but a deep conviction. Yet I never mean hereafter to be a politician, but quietly as a good citizen doing duty to my God, my family, my Country and myself.

Charley has left here about a week ago; I think however he is yet in New Orleans. You must write me a long, long letter and many of them and ask me ten thousand questions in every one and I will take them up one by one and answer them. This is the tirest place I ever was at, during my Soldier life, but the boys are so comfortable and feel so very well that I am not at all anxious to leave here. We had a negro woman cooking for us when Uncle Josey, Charley and Sinsheimer messed with us, but it is so far for them and they left us and we discharged our Cook and have only our boy. One of my men who deserted in Covington and was brought up by the Provost Marshal was tried by a Court Marshal and sentenced to forfeit all his pay and condemned for six months hard labor on Fort Espararox [Esperanza], Texas, with a Ball and Chain on his right leg, a very very hard sentence indeed; I would rather they would have shot him, for death is not so hard as degradation.

I am well and hearty and if I had my dear, dear little family here I would not wish anything better, but as it is my heart is ever yearning for home, home with all its blessings. I hope you are comfortable during this extreme awful cold weather, such as I see by the Papers you must have had; it makes me tremble to think you had to be there without me God grant all was right.

Hamlin must continue to be a good and obedient boy. It is about getting to be a youth and he must endeavor to learn well and make a man so he can aid and assist his father and mother when they get old. I hope soon to be at home when I can teach him and help him along . . .

Questions

1. What do you think Spiegel means by "the horrors of slavery"?

2. Why does he say that his new antislavery viewpoint "goes hard"?

━━━━━━━━━━

87. Abraham Lincoln, The Gettysburg Address (1863)

Source: **Abraham Lincoln: Letters and Addresses** *(New York, 1903), pp. 289–90.*

Probably the most famous single speech in American history, Abraham Lincoln's Gettysburg Address was delivered in November 1863 at the dedication of a military cemetery at the site of the Civil War's greatest battle. In fewer than 270 words, which took only three minutes to deliver, Lincoln distilled his conception of the war's meaning, and displayed his genius for linking the conflict with the deepest beliefs of northern society. At Gettysburg, he identified the nation's mission with the principle that "all men are created equal," spoke of the war as bringing about a "new birth of freedom" through the emancipation of the slaves, and defined the essence of democratic government. The sacrifices of Union soldiers, he declared, would ensure that "government of the people, by the people, for the people, shall not perish from the earth."

The speech also illustrated how the Civil War brought into being a new American nation-state. In his inaugural address in 1861, Lincoln had used the word "Union" twenty times, while making no mention of the "nation." But Union does not appear at all in the Gettysburg Address, while Lincoln referred five times to the "nation."

━━━━━━━━━━

FOUR SCORE AND seven years ago our fathers brought forth on this continent, a new nation, conceived in liberty, and dedicated to the proposition that all men are created equal.

Now we are engaged in a great civil war, testing whether that nation, or any nation so conceived and so dedicated, can long endure. We are met on a great battle-field of that war. We have come to dedicate a portion of that field, as a final resting place for those who here gave their lives that that nation might live. It is altogether fitting and proper that we should do this.

But, in a larger sense, we can not dedicate—we can not consecrate—we can not hallow—this ground. The brave men, living and dead, who struggled here, have consecrated it, far above our poor power to add or detract. The world will little note, nor long remember what we say here, but it can never forget what they did here. It is for us the living, rather, to be dedicated here to the unfinished work which they who fought here have thus far so nobly advanced. It is rather for us to be here dedicated to the great task remaining before us—that from these honored dead we take increased devotion to that cause for which they gave the last full measure of devotion— that we here highly resolve that these dead shall not have died in vain—that this nation, under God, shall have a new birth of freedom—and that government of the people, by the people, for the people, shall not perish from the earth.

Questions

1. Why does Lincoln date the foundation of the nation from 1776 (the date of the Declaration of Independence) rather than 1787, when the Constitution was written?

2. Why does Lincoln consider the Civil War a "new birth of freedom?"

88. Frederick Douglass on Black Soldiers (1863)

Source: Men of Color, to Arms, *Broadside, Rochester, March 21, 1863.*

At the beginning of the Civil War, the Union army refused to accept northern black volunteers. But as casualty rolls expanded, pressure mounted to allow blacks to serve. Although preliminary steps to enlist combat troops were taken in a few parts of the South in 1862, only after the Emancipation Proclamation of January 1, 1863, did the recruitment of black soldiers begin in earnest.

Some black units won considerable fame, among them the 54th Massachusetts Volunteers, a company of free blacks from throughout the North commanded by Robert Gould Shaw, a young reformer from a prominent Boston family. In March 1863, Frederick Douglass called on northern blacks to volunteer for this unit. "Liberty won by white men would lose half its luster," he wrote. Douglass realized that by serving in the army, black men would be placing the question of postwar black citizenship on the nation's agenda.

WHEN FIRST THE rebel cannon shattered the walls of Sumter and drove away its starving garrison, I predicted that the war then and there inaugurated would not be fought out entirely by white men. Every month's experience during these dreary years has confirmed that opinion. A war undertaken and brazenly carried on for the perpetual enslavement of colored men, calls logically and loudly for colored men to help suppress it. Only a moderate share of sagacity was needed to see that the arm of the slave was the best defense against the arm of the slaveholder. Hence with every reverse to the national arms, with every exulting shout of victory raised by the slaveholding rebels, I have implored the imperiled nation to unchain against her foes, her powerful black hand. Slowly and reluctantly that appeal is beginning to be heeded. Stop not now to complain that it was not heeded sooner. It may or it may not have been best that it should not.

This is not the time to discuss that question. Leave it to the future. When the war is over, the country is saved, peace is established, and the black man's rights are secured, as they will be, history with an impartial hand will dispose of that and sundry other questions. Action! Action! not criticism, is the plain duty of this hour. Words are now useful only as they stimulate to blows. The office of speech now is only to point out when, where, and how to strike to the best advantage. There is no time to delay. The tide is at its flood that leads on to fortune. From East to West, from North to South, the sky is written all over, "Now or never."

Liberty won by white men would lose half its luster. "Who would be free themselves must strike the blow." "Better even die free, than to live slaves." This is the sentiment of every brave colored man amongst us. There are weak and cowardly men in all nations. We have them amongst us. They tell you this is the "white man's war"; that you will be "no better off after than before the war"; that the getting of you into the army is to "sacrifice you on the first opportunity." Believe them not; cowards themselves, they do not wish to have their cowardice shamed by your brave example. Leave them to their timidity, or to whatever motive may hold them back. I have not thought lightly of the words I am now addressing you. The counsel I give comes of close observation of the great struggle now in progress, and of the deep conviction that this is your hour and mine. In good earnest then, and after the best deliberation, I now for the first time during this war feel at liberty to call and counsel you to arms. By every consideration which binds you to your enslaved fellow-countrymen, and the peace and welfare of your country; by every aspiration which you cherish for the freedom and equality of yourselves and your children; by all the ties of blood and identity which make us one with the brave black men now fighting our battles in Louisiana and in South Carolina, I urge you to fly to arms, and smite with death the power that would bury the government and your liberty in the same hopeless grave. I wish I could tell you that the State of New York calls you to this high honor. For the moment her constituted authorities are silent on the subject. They will speak by and by, and doubtless on the right side; but we are not compelled to wait for her. We can get at the throat of treason and slavery through the State of Massachusetts. She was first in the War of Independence; first to break the chains of her slaves; first to make the black man equal before the law; first to admit colored children to her common schools, and she was first to answer with her blood the alarm cry of the nation, when its capital was menaced by rebels. You know her patriotic governor, and you know Charles Sumner. I need not add more.

Massachusetts now welcomes you to arms as soldiers. She has but a small colored population from which to recruit. She has full leave of the general government to send one regiment to the war, and she has undertaken to do it. Go quickly and help fill up the first colored regiment from the North. I am authorized to assure you that you will receive the same wages, the same rations, the same equipments, the same protection, the same treatment, and the same bounty, secured to the white soldiers. You will be led by able and skillful officers, men who will take especial pride in your efficiency and success. They will be quick to accord to you all the honor you shall merit by your valor, and see that your rights and feelings are respected by other soldiers. I have assured myself on these points, and can speak with authority. More than twenty years of unswerving devotion to our common cause may give me some humble claim to be trusted at this momentous crisis. I will not argue. To do so implies hesitation and doubt, and you do not hesitate. You do not doubt. The day dawns; the morning star is bright upon the horizon! The iron gate of our prison stands half open. One gallant rush from the North will fling it wide open, while four millions of our brothers and sisters shall march out into liberty. The chance is now given you to end in a day the bondage of centuries, and to rise in one bound from social degradation to the plane of common equality with all other varieties of men. Remember Denmark Vesey of Charleston; remember Nathaniel Turner of Southampton; remember Shields Green and Copeland, who followed noble John Brown, and fell as glorious martyrs for the cause of the slave. Remember that in a contest with oppression, the Almighty has no attribute which can take sides with oppressors. The case is before you. This is our golden opportunity. Let us accept it, and forever wipe out the dark reproaches unsparingly hurled against us by our enemies. Let us win for ourselves the gratitude of our country, and the best blessings of our posterity through all time. The nucleus of this first regiment is now in camp at Readville, a short distance from Boston. I will undertake to forward to Boston all persons adjudged fit to be mustered into the regiment, who shall apply to me at any time within the next two weeks.

Questions

1. Why does Douglass believe that black service in the Union army will lead to an expansion of blacks' rights in the postwar world?

2. What does Douglass mean when he writes that black soldiers will "wipe out the dark reproaches" directed at blacks "by our enemies"?

89. Letter by the Mother of a Black Soldier (1863)

Source: Ira Berlin et al., eds., Freedom: A Documentary History of Emancipation, 1861–1867, Series 2 (New York, 1982), pp. 582–83.

Within the Union army, black soldiers were anything but equal to white. Serving in segregated units and ineligible, until the end of the war, to rise to the rank of commissioned officers, they were initially paid less than white soldiers. Even more alarming, the Confederacy announced that it would treat captured black soldiers not as prisoners of war but as fugitives who would be remanded to slavery.

One of the more remarkable letters of the Civil War era was written to President Lincoln by Hannah Johnson, the mother of a black soldier.

Although, as she notes, she had enjoyed but a "poor education," Mrs. John-son eloquently advised the president to insist that black prisoners be treated the same as white and resist pressures to rescind the Emancipation Proclamation. The fact that she felt she had a sympathetic recipient in the White House illustrates the enormous changes American society was un-dergoing as a result of the Civil War. Mrs. Johnson did not know that the day before she wrote the letter, Lincoln had ordered that, for every captured black soldier enslaved, a Confederate prisoner would be put to hard labor for the duration of the war.

BUFFALO [NEW YORK] July 31 1863

Excellent Sir

My good friend says I must write to you and she will send it[.] My son went in the 54th regiment. I am a colored woman and my son was strong and able to fight for his country and the colored people have as much to fight for as any. My father was a Slave and escaped from Louisiana before I was born morn forty years agone[.] I have but poor edication but I never went to schol, but I know just as well as any what is right between man and man. Now I know it is right that a colored man should go and fight for his country, and so ought to a white man. I know that a colored man ought to run no greater risques than a white, his pay is no greater his obligation to fight is the same. So why should not our enemies be compelled to treat him the same, Made to do it.

My son fought at Fort Wagoner but thank God he was not taken prisoner, as many were[.] I thought of this thing before I let my boy go but then they said Mr. Lincoln will never let them sell our colored soldiers for slaves, if they do he will get them back quck[.] he will ret-tallyate and stop it. Now Mr. Lincoln dont you think you oght to stop this thing and make them do the same by the colored men they have lived in idleness all their lives on stolen labor and made savages of the colored people, but they now are so furious because they are proving themselves to be men, such as have come away and got some edication. It must not be so. You must put the rebels to work in State prisons to making shoes and things, if they sell our colored soldiers, till they let them all go. And give their wounded the same treatment. it would seem cruel, but their [is] no other way, and a just man must do hard things sometimes, that shew him to be a great man. They tell me some do you will take back the Proclamation, don't do it. When you are dead and in Heaven, in a thousand years that action of yours will make the Angels sing your praises I know it. Ought one man to own another, law for or not, who made the law, surely the poor slave did not. so it is wicked, and a horrible Outrage, there is no sense in it, because a man has lived by robbing all his life and his father before him, should he complain because the stolen things found on him are taken. Robbing the colored people of their labor is but a small part of the robbery[.] their souls are almost taken, they are made bruits of often. You know all about this[.]

Will you see that the colored men fighting now, are fairly treated. You ought to do this, and do it at once, Not let the thing run along meet it quickly and manfully, and stop this, mean cowardly cruelty. We poor oppressed ones, appeal to you, and ask fair play.

Yours for Christs sake
Hannah Johnson

Questions

1. What is Mrs. Johnson's opinion of slavery and slaveholders?

2. How would you describe the tone Mrs. Johnson adopts in writing to the president?

90. Abraham Lincoln, Address at Sanitary Fair, Baltimore (1864)

Source: Abraham Lincoln: Letters and Addresses *(New York, 1903), pp. 295–96.*

Never was freedom's contested nature more evident than during the Civil War. Both sides fought in the name of freedom. "We all declare for liberty," Lincoln observed in a speech in Baltimore in 1864, "but in using the same *word* we do not all mean the same *thing*." He went on to explain the differences between the two sides' understandings of this word. Lincoln noted that Maryland, a slave state before the Civil War, had just adopted a new constitution abolishing slavery. And he announced his intention to investigate reports (later confirmed) that Confederate forces had massacred a number of black Union soldiers after they surrendered at Fort Pillow, Tennessee. The advance of emancipation and the service of black troops, for Lincoln, embodied "the advance of liberty."

THE WORLD HAS never had a good definition of the word liberty, and the American people, just now, are much in want of one. We all declare for liberty; but in using the same word we do not all mean the same thing. With some the word liberty may mean for each man to do as he pleases with himself, and the product of his labor; while with others the same word may mean for some men to do as they please with other men, and the product of other men's labor. Here are two, not only different, but incompatible things, called by the same name, liberty. And it follows that each of the things is, by the respective parties, called by two different and incompatible names— liberty and tyranny.

The shepherd drives the wolf from the sheep's throat, for which the sheep thanks the shepherd as his liberator, while the wolf denounces him for the same act, as the destroyer of liberty, especially as the sheep was a black one. Plainly, the sheep and the wolf are not agreed upon a definition of the word liberty; and precisely the same difference prevails to-day among us human creatures, even in the North, and all professing to love liberty. Hence we behold the process by which thousands are daily passing from under the yoke of bondage hailed by some as the advance of liberty, and bewailed by others as the destruction of all liberty. Recently, as it seems, the people of Maryland have been doing something to define liberty, and thanks to them that, in what they have done, the wolf's dictionary has been repudiated.

It is not very becoming for one in my position to make speeches at great length; but there is another subject upon which I feel that I ought to say a word.

A painful rumor—true, I fear—has reached us of the massacre by the rebel forces at Fort Pillow, in the west end of Tennessee, on the Mississippi River, of some three hundred colored soldiers and white officers, who had just been overpowered by their assailants. There seems to be some anxiety in the public mind whether the government is doing its duty to the colored soldier, and to the service, at this point. At the beginning of the war, and for some time, the use of colored troops was not contemplated; and how the change of purpose was wrought I will not now take time to explain. Upon a clear conviction of duty I resolved to turn that element of strength to account; and I am responsible for it to the American people, to the Christian world, to history, and in my final account to God. Having determined to use the negro as a soldier, there is no way but to give him all the protection given to any other soldier. The difficulty is not in stating the principle, but in practically applying it. It is a mistake to suppose the government is indifferent to this matter, or is not doing the best it can in regard to it. We do not to-day know that a colored soldier, or white officer commanding colored soldiers, has been massacred by the rebels when made a prisoner. We fear it,—believe it, I may say,— but we do not know it. To take the life of one of their prisoners on the assumption that they murder ours, when it is short of certainty that they do murder ours, might be too serious, too cruel, a mistake. We are having the Fort Pillow affair thoroughly investigated; and such investigation will probably show conclusively how the truth is. If after all that has been said it shall turn out that there has been no massacre at Fort Pillow, it will be almost safe to say there has been none, and will be none, elsewhere. If there has been the massacre of three hundred there, or even the tenth part of three hundred, it will be conclusively proved; and being so proved, the retribution shall as surely come. It will be matter of grave consideration in what exact course to apply the retribution; but in the supposed case it must come.

Questions

1. What does Lincoln identify as the essential difference between northern and southern definitions of freedom?

2. What is the purpose of Lincoln's metaphor about the wolf and the sheep and their differing views of liberty?

---

91. Mary Livermore on Women and the War (1883)

Source: Mary A. Livermore, **What Shall We Do with Our Daughters?** *(Boston, 1883), pp. 10–16.*

The Civil War opened new doors of opportunity for northern women. Some took advantage of the wartime labor shortage to move into jobs in factories and into previously largely male professions like nursing. Hundreds of thousands of northern women took part in organizations that gathered money and medical supplies for soldiers and sent books, clothing, and food to the freedmen. Women played a leading role in organizing sanitary fairs—grand bazaars that raised money for soldiers' aid. The suffrage movement suspended operations during the war to devote itself to the Union and emancipation. But from the ranks of this wartime mobilization came many of the leaders of the postwar movement for women's rights. Mary Livermore, the wife of a Chicago minister, toured military hospitals to assess their needs, cared for injured and dying soldiers, and organized two sanitary fairs. She emerged from the war with a deep resentment against women's legal and political subordination and organized her state's first woman suffrage convention. Looking back on her experience two decades later, Livermore concluded that the spirit of the age was emancipating women no less than slaves and creating new opportunities in education, employment, and the law.

THE CONTEMPTUOUS OPINION entertained of woman in the past has found expression, not alone in literature, but also in unjust laws and customs. "In marriage she has been a serf; as a mother she has been robbed of her children; in public instruction she has been ignored; in labor she has been a menial, and then inadequately compensated; civilly she has been a minor, and politically she has had no existence. She has been the equal of man only when punishment, and the payment of taxes, were in question."

Born and bred for generations under such conditions of hindrance, it has not been possible for women to rise much above the arbitrary standards of inferiority persistently set before them. Here and there through the ages some woman endowed with phenomenal force of character has towered above the mediocrity of her sex, hinting at the qualities imprisoned in the feminine nature. It is not strange that these instances have been rare: it is strange, indeed, that women have held their own during these ages of degradation....

• • •

Humanity has moved forward to an era where wrong and slavery are being displaced, and reason and justice are being recognized as the rule of life. Science is extending immeasurably the bounds of knowledge and power; art is refining life, giving to it beauty and grace; literature bears in her hands whole ages of comfort and sympathy; industry, aided by the hundred-handed elements of nature, is increasing the world's wealth; and invention is economizing its labor. The age looks steadily to the redressing of wrong, to the right-

ing of every form of error and injustice; and a tireless and prying philanthropy, which is almost omniscient, is one of the most hopeful
characteristics of the time....

• • •

It could not be possible in such an era but that women should share
in the justice and kindliness with which the time is fraught. A great
wave is lifting them to higher levels. The leadership of the world is being taken from the hands of the brutal and low, and the race is groping
its way to a higher ideal than once it knew. It is the evolution of this
tendency that is lifting women out of their subject condition, that is
emancipating them from the seclusion of the past, and adding to the
sum total of the world's worth and wisdom, by giving to them the cultivation human beings need. The demand for their education,—
technical and industrial, as well as intellectual,—and for their civil
and political rights, is being urged each year by an increasing host, and
with more emphatic utterance.

Colleges, professional schools, and universities, closed against them
for ages, are opening to them. They are invited to pursue the same
course of study as their brothers, and are graduated with the same
diplomas. Trades, businesses, remunerative vocations, and learned
professions seek them; and even the laws, which are the last to feel the
change in public opinion,—usually dragging a whole generation
behind,—even these are being annually revised and amended, and
then they fail to keep abreast of the advancing civilization.

All this is but prefatory, and prophetic of the time when, for
women, law will be synonymous with justice, and no opportunity
for knowledge or effort will be denied them on the score of sex....

• • •

It is for our young women that the great changes of the time promise the most: it is for our daughters,—the fair, bright girls, who are
the charm of society and the delight of home; the sources of infinite
comfort to fathers and mothers, and the sources of great anxiety also.
What shall we do with them,—and what shall they do with and for
themselves?

> "New occasions teach new duties,
> Time makes ancient good uncouth,"

and the training of fifty years ago is not sufficient for the girls of to-day. The changed conditions of life which our young women confront compel greater care and thought on the part of those charged with their education than has herefore been deemed necessary. They are to be weighted with heavy duties, and to assume heavier responsibilities; for the days of tutelage seem to be ended for civilized women, and they are to think and act for themselves.

Questions

1. How does Livermore explain the inequality in status and achievement between men and women?

2. How does Livermore understand freedom for women?

CHAPTER 15

"What Is Freedom?": Reconstruction, 1865–1877

92. "Colloquy with Colored Ministers" (1865)

Source: Journal of Negro History, *Vol. 16, January 1931, pp. 88–92. Reprinted with permission of the Association for the Study of African American Life.*

On the evening of January 12, 1865, twenty leaders of the local black community met in Savannah with General William T. Sherman and Secretary of War Edwin M. Stanton. Less than a month had passed since Sherman's army had captured the city, at the end of the March to the Sea. The group chose as its spokesman Garrison Frazier, a Baptist minister who had purchased the freedom of himself and his wife in 1856.

One of the most remarkable interchanges of those momentous years, the "Colloquy" offered a rare insight into African-Americans' ideas and aspirations at the dawn of freedom. Four days after the meeting, Sherman issued Special Field Order 15, which set aside the Sea Islands and a large area along the South Carolina and Georgia coasts for the settlement of black families on forty-acre plots of land. He also offered them broken-down mules that the army could no longer use. In Sherman's order lay the origins of the phrase, "forty acres and a mule," that would reverberate across the South in the next few years.

ON THE EVENING of Thursday, the 12th day of January, 1865, the following persons of African descent met, by appointment, to hold an interview with EDWIN M. STANTON, Secretary of War, and Major-General SHERMAN, to have a conference upon matters relating to the freedmen of the State of Georgia....

• • •

Garrison Frazier being chosen by the persons present to express their common sentiments upon the matters of inquiry, makes answers to inquiries as follows:

1. State what your understanding is in regard to the acts of Congress, and President Lincoln's proclamation, touching the condition of the colored people in the rebel States.

Answer. So far as I understand President Lincoln's proclamation to the rebellious States, it is, that if they would lay down their arms and submit to the laws of the United States before the 1st of January, 1863, all should be well; but if they did not, then all the slaves in the rebel States should be free, henceforth and forever; that is what I understood.

2. State what you understand by slavery, and the freedom that was to be given by the President's Proclamation.

Answer. Slavery is receiving by irresistible power the work of another man, and not by his consent. The freedom, as I understand it, promised by the proclamation, is taking us from under the yoke of bondage and placing us where we could reap the fruit of our own labor, and take care of ourselves, and assist the Government in maintaining our freedom.

3. State in what manner you think you can take care of yourselves, and how can you best assist the Government in maintaining your freedom.

Answer. The way we can best take care of ourselves is to have land, and turn in and till it by our labor—that is, by the labor of the women, and children, and old men—and we can soon maintain ourselves and have something to spare; and to assist the Government, the young men should enlist in the service of the Government, and serve in such manner as they may be wanted (the rebels told us that they piled them up and made batteries of them, and sold them to Cuba, but we don't believe that). We want to be placed on land until we are able to buy it and make it our own.

4. State in what manner you would rather live, whether scattered among the whites, or in colonies by yourselves.

Answer. I would prefer to live by ourselves, for there is a prejudice against us in the South that will take years to get over; but I do not know that I can answer for my brethren.

[*Mr.* [James] *Lynch* says he thinks they should not be separated, but live together. All the other persons present being questioned, one by one, answer that they agree with "brother *Frazier.*"]

5. Do you think that there is intelligence enough among the slaves of the South to maintain themselves under the Government of the United States, and the equal protection of its laws, and maintain good and peaceable relations among yourselves and with your neighbors?

Answer. I think there is sufficient intelligence among us to do so.

6. State what is the feeling of the black population of the South toward the Government of the United States; what is the understanding in respect to the present war, its causes and object, and their disposition to aid either side; state fully your views.

Answer. I think you will find there is thousands that are willing to make any sacrifice to assist the Government of the United States, while there is also many that are not willing to take up arms. I do not suppose there is a dozen men that is opposed to the Government. I understand as to the war that the South is the aggressor. President Lincoln was elected President by a majority of the United States, which guaranteed him the right of holding the office and exercising that right over the whole United States. The South, without knowing what he would do, rebelled. The war was commenced by the rebels before he came into the office. The object of the war was not, at first, to give the slaves their freedom, but the sole object of the war was, at first to bring the rebellious States back into the Union, and their loyalty to the laws of the

United States. Afterwards, knowing the value that was set on the slaves by the rebels, the President thought that his proclamation would stimulate them to lay down their arms, reduce them to obedience, and help to bring back the rebel States; and their not doing so has now made the freedom of the slaves a part of the war. It is my opinion that there is not a man in this city that could be started to help the rebels one inch, for that would be suicide. There was two black men left with the rebels, because they had taken an active part for the rebels, and thought something might befall them if they staid behind, but there is not another man. If the prayers that have gone up for the Union army could be read out, you would not get through them these two weeks.

Questions

1. Why do the black leaders believe that owning land is essential to freedom?

2. How do blacks understand their relationship to the national government as the Civil War draws to a close?

93. Petition of Committee on Behalf of the Freedmen to Andrew Johnson (1865)

Source: Henry Bram et al. to the President of the United States, October 28, 1865, P-27, 1865, Letters Received (series 15), Washington Headquarters, Freedmen's Bureau Papers, National Archives.

By June 1865, some 40,000 freedpeople had been settled on "Sherman land" in South Carolina and Georgia, in accordance with Special Field Order 15. That summer, however, President Andrew Johnson, who had succeeded Lincoln, ordered nearly all land in federal hands returned to its former owners. In October, O. O. Howard, head of the Freedmen's Bureau, traveled to the Sea Islands to inform blacks of the new policy.

Howard was greeted with disbelief and protest. A committee drew up petitions to Howard and President Johnson. Their petition to the president pointed out that the government had encouraged them to occupy the land and affirmed that they were ready to purchase it if given the opportunity. Johnson rejected the former slaves' plea. And, throughout the South, because no land distribution took place, the vast majority of rural freedpeople remained poor and without property during Reconstruction.

EDISTO ISLAND S.C. Oct 28th, 1865.

To the President of these United States. We the freedmen of Edisto Island South Carolina have learned From you through Major General O O Howard commissioner of the Freedmans Bureau. with deep sorrow and Painful hearts of the possibility of government restoring These lands to the former owners. We are well aware Of the many perplexing and trying questions that burden Your mind. and do therefore pray to god (the preserver of all and who has through our Late and beloved President (Lincoln) proclamation and the war made Us A free people) that he may guide you in making Your decisions. and give you that wisdom that Cometh from above to settle these great and Important Questions for the best interests of the country and the Colored race: Here is where secession was born and Nurtured Here is were we have toiled nearly all Our lives as slaves and were treated like dumb Driven cattle, This is our home, we have made These lands what they are. we were the only true and Loyal people that were found in posession of these Lands. we have been always ready to strike for Liberty and humanity yea to fight if needs be To preserve this glorious union. Shall not we who Are freedman and have been always true to this Union have the same rights as are enjoyed by Others? Have we broken any Law of these United States? Have we forfieted our rights of property In Land?—If not then! are not our rights as A free people and good citizens of these United States To be considered before the rights of those who were Found in rebellion against this good and just Government (and now being conquered) come (as they Seem) with penitent hearts and beg forgiveness For past offences and also ask if their lands Cannot be restored to them are these rebellious Spirits to be reinstated in their *possessions* And we who have been abused and oppressed For many long years not to be allowed the Privilege of purchasing land But be subject To the will of these large Land owners? God forbid, Land monopoly is injurious to the advancement of the course of freedom, and if Government Does not make some provision by which we as Freedmen can obtain A Homestead, we have Not bettered our condition.

We have been encouraged by Government to take Up these lands in small tracts, receiving Certificates of the same—we have thus far Taken Sixteen thousand (16000) acres of Land here on This Island. We are ready to pay for this land When Government calls for it. and now after What has been done will the good and just government take from us all this right and make us Subject to the will of those who have cheated and Oppressed us for many years God Forbid!

We the freedmen of this Island and of the State of South Carolina— Do therefore petition to you as the President of these United States, that some provisions be made by which Every colored man can purchase land. and Hold it as his own. We wish to have A home if It be but A few acres. without some provision is Made our future is sad to look upon. yess our Situation is dangerous. we therefore look to you In this trying hour as A true friend of the poor and Neglected race. for protection and Equal Rights. with the privilege of purchasing A Homestead—A Homestead right here in the Heart of South Carolina.

We pray that God will direct your heart in Making such provision for us as freedmen which Will tend to united these states together stronger Than ever before—May God bless you in the Administration of your duties as the President Of these United States is the humble prayer Of us all.—

In behalf of the Freedmen
           Henry Bram
Committee   Ishmael Moultrie.
           yates. Sampson

Questions

1. How important is it for the petitioners to obtain land on Edisto Island, as opposed to land elsewhere in the country?

2. What do they think is the relationship between owning land and freedom?

94. The Mississippi Black Code (1865)

Source: Walter L. Fleming, ed., Documentary History of Reconstruction *(Cleveland, 1906–07), Vol. 1, pp. 281–90.*

During 1865, Andrew Johnson put into effect his own plan of Reconstruction, establishing procedures whereby new governments, elected by white voters only, would be created in the South. Among the first laws passed by the new governments were the Black Codes, which attempted to regulate the lives of the former slaves. These laws granted the freedpeople certain rights, such as legalized marriage, ownership of property, and limited access to the courts. But they denied them the right to testify against whites, serve on juries or in state militias, or to vote. And in response to planters' demands that the freedpeople be required to work on the plantations, the Black Codes declared that those who failed to sign yearly labor contracts could be arrested and hired out to white landowners. The Black Codes indicated how the white South would regulate black freedom if given a free hand by the federal government. But they so completely violated free labor principles that they discredited Johnson's Reconstruction policy among northern Republicans.

VAGRANT LAW

Sec. 2. . . . All freedmen, free negroes and mulattoes in this State, over the age of eighteen years, found on the second Monday in January, 1866, or thereafter, with no lawful employment or business, or found unlawfully assembling themselves together, either in the day or night time, and all white persons so assembling themselves with freedmen, free negroes or mulattoes, or usually associating with freedmen, free negroes or mulattoes, on terms of equality, or living in adultery or fornication with a freed woman, free negro or mulatto, shall be deemed vagrants, and on conviction thereof shall be fined in a sum not exceeding, in the case of a freedman, free negro, or mulatto, fifty dollars, and a white man two hundred dollars, and imprisoned at the discretion of the court, the free negro not exceeding ten days, and the white man not exceeding six months. . . .

Sec. 7. . . . If any freedman, free negro, or mulatto shall fail or refuse to pay any tax levied according to the provisions of the sixth section of this act, it shall be *prima facie* evidence of vagrancy, and it shall be the duty of the sheriff to arrest such freedman, free negro, or mulatto or such person refusing or neglecting to pay such tax, and proceed at once to hire for the shortest time such delinquent tax-payer to any one who will pay the said tax, with accruing costs, giving preference to the employer, if there be one.

CIVIL RIGHTS OF FREEDMEN

Sec. 1. . . . That all freedmen, free negroes, and mulattoes may sue and be sued, implead and be impleaded, in all the courts of law and equity of this State, and may acquire personal property, and choses in action, by descent or purchase, and may dispose of the same in the same manner and to the same extent that white persons may: *Provided*, That the provisions of this section shall not be so construed as to allow any freedman, free negro, or mulatto to rent or lease any lands or tenements except in incorporated cities or towns. . . .

Sec. 2.... All freedmen, free negroes, and mulattoes may inter-marry with each other, in the same manner and under the same reg-ulations that are provided by law for white persons: *Provided*, That the clerk of probate shall keep separate records of the same.

Sec. 3.... All freedmen, free negroes, or mulattoes who do now and have herebefore lived and cohabited together as husband and wife shall be taken and held in law as legally married, and the issue shall be taken and held as legitimate for all purposes; that it shall not be lawful for any freedman, free negro, or mulatto to intermarry with any white person; nor for any white person to intermarry with any freedman, free negro, or mulatto; and any person who shall so intermarry, shall be deemed guilty of felony, and on conviction thereof shall be confined in the State penitentiary for life; and those shall be deemed freedmen, free negroes, and mulattoes who are of pure negro blood, and those descended from a negro to the third gen-eration, inclusive, though one ancestor in each generation may have been a white person.

Sec. 4.... In addition to cases in which freedmen, free negroes, and mulattoes are now by law competent witnesses, freedmen, free ne-groes, or mulattoes shall be competent in civil cases, when a party or parties to the suit, either plaintiff or plaintiffs, defendant or defen-dants; also in cases where freedmen, free negroes, and mulattoes is or are either plaintiff or plaintiffs, defendant or defendants, and a white person or white persons, is or are the opposing party or parties, plaintiff or plaintiffs, defendant or defendants. They shall also be competent witnesses in all criminal prosecutions where the crime charged is alleged to have been committed by a white person upon or against the person or property of a freedman, free negro, or mu-latto: *Provided*, that in all cases said witnesses shall be examined in open court, on the stand; except, however, they may be examined be-fore the grand jury, and shall in all cases be subject to the rules and tests of the common law as to competency and credibility.

Sec. 5.... Every freedman, free negro, and mulatto shall, on the second Monday of January, one thousand eight hundred and sixty-six and annually thereafter, have a lawful home or employment, and shall have written evidence thereof. . . .

Sec. 6. . . . All contracts for labor made with freedmen, free negroes, and mulattoes for a longer period than one month shall be in writing, and in duplicate, attested and read to said freedman, free negro, or mulatto by a beat, city or county officer, or two disinterested white persons of the county in which the labor is to be performed, of which each party shall have one; and said contracts shall be taken and held as entire contracts, and if the laborer shall quit the service of the employer before the expiration of his term of service, without good cause, he shall forfeit his wages for that year up to the time of quitting.

Sec. 7. . . . Every civil officer shall, and every person may, arrest and carry back to his or her legal employer any freedman, free negro, or mulatto who shall have quit the service of his or her employer before the expiration of his or her term of service without good cause. . . . *Provided*, that said arrested party, after being so returned, may appeal to the justice of the peace or member of the board of police of the county, who, on notice to the alleged employer, shall try summarily whether said appellant is legally employed by the alleged employer, and has good cause to quit said employer; either party shall have the right of appeal to the county court, pending which the alleged deserter shall be remanded to the alleged employer or otherwise disposed of, as shall be right and just; and the decision of the county court shall be final.

CERTAIN OFFENSES OF FREEDMEN

Sec. 1. . . . That no freedman, free negro or mulatto, not in the military service of the United States government, and not licensed so to do by the board of police of his or her county, shall keep or carry firearms of any kind, or any ammunition, dirk or bowie knife, and on conviction thereof in the county court shall be punished by fine, not exceeding ten dollars, and pay the costs of such proceedings, and all such arms or ammunition shall be forfeited to the informer. . . .

Sec. 2.... Any freedman, free negro, or mulatto committing riots, routs, affrays, trespasses, malicious mischief, cruel treatment to animals, seditious speeches, insulting gestures, language, or acts, or assaults on any person, disturbance of the peace, exercising the function of a minister of the Gospel without a license from some regularly organized church, vending spirituous or intoxicating liquors, or committing any other misdemeanor, the punishment of which is not specifically provided for by law, shall, upon conviction thereof in the county court, be fined not less than ten dollars, and not more than one hundred dollars, and may be imprisoned at the discretion of the court, not exceeding thirty days.

Sec. 3.... If any white person shall sell, lend, or give to any freedman, free negro, or mulatto any fire-arms, dirk or bowie knife, or ammunition, or any spirituous or intoxicating liquors, such person or persons so offending, upon conviction thereof in the county court of his or her county, shall be fined not exceeding fifty dollars, and may be imprisoned, at the discretion of the court, not exceeding thirty days....

Sec. 5.... If any freedman, free negro, or mulatto, convicted of any of the misdemeanors provided against in this act, shall fail or refuse for the space of five days, after conviction, to pay the fine and costs imposed, such person shall be hired out by the sheriff or other officer, at public outcry, to any white person who will pay said fine and all costs, and take said convict for the shortest time.

Questions

1. Why do you think the state of Mississippi required all black persons to sign yearly labor contracts but not white citizens?

2. What basic rights are granted to the former slaves and which are denied to them by the Black Code?

95. Sidney Andrews on the White South and Black Freedom (1866)

Source: Sidney Andrews, "Three Months among the Reconstructionists," Atlantic Monthly, *Vol. 17 (February 1866), pp. 237–45.*

Many northern journalists visited the South after the end of the Civil War to report on conditions there. One of the most influential was Sidney Andrews, who toured the Southeast late in 1865. Andrews offered a vivid description of how white southerners defined black freedom. Most, he reported, were convinced that the emancipated slaves equated freedom with idleness; they would not work except if compelled to do so. Andrews considered this a "cruel slander." The attitudes he encountered help explain the motives for the enactment of the Black Codes.

I SPENT THE months of September, October, and November, 1865, in the States of North Carolina, South Carolina, and Georgia. I travelled over more than half the stage and railway routes therein, visited a considerable number of towns and cities in each State, attended the so-called reconstruction conventions at Raleigh, Columbia, and Milledgeville, and had much conversation with many individuals of nearly all classes.

• • •

Going into the States where I went—and perhaps the fact is true also of the other Southern states—going into Georgia and the Carolinas, and not keeping in mind the facts of yesterday, any man would almost be justified in concluding that the end and purpose in respect to this poor negro was his extermination. . . . It is proclaimed everywhere that he will not work, that he cannot take care of himself, that he is a nuisance to society, that he lives by stealing, and that he is sure to die in a few months; and, truth to tell, the great body of the people, though one must not say intentionally, are doing all they well can to make these assertions true. If it is not said that any considerable number wantonly abuse and outrage him, it must be said that they manifest a barbarous indifference to his fate, which just as surely drives him on to destruction as open cruelty would.

There are some men and a few women—and perhaps the number of these is greater than we of the North generally suppose—who really desire that the negro should now have his full rights as a human being. With the same proportion of this class of persons in a community of Northern constitution, it might be justly concluded that the whole community would soon join or acquiesce in the effort to secure for him at least a fair share of those rights.... Unfortunately, however, in these Southern communities the opinion of such persons cannot have such weight as it would in ours. The spirit of the caste, of which I have already spoken, is an element figuring largely against them in any contest involving principle—an element of whose practical workings we here know very little. The walls between individuals and classes are so high and broad, that the men and women who recognize the negro's rights and privileges as a freeman are almost as far from the masses as we of the North are. Moreover, that any opinion savors of the "Yankee"—in other words, is new to the South—is a fact that even prevents its consideration by the great body of the people. Their inherent antagonism to everything from the North—an antagonism fostered and cunningly cultivated for half a century by the politicians in the interest of Slavery—is something that no traveller can photograph, that no Northern man can understand, till he sees it with his own eyes, hears it with his own ears, and feels it by his own consciousness. That the full freedom of the negroes would be acknowledged at once is something we had no warrant for expecting. The old masters grant them nothing, except at the requirement of the nation—as a military and political necessity; and any plan for reconstruction is wrong which proposes at once or in the immediate future to substitute free-will for this necessity.

Three fourths of the people assume that the negro will not labor, except on compulsion; and the whole struggle between the whites on the one hand and the blacks on the other hand is a struggle for and against compulsion. The negro insists, very blindly perhaps, that he shall be free to come and go as he pleases; the white insists that he shall come and go only at the pleasure of his employer. The whites seem wholly unable to comprehend that freedom for the negro means the same thing as freedom for them. They readily enough admit that the Government has made him free, but appear to believe that they still have the right to exercise over him the old control. It is partly their misfortune, and not wholly their fault, that they cannot understand the national intent, as expressed in the Emancipation Proclamation and the [Thirteenth] Constitutional Amendment. I did not anywhere find a man who could see that laws should be applicable to all persons alike; and hence even the best men hold that each State must have a negro code. They acknowledge the overthrow of the special servitude of man to man, but seek through these codes to establish the general servitude of man to the commonwealth. I had much talk with intelligent gentlemen in various sections, and particularly with such as I met during the conventions at Columbia and Milledgeville, upon this subject, and found such a state of feeling as warrants little hope that the present generation of negroes will see the day in which their race shall be amenable only to such laws as apply to the whites.

I think the freedmen divide themselves into four classes: one fourth recognizing, very clearly, the necessity of work, and going about it with cheerful diligence and wise forethought; one fourth comprehending that there must be labor, but needing considerable encouragement to follow it steadily; one fourth preferring idleness, but not specially averse to doing some job-work about the towns and cities; and one fourth avoiding work as much as possible, and living by voluntary charity, persistent begging, or systematic pilfering. It is true, that thousands of the aggregate body of this people appear to have hoped, and perhaps believed, that freedom meant idleness; true, too, that thousands are drifting about the country or loafing about the centres of population in a state of vagabondage.

Yet of the hundreds with whom I talked, I found less than a score who seemed beyond hope of reformation. It is a cruel slander to say that the race will not work, except on compulsion. I made much inquiry, wherever I went, of great numbers of planters and other employers, and found but very few cases in which it appeared that they had refused to labor reasonably well, when fairly treated and justly paid. Grudgingly admitted to any of the natural rights of man, despised alike by Unionists and Secessionists, wantonly outraged by many and meanly cheated by more of the old planters, receiving a hundred cuffs for one helping hand and a thousand curses for one kindly word—they bear themselves toward their former masters very much as white men and women would under the same circumstances. True, by such deportment they unquestionably harm themselves; but consider of how little value life is from their stand-point. They grope in the darkness of this transition period, and rarely find any sure stay for the weary arm and the fainting heart. Their souls are filled with a great, but vague longing for freedom; they battle blindly with fate and circumstance for the unseen and uncomprehended, and seem to find every man's hand raised against them. What wonder that they fill the land with restlessness!

Questions

1. Given that blacks had done all the work on plantations under slavery, how do you explain the widespread belief among whites that they would not work in freedom?

2. How do white understandings of freedom differ from those of the former slaves?

96. Elizabeth Cady Stanton, "Home Life" (ca. 1875)

Source: "Home Life," manuscript, ca. 1875, Elizabeth Cady Stanton Papers, Library of Congress.

Women activists saw Reconstruction as the moment for women to claim their own emancipation. With blacks guaranteed equality before the law by the Fourteenth Amendment and black men given the right to vote by the Fifteenth, women demanded that the boundaries of American democracy be expanded to include them as well. Other feminists debated how to achieve "liberty for married women." In 1875, Elizabeth Cady Stanton drafted an essay that demanded that the idea of equality, which had "revolutionized" American politics, be extended into private life. Genuine liberty for women, she insisted, required an overhaul of divorce laws (which generally required evidence of adultery, desertion, or extreme abuse to terminate a marriage) and an end to the authority men exercised over their wives.

Women's demand for the right to vote found few sympathetic male listeners. Even fewer supported liberalized divorce laws. But Stanton's extension of the idea of "liberty for women" into the most intimate areas of private life identified a question that would become a central concern of later generations of feminists.

WE ARE IN the midst of a social revolution, greater than any political or religious revolution, that the world has ever seen, because it goes deep down to the very foundations of society.... A question of magnitude presses on our consideration, whether man and woman are equal, joint heirs to all the richness and joy of earth and Heaven, or whether they were eternally ordained, one to be sovereign, the other slave.... Here is a question with half the human family, and that the stronger half, on one side, who are in possession of the citadel, hold the key to the treasury and make the laws and public sentiment to suit their own purposes. Can all this be made to change base without prolonged discussion, upheavings, heartburnings, violence and war? Will man yield what he considers to be his legitimate authority over woman with less struggle than have Popes and Kings their supposed rights over their subjects, or slaveholders over their slaves? No, no. John Stuart Mill says the generality of the male sex cannot yet tolerate the idea of living with an equal at the fireside; and here is the secret of the opposition to woman's equality in the state and the church—men are not ready to recognize it in the home. This is the real danger apprehended in giving woman the ballot, for as long as man makes, interprets, and executes the laws for himself, he holds the power under any system. Hence when he expresses the fear that liberty for woman would upset the family relation, he acknowledges that her present condition of subjection is not of her own choosing, and that if she had the power the whole relation would be essentially changed. And this is just what is coming to pass, the kernel of the struggle we witness to day.

This is woman's transition period from slavery to freedom and all these social upheavings, before which the wisest and bravest stand appalled, are but necessary incidents in her progress to equality. Conservatism cries out we are going to destroy the family. Timid reformers answer, the political equality of woman will not change it. They are both wrong. It will entirely revolutionize it. When woman is man's equal the marriage relation cannot stand on the basis it is to day. But this change will not destroy it; as state constitutions and statute laws did not create conjugal and maternal love, they cannot annul them.... We shall have the family, that great conservator of national strength and morals, after the present idea of man's headship is repudiated and woman set free. To establish a republican form of government [and] the right of individual judgment in the family must of necessity involve discussion, dissension, division, but the purer, higher, holier marriage will be evolved by the very evils we now see and deplore. This same law of equality that has revolutionized the state and the church is now knocking at the door of our homes and sooner or later there too it must do its work. Let us one and all wisely bring ourselves into line with this great law for man will gain as much as woman by an equal companionship in the nearest and holiest relations of life.... So long as people marry from considerations of policy, from every possible motive but the true one, discord and division must be the result. So long as the State provides no education for youth on the questions and throws no safeguards around the formation of marriage ties, it is in honor bound to open wide the door of escape. From a woman's standpoint, I see that marriage as an indissoluble tie is slavery for woman, because law, religion and public sentiment all combine under this idea to hold her true to this relation, whatever it may be and there is no other human slavery that knows such depths of degradations as a wife chained to a man whom she neither loves nor respects, no other slavery so disastrous in its consequences on the race, or to individual respect, growth and development....

• • •

By the laws of several states in this republic made by Christian representatives of the people divorces are granted to day for ... seventeen reasons.... By this kind of legislation in the several states we have practically decided two important points: 1st That marriage is a dissoluble tie that may be sundered by a decree of the courts. 2nd That it is a civil contract and not a sacrament of the church, and the one involves the other....

A legal contract for a section of land requires that the parties be of age, of sound mind, [and] that there be no flaw in the title.... But a legal marriage in many states in the Union may be contracted between a boy of fourteen and a girl of twelve without the consent of parents of guardians, without publication of banns.... Now what person of common sense, or conscience, can endorse laws as wise or prudent that sanction acts such as these. Let the state be logical: if marriage is a civil contract, it should be subject to the laws of all other contracts, carefully made, the parties of age, and all agreements faithfully observed....

Let us now glance at a few of the popular objections to liberal divorce laws. It is said that to make divorce respectable by law, gospel and public sentiment is to break up all family relations. Which is to say that human affections are the result and not the foundation of the canons of the church and statutes of the state.... To open the doors of escape to those who dwell in continual antagonism, to the unhappy wives of drunkards, libertines, knaves, lunatics and tyrants, need not necessarily embitter the relations of those who *are* contented and happy, but on the contrary the very fact of freedom strengthens and purifies the bond of union. When husbands and wives do not own each other as property, but are bound together only by affection, marriage will be a life long friendship and not a heavy yoke, from which both may sometimes long for deliverance. The freer the relations are between human beings, the happier....

• • •

Home life to the best of us has its shadows and sorrows, and because of our ignorance this must needs be.... The day is breaking. It is something to know that life's ills are not showered upon us by the Good Father from a kind of Pandora's box, but are the results of causes that we have the power to control. By a knowledge and observance of law the road to health and happiness opens before [us]: a joy and peace that passeth all understanding shall yet be ours and Paradise regained on earth. When marriage results from a true union of intellect and spirit and when Mothers and Fathers give to their holy offices even that preparation of soul and body that the artist gives to the conception of his poem, statue or landscape, then will marriage, maternity and paternity acquire a new sacredness and dignity and a nobler type of manhood and womanhood will glorify the race!!

Questions

1. How does Stanton define the "social revolution" the United States underwent after the Civil War?

2. How does Stanton believe that individual freedom within the family can be established?

97. Frederick Douglass, "The Composite Nation" (1869)

Source: Philip S. Foner and Daniel Rosenberg, eds., Racism, Dissent, and Asian Americans from 1850 to the Present *(Westport, Conn., 1993), pp. 217–30.*

Another group that did not share fully in the expansion of rights inspired by the Civil War and Reconstruction was Asian-Americans. Prejudices against Asians was deeply entrenched, especially on the West Coast, where most immigrants from Asia lived. When the radical Republican Charles Sumner, senator from Massachusetts, moved to allow Asians to become naturalized citizens (a right that had been barred to them since 1790), senators from California and Oregon objected vociferously, and the proposal was defeated.

Another advocate of equal rights for Asian-Americans was Frederick Douglass. In his remarkable "Composite Nation" speech, delivered in Boston in 1869, Douglass condemned anti-Asian discrimination and called for giving them all the rights of other Americans, including the right to vote. Douglass's comprehensive vision of a country made up of people of all races and national origins and enjoying equal rights was too radical for the time, but it would win greater and greater acceptance during the twentieth century.

THERE WAS A time when even brave men might look fearfully at the destiny of the Republic. When our country was involved in a tangled network of contradictions; when vast and irreconcilable social forces fiercely disputed for ascendancy and control; when a heavy curse rested upon our very soil, defying alike the wisdom and the virtue of the people to remove it; when our professions were loudly mocked by our practice and our name was a reproach and a by word to a mocking earth; when our good ship of state, freighted with the best hopes of the oppressed of all nations, was furiously hurled against the hard and flinty rocks of derision, and every cord, bolt, beam and bend in her body quivered beneath the shock, there was some apology for doubt and despair. But that day has happily passed away. The storm has been weathered, and the portents are nearly all in our favor.

There are clouds, wind, smoke and dust and noise, over head and around, and there will always be; but no genuine thunder, with destructive bolt, menaces from any quarter of the sky.

The real trouble with us was never our system or form of Government, or the principles under lying it; but the peculiar composition of our people; the relations existing between them and the compromising spirit which controlled the ruling power of the country.

We have for a long time hesitated to adopt and may yet refuse to adopt, and carry out, the only principle which can solve that difficulty and give peace, strength and security to the Republic, *and that is* the principle of absolute *equality.*

We are a country of all extremes, ends and opposites; the most conspicuous example of composite nationality in the world. Our people defy all the ethnological and logical classifications. In races we range all the way from black to white, with intermediate shades which, as in the apocalyptic vision, no man can name a number.

In regard to creeds and faiths, the condition is no better, and no worse. Differences both as to race and to religion are evidently more likely to increase than to diminish.

We stand between the populous shores of two great oceans. Our land is capable of supporting one fifth of all the globe. Here, labor is abundant and here labor is better remunerated than any where else. All moral, social and geographical causes, conspire to bring to us the peoples of all other over populated countries.

Europe and Africa are already here, and the Indian was here before either. He stands to-day between the two extremes of black and white, too proud to claim fraternity with either, and yet too weak to with stand the power of either. Heretofore the policy of our government has been governed by race pride, rather than by wisdom. Until recently, neither the Indian nor the negro has been treated as a part of the body politic. No attempt has been made to inspire either with a sentiment of patriotism, but the hearts of both races have been dili-gently sown with the dangerous seeds of discontent and hatred.

The policy of keeping the Indians to themselves, has kept the tom-ahawk and scalping knife busy upon our borders, and has cost us largely in blood and treasure. Our treatment of the negro has slacked humanity, and filled the country with agitation and ill-feeling and brought the nation to the verge of ruin.

Before the relations of these two races are satisfactorily settled, and in spite of all opposition, a new race is making its appearance within our borders, and claiming attention. It is estimated that not less than one-hundred thousand Chinamen are now within the lim-its of the United States. Several years ago every vessel, large or small, of steam or sail, bound to our Pacific coast and hailing from the Flow-ery kingdom, added to the number and strength of this element of our population.

Men differ widely as to the magnitude of this potential Chinese immigration. The fact that by the late treaty with China, we bind ourselves to receive immigrants from that country only as the sub-jects of the Emperor, and by the construction, at least, are bound not to naturalize them, and the further fact that Chinamen themselves have a superstitious devotion to their country and an aversion to permanent location in any other, contracting even to have their bones carried back should they die abroad, and from the fact that many have returned to China, and the still more stubborn that resis-tance to their coming has increased rather than diminished, it is inferred that we shall never have a large Chinese population in America. This however is not my opinion.

It may be admitted that these reasons, and others, may check and moderate the tide of immigration; but it is absurd to think that they will do more than this. Counting their number now, by the thou-sands, the time is not remote when they will count them by the mil-lions. The Emperor's hold upon the Chinaman may be strong, but the Chinaman's hold upon himself is stronger.

Treaties against naturalization, like all other treaties, are limited by circumstances. As to the superstitious attachment of the Chinese to China, that, like all other superstitions, will dissolve in the light and heat of truth and experience. The Chinaman may be a bigot, but it does not follow that he will continue to be one, tomorrow. He is a man, and will be very likely to act like a man. He will not be long in finding out that a country which is good enough to live in, is good enough to die in; and that a soil that was good enough to hold his body while alive, will be good enough to hold his bones when he is dead.

Those who doubt a large immigration, should remember that the past furnishes no criterion as a basis of calculation. We live under new and improved conditions of migration, and these conditions are constantly improving. America is no longer an obscure and inaccessible country. Our ships are in every sea, our commerce in every port, our language is heard all around the globe, steam and lightning have revolutionized the whole domain of human thought, changed all geographical relations, make a day of the present seem equal to a thousand years of the past, and the continent that Columbus only conjectured four centuries ago is now the center of the world.

• • •

I have said that the Chinese will come, and have given some reasons why we may expect them in very large numbers in no very distant future. Do you ask, if I favor such immigration, I answer *I would*. Would you have them naturalized, and have them invested with all the rights of American citizenship? *I would*. Would you allow them to vote? *I would*. Would you allow them to hold office? *I would*.

But are there not reasons against all this? Is there not such a law or principle as that of self preservation? Does not every race owe something to itself? Should it not attend to the dictates of common sense? Should not a superior race protect itself from contact with inferior ones? Are not the white people the owners of this continent? Have they not the right to say what kind of people shall be allowed to come here and settle? Is there not such a thing as being more generous than wise? In the effort to promote civilization may we not corrupt and destroy what we have? Is it best to take on board more passengers than the ship will carry?

To all this and more I have one among many answers, altogether satisfactory to me, though I cannot promise that it will be so to you.

I submit that this question of Chinese immigration should be settled upon higher principles than those of a cold and selfish expediency. There are such things in the world as human rights. They rest upon no conventional foundation, but are external, universal, and indestructible. Among these, is the right of locomotion; the right of migration; the right which belongs to no particular race, but belongs alike to all and to all alike. It is the right you assert by staying here, and your fathers asserted by coming here. It is this great right that I assert for the Chinese and the Japanese, and for all other varieties of men equally with yourselves, now and forever. I know of no rights of race superior to the rights of humanity, and when there is a supposed conflict between human and national rights, it is safe to go to the side of humanity. I have great respect for the blue eyes and light haired races of America. They are a mighty people. In any struggle for the good things of this world they need have no fear. They have no need to doubt that they will get their full share.

But I reject the arrogant and scornful theory by which they would limit migratory rights, or any other essential human rights to themselves, and which would make them the owners of this great continent to the exclusion of all other races of men.

I want a home here not only for the negro, the mulatto and the Latin races; but I want the Asiatic to find a home here in the United States, and feel at home here, both for his sake and for ours. Right wrongs no man. If respect is had to majorities, the fact that only one fifth of the population of the globe is white, the other four fifths are colored, ought to have some weight and influence in disposing of this and similar questions. It would be a sad reflection upon the laws of nature and upon the idea of justice, to say nothing of a common Creator, if four-fifths of mankind were deprived of the rights of migration to make room for the one fifth. If the white race may exclude all other races from this continent, it may rightfully do the same in respect to all other lands, islands, capes and continents, and thus have all the world to itself. Thus what would seem to belong to the whole, would become the property only of a part. So much for what is right, now let us see what is wise.

And here I hold that a liberal and brotherly welcome to all who are likely to come to the United States is the only wise policy which this nation can adopt.

• • •

I close these remarks as I began. If our action shall be in accordance with the principles of justice, liberty, and perfect human equality, no eloquence can adequately portray the greatness and grandeur of the future of the Republic.

We shall spread the network of our science and civilization over all who seek their shelter whether from Asia, Africa, or the Isles of the sea. We shall mold them all, each after his kind, into Americans; Indian and Celt, negro and Saxon, Latin and Teuton, Mongolian and Caucasian, Jew and Gentile, all shall here bow to the same law, speak the same language, support the same government, enjoy the same liberty, vibrate with the same national enthusiasm, and seek the same national ends.

Questions

1. What does Douglass mean by the term "composite nation"?

2. Why does he believe that people should be allowed to move freely from one country to another?

98. Robert B. Elliott on Civil Rights (1874)

Source: Civil Rights. Speech of Hon. Robert B. Elliott, of South Carolina, in the House of Representatives, January 6, 1874 *(Washington, D.C., 1874), pp. 1–8.*

One of the South's most prominent black politicians during Reconstruction, Robert B. Elliott appears to have been born in England and arrived in Boston shortly before the Civil War. He came to South Carolina in 1867, where he established a law office and was elected as a delegate to the state's constitutional convention of 1868. During the 1870s, he served in the legislature and was twice elected to the United States House of Representatives.

In January 1874, Elliott delivered a celebrated speech in Congress in support of the bill that became the Civil Rights Act of 1875. The measure outlawed racial discrimination in transportation and places of public accommodation like theaters and hotels. Thanks to the Civil War and Reconstruction, Elliott proclaimed, "equality before the law" regardless of race had been written into the laws and Constitution and had become an essential element of American freedom. Reconstruction, he announced, had "settled forever the political status of my race."

Elliott proved to be wrong. By the turn of the century, many of the rights blacks had gained after the Civil War had been taken away. It would be left to future generations to breathe new life into Elliott's dream of "equal, impartial, and universal liberty."

═══════════

SIR, IT IS scarcely twelve years since that gentleman [Alexander H. Stephens] shocked the civilized world by announcing the birth of a government which rested on human slavery as its corner-stone. The progress of events has swept away that *pseudo*-government which rested on greed, pride, and tyranny; and the race whom he then ruthlessly spurned and trampled on are here to meet him in debate, and to demand that the rights which are enjoyed by their former oppressors—who vainly sought to overthrow a Government which they could not prostitute to the base uses of slavery—shall be accorded to those who even in the darkness of slavery kept their allegiance true to freedom and the Union. Sir, the gentleman from Georgia has learned much since 1861; but he is still a laggard. Let him put away entirely the false and fatal theories which have so greatly marred an otherwise enviable record. Let him accept, in its fullness and beneficence, the great doctrine that American citizenship carries with it every civil and political right which manhood can confer. Let him lend his influence, with all his masterly ability, to complete the proud structure of legislation which makes this nation worthy of the great declaration which heralded its birth, and he will have done that which will most nearly redeem his reputation in the eyes of the world, and best vindicate the wisdom of that policy which has permitted him to regain his seat upon this floor. . . .

• • •

Sir, equality before the law is now the broad, universal, glorious rule and mandate of the Republic. No State can violate that. Kentucky and Georgia may crowd their statute-books with retrograde and barbarous legislation; they may rejoice in the odious eminence of their consistent hostility to all the great steps of human progress which have marked our national history since slavery tore down the stars and stripes on Fort Sumter; but, if Congress shall do its duty, if Congress shall enforce the great guarantees which the Supreme Court has declared to be the one pervading purpose of all the recent amendments, then their unwise and unenlightened conduct will fall with the same weight upon the gentlemen from those States who now lend their influence to defeat this bill, as upon the poorest slave who once had no rights which the honorable gentlemen were bound to respect. . . .

No language could convey a more complete assertion of the power of Congress over the subject embraced in the present bill than is expressed [in the Fourteenth Amendment]. If the States do not conform to the requirements of this clause, if they continue to deny to any person within their jurisdiction the equal protection of the laws, or as the Supreme Court had said, "deny equal justice in its courts," then Congress is here said to have power to enforce the constitutional guarantee by appropriate legislation. That is the power which this bill now seeks to put in exercise. It proposes to enforce the constitutional guarantee against inequality and discrimination by appropriate legislation. It does not seek to confer new rights, nor to place rights conferred by State citizenship under the protection of the United States, but simply to prevent and forbid inequality and discrimination on account of race, color, or previous condition of servitude. Never was there a bill more completely within the constitutional power of Congress. Never was there a bill which appealed for support more strongly to that sense of justice and fair-play which has been said, and in the main with justice, to be a characteristic of the Anglo-Saxon race. The Constitution warrants it; the Supreme Court sanctions it; justice demands it.

Sir, I have replied to the extent of my ability to the arguments which have been presented by the opponents of this measure. I have replied also to some of the legal propositions advanced by gentlemen on the other side; and now that I am about to conclude, I am deeply sensible of the imperfect manner in which I have performed the task. Technically, this bill is to decide upon the civil status of the colored American citizen; a point disputed at the very formation of our present Government, when by a short-sighted policy, a policy repugnant to true republican government, one negro counted as three-fifths of a man. The logical result of this mistake of the framers of the Constitution strengthened the cancer of slavery, which finally spread its poisonous tentacles over the southern portion of the body-politic. To arrest its growth and save the nation we have passed through the harrowing operation of intestine war, dreaded at all times, resorted to at the last extremity, like the surgeon's knife, but absolutely necessary to extirpate the disease which threatened with the life of the nation the overthrow of civil and political liberty on this continent. In that dire extremity the members of the race which I have the honor in part to represent—the race which pleads for justice at your hands to-day, forgetful of their inhuman and brutalizing servitude at the South, their degradation and ostracism at the

North—flew willingly and gallantly to the support of the national Government. Their sufferings, assistance, privations, and trials in the swamps and in the rice-fields, their valor on the land and on the sea, is a part of the ever-glorious record which makes up the history of a nation preserved, and might, should I urge the claim, incline you to respect and guarantee their rights and privileges as citizens of our common Republic. But I remember that valor, devotion, and loyalty are not always rewarded according to their just deserts, and that after the battle some who have borne the brunt of the fray may, through neglect or contempt, be assigned to a subordinate place, while the enemies in war may be preferred to the sufferers.

The results of the war, as seen in reconstruction, have settled forever the political status of my race. The passage of this bill will determine the civil status, not only of the negro, but of any other class of citizens who may feel themselves discriminated against. It will form the cap-stone of that temple of liberty, begun on this continent under discouraging circumstances, carried on in spite of the sneers of monarchists and the cavils of pretended friends of freedom, until at last it stands in all its beautiful symmetry and proportions, a building the grandest which the world has ever seen, realizing the most sanguine expectations and the highest hopes of those who, in the name of equal, impartial, and universal liberty, laid the foundation stones.

Questions

1. How does Elliott defend the constitutionality of the Civil Rights Bill?

2. Why does Elliott refer to the "cornerstone speech" of Alexander H. Stephens in making his argument?